Elizabeth Ward   Photo: Jenny Green

Born in Sydney in 1942, Elizabeth Ward has been a teacher, co-ordinator of the government alternative School Without Walls in Canberra, creative writing teacher for adults, a tutor in Teacher Education, Women's Refuge worker and full-time writer. She is currently teaching English literacy to Aboriginal people in Alice Springs, writing poetry and working on a novel. She is also a very active member of Women for Survival – the group which recently organised the two week women's camp at the US military installation at Pine Gap, near Alice Springs.

ELIZABETH WARD

Father–Daughter Rape

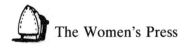 The Women's Press

For Chrissi

First published by The Women's Press Limited 1984
A member of the Namara Group
124 Shoreditch High Street, London E1 6JE

British Library Cataloguing in Publication Data

Ward, Elizabeth
    Father/daughter rape
    1. Incest
    2. Fathers and daughters
    I. Title
    306.7'77   HQ71
    ISBN 0-7043-3924-2

Typeset by MC Typeset, Chatham, Kent
Printed in Great Britain by Nene Litho
and bound by Woolnough Bookbinding
both of Wellingborough, Northants

Contents

Acknowledgements

I first came across the widespread phenomenon of Father–Daughter rape when visiting the United States in 1978. This was in the form of close contact with psychologists who worked in an incest clinic. Upon returning to Australia, I began working in a women's refuge. Within a few weeks I met Chrissi, to whom this book is dedicated. Suddenly the group of us working there realised that not a small number of the women and families we were spending time with in the refuge were escaping from Father–Daughter rape, or had been 'incest' victims as children. The American experience had 'taken the scales from my eyes'.

From this grass-roots involvement, I was provoked into library research because nothing was readily available on the subject – nothing in written form and nothing useful from the counselling and mental health professionals. I became deeply immersed in the research and the world of the women I met because of it, and wrote *Father–Daughter Rape* as a result.

My sister-workers at the Canberra Women's Refuge during 1979–1982 were an integral part of the development of my ideas. I particularly honour the trust and sharing which took place in the 'incest group' which we formed in 1979.

The workers at the Sydney Rape Crisis Centre, 1979–1981, and the Canberra Rape Crisis Centre, 1981–1982, were always helpful with resources and available for discussion time.

Liz O'Brien shared home and family and gave me encouragement, support and ideas which were very important during the early research. For unfailing assistance in the face of the most obscure requests, I thank Rod Stroud of the Australian National Library and Shirley O'Reilly of the Menzies Library (Australian National University). For the same things, and also for bringing the august halls of the Australian National Library into the laughter- and anger-filled world of feminist researching, I thank Margaret Crawford.

For thoughtful reading, constructive criticism and the warmth of their emotional reactions, I gratefully thank Julia Ryan, Pam Leddon, Carole Deagen, Alison Lyssa, Lesley de Haviland, Dottie Broom, Jessica Aan and Cora Gilbert. Rosemary Pringle and Liz Fell were particularly helpful with the chapter on Freud.

Gill Shaw and Pat Walker very lovingly gave me financial assistance without which I would not have been able to write this book. Judy Morris was a most participatory typist: the best kind.

Sarah Gibson, Merrilee Moss, Armide Hill, Sarah Parry, Druscilla Mojeska, my father Russel Ward and my daughter Genna Claire gave unending support, encouragement, love and friendship throughout. So did Jill Matthews and Sara Dowse: each was writing her own book at the same time, and we shared deadlines, breakthroughs, angst, love, encouragement, wine and fresh eggs.

Obi Olgrin shared home and family throughout the writing of this book. Her support was practical, spiritual, psychic and caring – and it was there every day. Her contribution to this book cannot begin to be measured.

And lastly, I thank the Goddess or my stars or the lines on my palm daily that I was born in a time and place that have enabled me to be part of the women's liberation movement. That is what has made everything about this book possible.

The author acknowledges with thanks permission from the following:

Marge Piercy for the quotation from *The Moon is Always Female* © Marge Piercy 1980;

WW Norton, New York, for lines from 'Natural Resources', *The Dream of a Common Language, Poems 1974–77* by Adrienne Rich © WW Norton and Co Inc., 1978;

Alta for lines from *The Shameless Hussy*;

Robin Morgan for the quotation from *Lady of the Beasts*, Random House, New York, 1976, © Robin Morgan 1976;

Bright Music Ltd, London, for the lines from 'Oh Daddy' by Christine McVie; Tina Reid and Sheba Feminist Publishers for 'Dear Sophie: Letter to an Ill Child', from *Smile Smile Smile Smile*, 1980.

I · EXPOSITION

Experience

Repeat the syllables
each cell has unforgotten:
There was the Word before their word
The Silence came.
The Name was changed

ROBIN MORGAN, *from*
The Network of the Imaginary Mother,
in Lady of the Beasts

Naming

> Eve is born of Adam for him to usurp 'the natural superiority
> of women' and, since Eve is then the child of Adam, she is
> created to become his daughter-wife, the ultimate child bride,
> and to symbolize the unconscious longings of men, as well as
> the power base inherent in a marriage in which one partner is
> both older, wiser, and the parent of the other . . .
>
> Nelson and Ikenberry, *Psychosexual Imperatives:*
> *Their Role in Identity Formation*

When I began the research that is the subject of this
book, I used the term 'child sexual abuse'. That quickly changed to
'incest', since the vast bulk of child sexual abuse occurs within the
family and the largest single group of offenders is comprised of
natural fathers. However, the more I read, and the more that
women talked to me about their experiences, the more it became
clear to me that not only was I looking at father–daughter rape, but
also at a phenomenon of epic proportions, which could only be
named by the capitalised form: Father–Daughter Rape.

In the foreground of the picture that emerged I found an
enormous proportion of girl-children raped, molested, abused and
used by their father, stepfather, de facto father, grandfather, uncle,
brother; the whole hidden from view by the resounding silence of
the 'incest taboo'. Until recently, the victims, if they 'told', were
mostly disbelieved, ignored, declared 'sick'; nowadays, they will
most probably be questioned, doubted, cross-examined, psychiatri-
cally examined, medically examined, and perhaps 'helped' by a
bewildering array of therapies delivered by a bewildering array of
service agencies, most of whose personnel openly state that they
don't know what to do.

Swirling through these facts I found myself conscious of images of
the Rape of The Daughter by The Father in the dawn of history.
The Biblical myth of creation has God take a rib from Adam, the

3

original person (male), and thereby create a female, Eve. And so Eve is created out of Adam: she comes from his body: Eve is born of Adam. Adam's daughter, Eve, then becomes his wife. Thus, not only do we have the male persona being creatrix, with the power to reproduce, but also father–daughter incest as the original sexual union. At a deeper level, we can also perceive that God as Father has created Adam, who is therefore a Son. Within this configuration, he is also Brother to Eve. Eve remains merely and essentially female: there to be sexually taken by the triptych of Father, Brother and Son, sanctioned by God, the ultimate Father, the male creator.

The deep and pervasive power of all myths of creation (and every society has one, or more, in some form) is only matched by the significance of the actual details of the myth. In the simplified realm of symbolism, only the essential message is retained. Christian mythology has emphasised Eve's eating of the fruit from the Tree of Life as the symbol of woman as temptress, thus diverting our attention from the social–sexual relationship between Adam and Eve by instituting Eve (woman) as the initiator of choiceless sexual union (rape) and establishing the myth of the child-bride (girl-child) as Seductress.

Our culture abounds with images of older men and younger women as couples. A man 'taking' a younger mistress, a man 'taking' a younger second wife, and then perhaps a third, is an accepted everyday occurrence. Aging male media personalities promote cigarettes, whisky, cars, swimming pools: each with a woman young enough to be his daughter draped on his arm, smiling with sexual innuendo.

Father–Daughter sexual union is implicitly sanctioned, from the Bible to the latest movie-star marriage. When this is integrated with the fact that an enormous number of girl-children are raped by men within their own families, then the reality of existence for The Daughter becomes plain. To be born female is to be a (potential) rape victim, from that moment on. Girl babies are raped. Girl toddlers are raped. Girl children are raped. And grown women are raped.

The Father to The Daughter: My little princess, My little girlie, Lass, Blossom, Flossie, Dolly, Sweetheart, Mine. Bring Daddy his paper, Blossom. My little girl's not old enough to go out with boys yet! Why were you late home from school? Who were you talking to?

The Father to The Daughter: lollies, lacy dresses, rides in the car, special cuddles, rape.

4

Fathers, mothers, teachers, police, clergymen, girl-guide leaders – all tell girl-children about Stranger Danger. Don't speak to strange men. Don't accept lifts from strange men. Don't take lollies from strange men. Don't sit near strange men in the movies. Watch out for strange men in the park. Beware. Of men.

But Daddy is different. Daddy will look after me. Daddy will protect me – from men.

The fact that Daddy is The Stranger to all the other little girls is one of the mindbinds of patriarchy. As little girls, we never quite see other girls (our friends) seeing Daddy as The Stranger. But he is. And some are raped by The Stranger who is her friend's father.

The daughter-rapers, child molesters, dirty old men, creepy uncles, and sticky-fingered grandfathers, are men who are in our families, next door, across the street, in grandma's house. The myth that there is a difference between The Father and The Stranger helps create the passivity of Daughter-victims. No one tells The Daughters (all girl-children) to beware of The Fathers (all male relatives, and male adult friends, trusted by the family). No one tells The Daughters how to say No to The Fathers.

The stories that follow are from interviews I had with women who were raped as children. In them, one hears/sees, over and over again, these images from the background: The Father as rapist; the conditioned blindness of The Mother (grandmother, aunt, sister, friend) who does not see because she cannot see what she has been told does not happen; and the helplessness, the passivity, the hope, and the anger-with-nowhere-to-go, of the raped Daughters. We see Adam, The Father, rape Eve, The Daughter, whom he created for his own use.

And finally, in these stories, we see The Daughters surging forward; rising, tentatively or wholeheartedly: the Sunday school images of Adam and Eve fade, as women find their own true power, and re-claim their sexuality and being for themselves.

Hearing

I interviewed many women who had been victims of sexual abuse by male members of their own families. The women I talked with had either read an article I had written, heard me speak, heard via grapevines of what I was doing, or they were friends or acquaintances. They live in various parts of Australia. I chose nine of the stories I was given.

Each 'interview' was informal: two women talking, with the tape recorder weaving its little circles nearby. Afterwards, I transcribed every word on to paper, in pencil. Then I read, and re-read; edited bits out that were repetitive or irrelevant; reorganised for chronological, ease-of-reading purposes; and then I typed each story in its final form.

In every case, the names of people and places have been changed. Since all the stories are told in the first person, many do not have any names in the text, since family members are virtually always named by their relationship to the speaker. But each woman has a name: it is in the ownership of her story.

All these women live vividly in my mind, with all the gestures, facial expressions, and intonations that could not reach the typed page. I have used punctuation and italics fairly liberally to try to convey some of these missing elements.

Virtually all the text, in every story, is the exact words used by the woman concerned. In a very few instances, I have edited two sentences into one; or summarised the description of the family numbers and relationships; or made other similar minor editorial alterations.

Sonia's Story

I was about twelve (I can't remember exactly) when it started. The situation was a fairly isolated one in terms of our nuclear family life. I had a brother eighteen months younger than I.

My father and I were fairly close; we would do things together, like the shopping (because my mother always worked), and I would read to him and things like that. He didn't read much – it was poetry that I first started reading to him. So we were fairly close then.

Then . . . I find bits difficult to recall. I can remember the gradual feeling-up, and I can remember it starting in places like the laundry out the back: I'd go to get something and he'd come in after me and start feeling me up, and rubbing himself up against me, and all that sort of stuff. Just recently I've remembered this part . . . it was on *every* occasion that my mother wasn't around. For example, he and I got up at six o'clock in the morning to get the breakfast (he'd take breakfast to my mother because she didn't like getting up), and so it would often happen when we were in our dressing-gowns and pyjamas . . .

I remember not liking the touching-up part, and being aware, even then, that it wasn't right.

I literally cannot remember the first time we ever fucked. So there is a gap in between. The touching-up . . . and then the recollections of the one night a week when my mother went out to bingo. I've got visual images of some of it: it always happened in the lounge-room, on the lounge, or on the floor, after my brother went to sleep. And he always used a condom – until much later when I went on the pill.

I have a much more visual memory of something that happened with someone else. I suppose I see it as the first sexual thing that happened to me. It was a man who came to paint some rooms – he was there for a few days when we came home from school – and one day he touched me up and he *kissed* me. I've got a clear memory of that. I rushed next door and told the neighbours who told my parents, and they *did* something about it, but I never knew what. I have a much clearer recollection of feeling strange about that, and of connecting it with my father – so it perhaps happened about the same time. And the same sort of feeling that this is wrong, this shouldn't be happening.

I wasn't titillated by what happened with that man . . . but I must have been when my father and I actually had intercourse. Because I did enjoy it . . . I mean, I remember mostly enjoying it in later years . . . but I remember mostly not feeling good about it at first, and spending all those years trying to avoid him. Trying to avoid being alone with him.

What actually happened was that we watched certain programmes on Thursday nights, when my mother went out. We would have dinner, then my brother would go to bed about 7.30 (my father always sent him to bed), and my father and I would sit up watching these programmes – sitting together on the lounge. He would be in his pyjamas, and I would often be in my pyjamas too . . . and he would start the whole touching-up thing – Oh, it's all so sordid! . . . I used to get that excited feeling in the pit of my stomach. It only ever happened once a night – always the missionary position. He used to make me feel his penis which I found fairly revolting. He only ever took his pyjama pants off – it wasn't a completely sensuous experience, there was a sense of furtiveness about it *all* the time. And I never got completely undressed either. He used to feel up my breasts but he never sucked them or anything like that; and he used to stimulate my clitoris with his finger. It was always a very short time – then he would come in . . . and he would come . . . and that would be it.

7

The furtiveness was partly because my brother was always there, just in the next room – so his coming was always fairly silent . . . he didn't do much more than, you know, pant and stuff. And we always got ourselves back together again, afterwards, fairly quickly. It was always a very short business. I guess it must have been a fairly dangerous business, for him, in those early years, with my brother always there, just through the wall.

I don't think . . . I had orgasms . . . No, I didn't. Because when I did with a lover, I had a sense that I had never felt this before – I'd never come. I realised afterwards that I quite deliberately didn't – that it was the one exposure thing that I kept to myself.

After a while I began masturbating – always in bed, alone – but that seemed apart from what happened with him. I remember feeling that the whole thing was the art of servicing him . . . But I was aware enough to know that it was important that I was lubricated – that must be because it hurt a few times. But I remember enjoying masturbating – in spite of the fear of going blind and so on!

To me, it's really significant that we never did it in the marital bed, *or* my bed, we *always* did it in the lounge-room. It was always the missionary position and I have a memory of that in terms of his weight – always this weight on me. He's not a big man, but he's stocky, and always there was this weight.

I can remember wanting to be affectionate, but pulling back . . . [very long silence] . . . I did start to come, I did have orgasms. I remember now, I did start to come because that's where the guilt came from: I started looking forward to it. I must have blotted it out completely . . . you must understand that the whole thing was part of this repressed life, often barely conscious . . . I'd blotted it out so that I'd forgotten by the time it started to happen with other blokes. I don't know how old I was when the orgasms started to happen. So, the affection . . . was because I felt that . . . well, you're fucking with someone, you know . . . but I withheld it. But I remember feeling that I'd like to be affectionate.

As I got older, the desire to avoid him meant that I started fighting with him, wanting to go out, and feel freer and things like that. And he became extremely possessive of me, and . . . so the battles became, on the surface, about teenage things, about wanting to go out and not being allowed to go out. He wouldn't let me wear jeans – even silly things like telling me what to wear. He was *incredibly* possessive.

The fights between him and me got worse . . . I was about

sixteen then. They were not all on the level of 'ordinary' father–daughter fighting. I started trying to withdraw from him and I remember one occasion where he took me for a drive and wanted a fuck in the car and I wouldn't and we ended up physically fighting and he ended up with a great big mark across his face – it was my nails I think – and he was bleeding. When we went home, my mother asked him what had happened, and he said he fell against something.

Then what happened was that I did get a boyfriend. There was a girl, Martha, who went to the same school: she had an enormous impact on me. I'd been brought up entirely cloistered – amazingly enough, Martha showed me a whole other world. She took me to Resistance [a radical youth centre in the late 60s] and I started meeting people. So – just as I was leaving school, I met this guy through Martha and I started going with him. I pretended I was a virgin and I pretended that I'd gone on the pill for him. My father didn't know (I didn't tell him), but the fights had got really bad between the two of us – he was sexually jealous, very jealous . . . it was all tied up with me trying to break out in a whole lot of ways.

I went to first-year university and I was still living at home and it was still going on. I left home sometime during that first year – I can't remember exactly when. I used to go and stay with some people in the country, friends near Bathurst, and this time, my father tried to stop me going. In amongst that, I'd gone and got a room in a house – a bed-sit type flat – without him knowing, so I felt strong and I said I was going to go to stay with my friends. There was a huge fight – he tried to strangle me. Why he stopped strangling me, I'll never know, but he did. He's totally irrational when he gets going – but anyway, he stopped. So I left – and I never went back . . . to live there. My mother stood by and watched him doing that – I will never forgive her for that.

I went to some friends, and then came back to get my things and he threw me out, lock, stock and barrel, just threw me out of the house. All my possessions and everything. I remember standing there, with no one else around . . . But all of that was explicable to friends, because it was just the business of leaving home and a parent freaking out.

But there's worse. After that, he . . . gradually . . . started to come around. This is when he really started to apply the pressure. Relations were very strained, but at some point he threatened that he would beat me up if I didn't go home . . . home! So I started going home, visiting . . . and it still went on. This is hazy – I don't remember how long I did that for, but it was at least a few months. (I've never told anyone this part before.)

About the middle of my second year, I must have really needed to do something about it, because I went to see a counsellor at the university – a man. I didn't tell him the full story – I told him my father had been difficult and over-sexed. I didn't tell him I'd been fucking my father. He insisted that I must tell my mother. Now I knew that my mother would commit suicide, because she had attempted suicide several times. I knew she wouldn't be able to cope with it. So I couldn't face this, but he kept pressing me when I went to see him.

I myself then did the usual undergraduate attempt and tried to commit suicide which was all rather farcical. I took something – antibiotics and other pills – and slept for three days. I didn't go back to that counsellor.

It was not long after that, I met John, whom I've been with ever since. It was about then that I did it – I got incredibly drunk and told a whole lot of friends . . . everything. They were extremely supportive, and really beaut, at the time. *But* – I also told this other guy, a medical student that I'd been going out with for some time. And he couldn't cope with it at all – he told the whole medical faculty. He said, 'You've had another lover all the time I've known you!' which I just couldn't believe. He told everyone he knew – which was awful. I didn't see him again.

I'd had this desperate fear that I didn't want the family to come apart, and that if I stopped going home to see them – which meant fucking with him – then somehow the family would break down. I cared about my mother and I couldn't bear this fear. But after telling those people, I had the strength to say, No more! That's it! and there wasn't any more, ever again. He obviously got very upset and tried to persuade me, he didn't stop doing that . . .

I realised I really was in a bit of a mess, so I went to a clinical psychologist at one of the big hospitals. I went to him and told him the story, and about the third time I went to him, he said, 'I don't think I can go on with this, because I find you physically attractive.' I just couldn't believe it! It was un-be-liev-able! But I said all right . . . then he said, 'Come back another time.' So I went back again and he said, 'I think I've overcome this' . . . I don't remember much else about what he said I guess because I remember being completely dissatisfied with what he said. He kept saying he couldn't do anything unless he saw the whole family, and that he couldn't do anything for me. I said that seeing the family was not on, and he could then offer nothing. One thing I do remember, he said that he thought I was looking for 'the golden cock'. I got very angry then, and stopped seeing him. What I really needed was to talk it all out – I felt I couldn't put that on my friends.

So then I had this thing about being neurotic. I remember on one occasion feeling as though I was on the edge of this really dark hole and if anyone pushed me any further, I wouldn't be responsible for what I did. I managed . . . to stay out . . . How I ever got through, I'll never know.

After that, I insisted on going to visit the family, which, for years, was quite strained. My father kept trying to get me alone – and I realised that, apart from fucking me on Thursday nights, *all through*, always, there had been the touching-up business – whenever he could get me alone, within the small confines of a house, it would be an occasion for touching me up. I really *hated* that. So, I told my brother – really rashly, I think now – because I needed someone in the house to know, so that I didn't have to be alone with my father. And he did exactly that: he wouldn't leave me alone in a room if my father was there. And I remember that as some real relief and protection. But my brother and I never discussed it after that, and he's never mentioned it since. I think he's just completely repressed it. He doesn't get on with my father – that may have contributed to why he helped me. He and I don't have much in common now anyway . . .

But there were still occasions when my father would try – and I rarely had the courage or strength . . . I used to say No and so on, but I would have had to scream the house down to stop him . . . So there was an endurance of the touching even when I was twenty and twenty-one. He never actually gave up. And so I tried to avoid situations in which I'd be alone with him, but I did keep going home . . . because I felt I should.

Then I met John, and I moved in with him quite soon after. My father would not accept the legitimacy of that relationship. Eventually we got married, and one of the reasons we got married was that in my father's terms it was the only legitimacy he would accept . . . and he did accept it. And after that he went cold – I had become someone else's wife – and that was the only thing he would accept.

Quite recently, a month or so ago, I went home to 'spend an evening' with them and found my mother all set to go out. And I completely freaked out, I yelled, 'You can't go.' And she couldn't understand . . . and it brought up all the old fear. Then I realised

11

that I could go, I didn't have to stay, so I told her it was OK. She went and he and I sat there . . . and he didn't touch me. Nothing happened. So in a way that was important . . . it was clearly the end. And I am now thirty.

I'm quite sure my mother must have known. Quite often I couldn't believe she didn't know. During those years, there were times when my father was caught in the act of touching me up . . . when she came back from somewhere . . . it would happen when she went to the toilet. I remember on one occasion she said something like, 'What are you doing? Leave her alone!' I think she must know . . . but fairly sensibly she can't face it, so she represses it.

She implies that he goes with other women, but she can cope with that. I always thought, How could any woman cope with the notion of her husband fucking her daughter? But, on second thoughts, I wonder if literally keeping it in the family was more acceptable to her – to be frank.

I find it hard to remember how I felt about my mother. He and she used to fight – throw things at each other, scream . . . She'd win though, she used to lock herself in the bathroom and take tablets and threaten to kill herself. I hated the conflict: I'd be kept awake for hours by their yelling. I just wanted it to stop. They'd get knives out, and throw things, and smash things . . . I just used to feel pain for her. I can't remember anything else: just the pain I felt. I suffered for her.

When I thought/felt that she must know, I used to have a sense that . . . she betrayed me . . . and that it's always been that way because her loyalty to him was stronger than anything else, and I think I probably always knew that. So that no matter what happened . . . they somehow got on. All those years of violence are part of the way they've related to each other. I feel, quite irrationally, that she should somehow have helped me . . . and she didn't. She tried to combat his authoritarianism sometimes – but that always meant a battle for her too. She was physically violent too: she'd hit him back, throw things, bash him up. And she did that to me too.

I also feel a certain amount of contempt for her. She's one of those women who, because she's powerless, has developed a whole mechanism for coping with that, by being . . . subtly powerful, I suppose you'd call it. Using her powerlessness . . . it's a sort of manipulation. I've tried to influence my mother in recent years . . . and she has been affected by the changing status of women. I sometimes take her out to things, films and meetings. And he's very possessive of her: he hates me taking her out, hates her going out anywhere, which is a very special part of why I do it. I find her irritating and irrational as a person, but I also have very strong loyalties to her.

It would have been much easier if I could hate him, you see, but I can't. I guess the truth is that there's a very strong emotional bond there. I think he's a very vulnerable, insecure person. I think he's a victim in all sorts of ways. I hate the fact that he's a pig and an authoritarian, and that he's intolerant – but my main feeling for him is a kind of incredible suffering for him because he's so deluded, he's so . . . he thinks he's upwardly socially mobile, but he hasn't got the attributes he's trying to emulate. He's regarded as something of a joke by his fellows.

I know he's a bastard, but that's too easy. I'm certainly very angry – but most of the time I just find him a *bore*. I do respect him in some sort of way.

I say 'we' did it, and other times 'he'. That's part of the conflict. In the early years when I felt that it wasn't only sex, it was my whole life that he had control over – that was when I really started feeling powerless. The conflict was about knowing it was wrong, knowing he was my father . . . and, at the same time, enjoying sex. And knowing that he'd love me if I did this. I felt guilt for a long time. I can now accept the fact that it *was* rape . . . but I still can't help feeling that I'm responsible . . . why didn't I get out, otherwise? And because I enjoyed it sometimes.

If I really face up to it, the guilt stems from two things: one, that I allowed it to go on, and, two, that I enjoyed it. And I don't know if I'll ever come to terms with that guilt . . . I really don't. It's *so* internalised, and *so* deep. Intellectually, I can accept everything, but emotionally I can't. There's a sense in which if you're conditioned to be exploited, you enjoy the power given to that exploited state.

Ever since then I've had problems with older men – the teachers and academics I've come into contact with. They try to get off with me – it's only in recent years that I've realised, with *absolute* clarity, that I'm putting out vibes. It's quite unconscious – but I must be doing something.

I had always accepted, without question, that men had absolute legitimacy. Their power was legitimate . . . and over the years, I've talked the trappings of feminism, but only in recent years realised that *that's* what it's about and that's caused a personal revolution for me. It's also meant that I'm much stronger than I was. And it was related to sexual power . . . for me, it ran through a whole series of patrons, thesis supervisors. There was one . . . he had dreamed about fucking his daughters . . . and he and I became friends. Then he started the same sorts of things that my father started doing to me. He used to feel me under the table when I was there for dinner. All that dirty man, furtive thing . . . a whole thing that men who were young in the 50s do – using sex – and such people were powerful referees for me.

I had a victory this year, because, having believed that way of behaving was acceptable, through my own insecurities . . . I had a victory in that I wrote to the latest one who started to do it to me, and said, No. Go away. Leave me alone. I don't want this.

I hate my body. One of my biggest battles is that for years I blamed anything that happened to me on my father. I'd say to myself, This is why you are a hopeless human being. Then a friend said to me, in terms of herself, that you can't go on blaming your parents for everything. At some point, you have to take responsibility for yourself. And I think that's really true . . . But I still do get angry when I think about it. I feel very intense about it and get all churned up inside. But it's not so much against him – maybe it should be – it's more, How could this happen to me? Why did this happen to me? But the family itself – I feel that the very structure was part of it all and what happened to me.

I haven't worked it out enough to know if it's this individual who's responsible. Like I used to think it was because my father was working class, that he didn't have the civilising restraint of the middle class. I know now that it's a cross-class thing, so I have no answers. Why did he do it? Because he was powerless? I used to try and say it to him: Don't you see what you've done to me? And he'd say, I've done nothing. I merely loved you. Maybe the truth would be: Because you're a woman, because you're accessible.

I see that what happened to me is only a step beyond what most women go through. The sexual element is there in lots of relationships between fathers and daughters . . . a lot of women have been through that kind of possessiveness: it's just sexual jealousy. So I want to know what happened, what peculiar things operated in my situation and for other women like me, that caused it to go that extra bit. I don't understand yet.

I used to tell people this story and it had a very confessional element in it. I feared being rejected so much I almost wanted it, and at the same time didn't want to be rejected. If they rejected me,

14

it was society's punishment; if they didn't, it only made me feel worse, because of the guilt. The expectation of rejection is the reason for the confessional element . . . deliberately putting myself down. But it was ambivalent: I really wanted the people I told to understand. And I'm still terrified that those people I told who tucked it away and don't want to talk about it, really think that ultimately the guilt is mine.

But it's all changing . . . because I've been thinking about it in trying to come to terms with my relationship to men in power; and also because I've had a lot of support from feminists that I've talked to, and become friends with. Most other people – even the older, closer friends – hear the confessional, and then that's it, it's never mentioned again. Whereas my feminist friends hear, and they talk about it . . . they raise it in the course of other conversations, it's part of their on-going relationship with me, it's not something that's a compartment of your life that's put away . . . and that's really good. I guess it's really acceptance, it's saying this is part of you, your experience as a woman. Over the years, I've got my head together and managed to survive . . . but there's always a sense in which I've known deep down that I had to really work through what happened to me . . . getting drunk and 'confessing' to someone wasn't enough. So doing that, the working through, and getting involved in feminism, have become one and the same process.

I'm not there yet, but it's much closer.

Jude's Story

I didn't see much of my father before I was thirteen. He was a businessman in Asia, so my mother and I lived for a long while with my grandmother – my mother's mother, that is.

When I was four we went to live with him, over there. I didn't like him much; he was a selfish and domineering man. He took my mother around a lot, and I was left alone often. Eventually I was sent to Australia, to live with my grandmother, which was a sort of extended household with other relatives as well.

My parents visited very infrequently. He came when I was nine, for a few days – that's my happiest memory of him. He was mad keen on movies and he seemed to take me everywhere with him in those days. We went to all the movies, to the beach; he bought me chocolates, talked to me about Charles Darwin and all sorts of things I hadn't heard of. I was fascinated, and really sorry when he left. We slept in the same bed – he told me stories, it was a great time. I cried and cried when he left.

My parents came back, with a baby sister, when I was thirteen, to set up a nuclear family, buy a house, all that. That's when the real oppression began, for me.

When they first came back and were staying in my grandmother's house, in places where anyone could have walked in and seen us, he started to fondle me. I remember my grandmother saying things like, 'Tom, you shouldn't . . . ' I have a vague memory that she rebuked his actions behind his back to my mother. I was fairly physically mature by then – I looked more like a woman than a girl.

He would say things like, 'Kiss me properly on the mouth. Give me a proper kiss' . . . giving me many hugs. I *hated* giving him proper kisses. I hated it. Your Freudians try to tell me that I really liked it, I really wanted him, and that angers me when I think of the hate in me . . . at those moments especially.

When we got our nuclear house . . . it was an awful way to live because whenever he was in the house I felt I had to keep moving from room to room. I felt I couldn't stay at whatever I was doing. If I was writing or listening to something, or reading a book, if I heard him coming, I'd get up and take my book or whatever it was with me and settle down somewhere else, like the hallway, then I'd hear him coming and go to the bedroom. I was forever moving because I knew when he found me it meant the fucking come-on and a 'proper kiss', as he called it.

It all went on for about seven years, because I left home when I was twenty.

There were still outings to the movies, much less, but masses and masses of chores were put on me as well. He was the full capitalist bastard, I guess. He felt, I think, that he owned *every*thing – he owned my mother, he owned me. He could ask anything of us because we were his possessions. Mum and I always fitted in with him and his life – that was the pattern. He *never* fitted in with anything we might want to do.

He used to do other things. He used to tickle me; go for my tummy-button with his finger through my clothes as he walked past. He was very accurate – and hard. When we had these tickling sessions I used to scream to Mum for help. I'd say, 'Help, help, Mum – I'm going to wet my pants', but I couldn't get away from him – you know how it is when you're giggling hysterically. But she'd say, 'It's between you and Daddy, dear. I'm not interfering.'

He used to play games, like hiding my six-guns (I loved playing cowboys) somewhere on his body, and I'd have to feel him all over to find them. He'd even do it in front of my grandmother. And of course sometimes I'd grab his penis – I didn't know what it was really – and he'd laugh, 'Oh, no, no, dear, that's not it!' I'm amazed now at how open he was, how he used these really devious ways to get me to feel him up.

He even stopped me from doing my homework. They called me dumb anyway. If I was doing a project for school, he'd pull me away from the table, slap a paint brush in my hand and make me help with painting the house.

He wanted a companion to play golf with, so he paid for my lessons and after that I *had* to play golf with him on Sundays. Mum would say, 'Keep him company, dear. If you keep Daddy happy, the family'll stay happy. And family harmony is very important.' And I'd say, 'But I hate him. I hate him! I want you to know. I want everyone to know that I hate him.' And she'd say, 'Oh, you don't really, dear. He's a wonderful provider. He's a good man. You know you don't hate him really.' And that's the way it went on.

I know it's a popular theory that the mother colludes – I really feel it's accurate. A counsellor that I saw years and years later, told me that I made a deal with my mother – the biggest deal of my life – to let my father be like this, so that I'd get her love. I kind of agree with that, except that I think there's another factor. I feel I had no choice. What else was I to do? I wasn't sure she loved me, because she'd left me for so long.

He had businesses which needed servicing – he was always going off in the car on work. I'd often have to go with him. I was everything: a friend, someone to do the work, someone for him to play with, someone for him to bawl out when he felt like it. I always think I was married, then, in a way, because my life was not my own.

The sex part was the worst part of being ordered around. I was scared of him – I couldn't state what I wanted to do. He'd trivialise any interest of mine – listening to Elvis, any television show I wanted to watch, when I wanted to read a book. The only important things were things he agreed with.

He used to call me in to discuss actresses on TV – their physical attributes. Like 'Hasn't she got a lovely mouth?' or 'Look at *her* beautiful eyes' or 'Isn't she sexy?' I was always being made to share in his appreciation of women – the way you imagine a father might call a son in, I suppose.

He used to regularly call me a fool . . . and he had a special name for me, which he was so proud of because he'd made it up, and that was Bugwit – inferring that I had the wit of a bug. That got shortened to Buggie and then to Gwit, and everybody used it. I was meant to appreciate the humour in it . . . so I used to laugh and tell him he was clever.

Anyway . . . I was pretty green, even when I was older. I didn't date men much; I didn't know about erections – I mean I sort of knew about them, but I never thought about it.

And so, what happened was that when I was nineteen, I smashed his car. He loved his car – I did too. I'd spend hours washing it and so on, and he used to let me drive it. Anyway, I had this crash, and I think that then he thought he had every right to violate me, because I'd smashed his car, and I was more in his debt than ever.

That weekend, he wanted me to sit on his lap while he was watching television. I still did that – it's incredible to me now – so I did it on this occasion. Then I wanted to get up because the kettle was boiling, and he wouldn't let me up. He clasped me round the waist, and I thought, 'Gee, this is odd! What's going on?' And then he started to tremble and shake, every part of him. I didn't recognise it as passion, but I knew something was pretty wrong. I forced myself up, and he shot up and went in one direction and I went in another. For some reason I followed him to check him out and I found him in the bedroom, doing something with a drawer, and I could see that his penis was erect in his trousers. And that stunned me. And suddenly I had the whole realisation of what had been going on for years. Somehow I'd been able to deny all that sexuality.

I mean . . . for example, as I got older, he and I used to tickle each other, instead of just him tickling me. I specially loved my back being tickled, slowly and gently. And he and I did that for years – and we'd talk about it – the technique, how we'd pick an area to miss, like a shoulder or something, so you were absolutely dying to have that area touched . . . then, really like a climax, you'd do it. Now, even today, it doesn't turn me on – if my lover does it to me, I appreciate it as a nice thing, but it's having my back tickled. I have no sexual arousal. I can still enjoy it, almost as much . . . but it just ain't sexual, you know. And that's even though I'm a lesbian, and my lovers are women.

So . . . the erection – well, after I saw that, I said nothing and did nothing until my mother came home. I got her alone, and said, 'Dad's just had an erection. He'd been cuddling me.' And she said, 'Oh, that's nothing, dear, that's been going on for years!' I really sort of shrieked: I said, 'What do you mean?' She said, 'Well, I think it was when you were about sixteen, and Daddy was giving you a cuddle, I saw that happen. And I just thought, "Well, Jude's a big girl now and Daddy's a man".'

And that's how she was able to ignore it! She also said not to say anything, not to take it any further, so I didn't because I always wanted to protect her. I wanted her love – that's pretty important. I was making some kind of bargain with her by letting them both use me, I guess.

Three weeks went past . . . then one day I was with him on one of the work trips to the shops and factories, and a manager complained about not having enough stock, and he said, 'Oh, those buggers at home won't do anything.' I was absolutely infuriated because I knew how much we did help him, we were always working for him – preparing things for the machines, counting the money . . . That night, he asked us to do some work, as usual . . . And my rage was so immense, I kind of yelled, 'Are you sure you want one of your buggers to help you?' He went into an immediate rage, which was typical of him, and said, 'How *dare* you talk to me like that!'

And then I did it. I said, 'How dare you go around having erections on me!' At which he jumped up and tore out of the room and went to water the garden. I followed him out . . . and he said all this stuff. He said, 'Dear, I've been wanting to talk to you about this for such a long time. I've wanted to offer you money, a thousand pounds if you'd go to bed with me . . . I'd send you on an overseas trip, if you would.' For him . . . to talk of giving money away . . . money was what he valued most. Everything was subordinate to that. So for him to be thinking of offering me money – that was the biggest sacrifice he could make.

I was stunned and shocked . . . and I called him abnormal and sick, and in no way was sympathetic, and in fact I was quietly triumphant. Because this god that my mother had insisted we both put on a pedestal, had finally crashed, and *I'd* brought him down! It was a great moment of revenge actually, because of all the hate . . . and never being able to get at him, ever. And there he was, undone. It was fantastic.

So then I told my mother. She became very angry with him, because she said I was the 'other woman'. As if she didn't know all along! It's really odd. The denial that must have been going on for her too! She was feeling cheated . . . and then she told me that he had for *years* not bothered about her orgasms.

19

You see, he'd told me, out in the confession scene, that he'd been dreaming of making love to me, and that then he'd wake up and make love to my mother. Which explained to her, then, what had been happening, why he'd wake up at 2.30 in the morning, roll over, take her, and go back to sleep again. And she of course had not come, had no stimulation or anything. She'd believed some hocus-pocus reason he gave her about not being able to hold his erection any more, and she said, 'I always thought it was that! I had no idea he was dreaming of you!' She said that he'd been a great lover when they were younger and then there'd been this change.

There was so much bitterness . . . they stopped communicating altogether. I was the messenger. They'd give me messages for each other, and there I was, running between them, taking messages. I did it, thinking they'd eventually start talking. There was she, sitting in bed, drinking sherry and chain-smoking, and him making his own meals . . . and I was the only one anyone would talk to.

I remember he talked a lot about sex then – even though I was disgusted by it all and he was disgusted by himself, he'd start up these conversations about how well it was all designed: how the vagina was so perfect for the penis to go into, and the penis was such a perfect shape for the vagina, and who could have designed it better, and the fact that it had evolved this way seemed miraculous . . . and on and on it would go.

Being intimidated still – even in my victory I hadn't lost that! – I'd say Yes, Dad, and No, Dad, and try to change the subject. But it seemed that he was giving vent, verbally, to all kinds of things. He'd say he'd make love to me in any way he could, and this was one way of doing it, with words, by instructing in sex. Even today, if he says he's heard a good joke, which means a dirty one, he'll tell it to my mother, or whoever's around, and I can never raise a laugh. I feel that he's intruding still. I can't *bear* to talk about sex with him, in any way, shape, or form. Because I think he's getting off on it; I'm being used – I can't get rid of that feeling.

Anyway, this going backward and forward went on – I was running backwards and forwards with accusations and defences about their past sexual histories, and it went on and on. Finally, I couldn't stand it any more – I felt as if the whole world was crazy, as if I was simply falling apart . . . so I went to a phone box and looked up a psychologist in the pink pages (I chose a woman), and took myself down there the very next morning.

I'd told my auntie and she said that I must leave home, so when the pyschologist said, 'You know what you must do, don't you?' I

20

plucked that out of the air and said that I must leave home. She said Yes!, thinking that I'd come to that conclusion for myself; and she also said that only by my leaving home would my parents come back together, and that one day they would thank me.

Well, they never have! They've always blamed me for disrupting the home; that I'm the black sheep, that I ran out when they needed me most. I can't imagine, now, when they thought I was going to leave home, in the normal course of events. I've always had all this stuff laid on me.

I wanted to live alone, and even arranged for a room, but my grandmother insisted that I go to live with her. When I told her what had happened, she had a terrible mental blackout . . . she couldn't remember *anything* for two days, not even how to get around her own house. The doctors said she must never be worried like that again. So in subsequent years, when abuse has been hurled at me by my family, the very one who would have stood up for me, can't.

My cousin and I think that the same thing may have happened to my grandmother. Her father was an alcoholic; her mother had lots and lots of children, so she was always pregnant and tired. My grandmother used to look after her father when he came home drunk. She used to talk about how she'd put him to bed, and he'd ask her to sing and she'd sing him to sleep. We think that that drunk man, coming home to his tired wife, using his eldest daughter like that, might well have done things . . . that's why her mind did that incredible flip, perhaps. Possibly, she really doesn't remember, she's repressed it, but to have her favourite granddaughter go through the same thing was too much to bear.

Round when I left home this first time, he was so frustrated – by wanting me, or something – that he became physically violent, started hitting me, or making gestures to do so. Now it was out in the open, he'd talk about boys I went out with, asking what did so-and-so do to you on the porch last night. He asked me to let him know when . . . I had my first . . . fuck . . . he wanted to know about it. He said that no matter how far off in the future, I must remember to come and tell him when it happened.

After I moved, he came to see me, to tell me that my mother had gone to pieces; and also that he'd debased himself in front of me, but now he was cured, and to please come home for your mother's sake! And I sort of thought, if he is cured . . . if my mother is in a bad way . . . I'll give him a chance. So I went home . . .

He always had lots of money around the house because of the

21

nature of his business, and he suddenly decided that he needed a secret place for his money. So he measured up this panel, inside the cupboard, between my sister's room and the bathroom. He was even measuring on the wall, in the bathroom one night – the opposite side of the wall from where the panel was to be . . . it was all so blatant, and yet it never occurred to me . . .

So then, one night – my mother was out – I ran a bath and asked him if he wanted it first and he was terribly, terribly nice and said that I could have the first one – which made me suspicious. You see, he was such a selfish man that whenever he was nice, you could see he was after something. But I thought, Oh, well, he says he's changed . . . so I went off to have the first bath. As I undressed, I felt I wasn't alone. I felt that nothing of what I was doing was private. I felt insane! It was ludicrous, because I *was* alone – but I kept looking at the door and the window. I thought, You're going off your head! So I made myself get undressed and get in the bath – and almost to prove to myself that I was alone, I masturbated, which I only ever did in the bathroom because it was the only place I felt private. I did it to prove to myself that the notion, or feeling, that I was being watched, was ludicrous.

As I was drying myself, I heard these heavy footsteps running through the house – a sort of instinct put me on guard, and I went to find him. He was sitting in bed, 'reading' a book, upside down! and he had this *glazed* expression on his face – I'd never seen an expression like it before, I haven't seen one since. His eyes were just . . . glazed . . . that's the only word I can use. And full of gratitude . . . some sort of admiration . . . he was looking at me as though I was some sort of divine creature. It was really spooky.

So then I realised . . . I went and investigated my sister's bedroom and found his so-called secret panel for the money, and there were two pinpricks where you could stand and look directly at the bath. I realised that that entire bit of intuition I'd had about being watched was true . . . I can't tell you how I felt about being watched . . . there are just no words.

So . . . when my mother came home, I showed her the 'secret panel'. And she wouldn't believe it had been deliberate, and she said not to mention it to him. I think she said she'd think about it. And I deferred to her again.

The next day was Sunday: we didn't get up early usually. But I did that day, and he was up before me. He was puttying up the eye-holes, on the bathroom side of the wall. So openly! Such an admission of guilt! And . . . he just handed me . . . five pounds or whatever . . . just handed it to me. I said, 'I don't want this.' And he had that same glazed look on his face, like gratitude . . . I don't know how else to explain it. And he said, 'Keep it.'

So, I went back to the psychologist, and told her I must go, and this time go for good. I was just totally sick of it – the fact that he wasn't 'cured' as he put it, was the end for me. I couldn't wait around for him to 'be cured'; I couldn't 'help' him be cured . . . I just had to run. He kept asking why I was going, and I'd just say, 'I've had enough. I've got to go.' I couldn't refer to it.

So I left again, went to my grandmother's again. I was about twenty then. And I kept it bottled up inside me, for several years. Until one day, I was setting up house with a friend, and we needed a fridge – so I went home and asked for money for a fridge. I felt I deserved something after all those years, working for him . . . I felt so ripped off . . . and he said No. It developed into a flaming row, and I mentioned the holes in the bathroom wall – he went crimson in the face. He yelled . . . 'Get out! That subject is not to be mentioned – in this house.'

I think he said 'in this house' because he knew I'd told people. I'd told some friends and the family doctor. It could have got back to him through the family doctor. The doctor, by the way, advised me to stay home; that it was a thing that 'happened'; that it happened all the time in different parts of the world; that it always had; not to worry about it; even that a baby produced by a father and daughter union would be OK – the notion that it would be retarded or something had been proved to be ill-founded. He and Dad got on quite well – they were kind of friends – so it's on the cards he told him.

And that's the story.

It's interesting that now, when this is becoming a publicised subject, I read an article of yours about how widespread it is and that ordinary average family men do it – and that made me feel incredibly depressed, and sorry for myself, and even more ripped off than I'd felt before – because somehow there was a safeness about the fact that my father might have been a bit odd, or a bit unusual – somehow that thought was comforting.

We didn't talk for ten years or so. You know – terrible embarrassment on Christmas Day, because everyone knew that Dad and I didn't get on. We do talk now – we even have a few things in common, a little bit – but I find him rather boring. He generalises wildly, says stupid things. He's pathetic in the things he finds amusing – and how he wants other people to be amused by him.

I mostly remember the hate; how I'd get to bursting point – walking around and around the house thinking, I'll kill him! And the explosive feeling – the bursting point – when I told my mother. And her shock and dismay – those are the things I remember strongly.

Kim's Story

My mother and father separated when I was about seven. She was pretty much alone for about three years and then she met this man and started going out. He was living with us quite soon after that – he had his own place somewhere, but he always seemed to be with us. Then he got a job right across the country – my mother and I packed up and moved to be with him.

I was the only child. I remember when they first met, I must have thought he was pretty hot stuff too – because he used to spend a lot of time sitting and chatting with me and I was extremely flattered by all of that. I think it was just because it was a man who took notice of me – I hadn't had a father-figure for a long while. At the beginning there was a lot of friendship and affection, I suppose, between him and me.

I desperately wanted a father. I wanted them to get married, so I could have a father. He let me talk – most adults didn't give me that feeling that they cared about what I had to say. But now I don't actually think it was a lot to do with me – he started talking to me as a way of getting in with my mother.

The relationship was a big thing for both of them I think. It was very sexual – passionate, I suppose. He sort of kept her on edge by hinting at other women all the time. I think that was very confusing for my mother because I'm sure it was her first really satisfying sexual relationship, and she gave herself to it utterly.

It all started with me when I was ten, before we even moved. It went on for two years.

The first incident I remember was before going to school one day. My mother left home about eight o'clock – she was a teacher then – and I didn't leave till about eight-thirty. When he was around, he always seemed to be there in the morning as well.

This time was one of those instances when I sat on his knee while he was reading me a story – and then he started rubbing his hand over my clothes, round my crotch. I was a bit shocked; it felt strange. You know – when men are in that situation they get all sort of short-breathed and so on, so as a kid, I thought, What's wrong with him? What's going on? – and I had a sense of all those furtive things.

You see, he was doing that to me, and at the same time going on reading the story – so on the one hand he's pretending there's nothing going on, and you in a way have to pretend nothing's going on, though something is. What can you say about it? And then I got up and went to school.

Somehow, we progressed from that day to lying in bed together – now how it came to that point I can't remember, but I think it only happened before we moved, so it was in the early days. At that stage of lying in bed, he used to try and penetrate and I'd say, No, no, you're too big – and he either respected that or thought he'd get to do it anyway, because he didn't force it.

It was only much much later that I had a desire to talk to people about it and things like that – when I started to feel I couldn't stop it . . . I do recall trying to raise it with my mother one day – that one morning he had done this funny thing and felt me over my clothes – and she just immediately got almost hysterical and said, 'If ever this happens again tell me straight away – it mustn't mustn't mustn't happen.' And, of course, by then it had already progressed way past that point. I simply couldn't tell her. I was afraid of her wrath. I guess I was afraid of lying too – my mother always said that she could always tell when I was lying – so lying did not sit at all comfortably between me and my mother: we were really quite close.

I felt if I told her the rest, she would be angry and disgusted – which is ultimately what did happen. Her reaction was all of those things I'd been afraid of. But by then I was so relieved that she knew, that the bad things, like her disappointment in me, were pale by comparison.

I adored my mother, particularly in those years after my father left: there are photos of me looking up at her with adoration. This was from when I was five or so, on up – so upsetting her was a very big thing to me.

I was aware of her being happy with him, and of the sexuality of their relationship. They frolicked a lot in front of me – I think she thought it was good and healthy for me to see a happy relationship. So when she found out, she took all that openness on herself and saw herself as being partly responsible. I think it was a really amazing thing for her to have had a relationship like that – a fully sexual joy – as a single 'divorcee', in the 50s, and I wish she could see it like that now.

What I next remember was after we moved – this sexual stuff had become quite oppressive for me. He'd use it as a punishment, like he'd come home when I was there after school, before my mother came home, and it meant he could have a bit of a play with me. I would rush home and try to grab my bike to go and play with friends, and he'd get really stroppy and tell me I had to go to the bedroom and wait for him. Then he'd come in and masturbate into a hanky in front of me, into which I'd dry-retch, which meant it was finished and then I could go.

Also, he'd come into my room at night, saying he wanted to read stories to me, which meant basically he wanted to masturbate me. That's when I remember feeling the real stress. I didn't want him to come in, but if I said I didn't, my mother would want to know why. It was sort of like she really knew, and she did sort of know, but I couldn't tell her and she didn't want to ask. That sense was always there when he and I were alone.

And so I would lie in the bed, with him reading a story, and trying at the same time to put his hand in the bed, or putting his hands in the bed, and me lying with my legs crossed as tight as I could hold them, trying to fight it off – but ultimately having my clitoris manipulated so that it did start to turn me on, and always giving in and always coming. So I was caught in that total dilemma of, I don't want this to happen and then I do want it, over and over again, and trying to fight it off, and getting into it. I was trying to fight off an adult man who had all this sexual experience, and I knew nothing of what you do, or how you say No, or whatever.

Sometimes it seemed like it happened all the time; other times he'd leave me alone for a few days, or there wouldn't be the opportunity – it's hard to recall clearly.

He'd also take me for drives in the car, going to pick something up, and it would be quite pleasant for a while, then on the way back he'd want to stop and have a bit of a feel, and I would be clinging to the door waiting to jump out, and argue with him and say, 'No, no, we have to go home. Mum'll be expecting us.' And all the time thinking, Why did you come out here? Did you really think it would be any different? You knew he'd do it again. So I felt responsible for it in a funny kind of way.

It all started around age ten, at the period of my life when I would normally have started masturbating, but someone else did it for me. So when I did start masturbating around twelve or thirteen, I was riddled by guilt that I had been taught all this stuff, and I had no sense of it having come from within me, and so I would again do the thing of battling with myself about wanting to do it and not wanting to do it. I know that's what lots of kids go through anyway, but for me it was a duplication of the scene with him, about I mustn't do this – then doing it anyway, and feeling both pleased and disappointed.

So it was mainly him masturbating me, to orgasm, and these other scenes of him making me watch him masturbate.

The only other 'grim' incident – and it's the only one that has carried on into my adult life, that I'm aware of – was one morning when I went into the bedroom to tell him that breakfast was ready: he grabbed me and pulled me over and pulled my pyjama pants down and started licking my cunt. He said that that's what he'd done to my mother the night before, and she'd done it to him, too – and all I could envisage was this sperm coming out of his penis like I'd seen it, which made me sick to think of. I was shocked and horrified. I remember being amazed at my mother and wondering why anyone would want to do that – having absolutely no understanding of why anyone would kiss genitals – and it made me feel really shocked at my mother. I thought that it was really going a bit far . . . It's taken me years and years to cope with sucking my lover's penis, whereas I love it being done to me.

His masturbating in front of me often felt like a form of punishment – there was aggression in it – and I thought of the semen as yucky, smelly. So that incident really stayed with me. I don't recall any pleasure out of what he did; it was what he said that stuck.

I don't understand why I couldn't say No. I mean, what on earth could he have done in mid-erection or mid-ejaculation, if I'd run out of the room? But I felt compelled to stay. I think I always had the fear that if I told my mother, all he had to do was deny it, and then I'd have become a total fool and I'd certainly never have got out of the situation.

He used to use 'It's our little secret', which is very seductive. He'd say, 'You're a big girl now: you can share a secret with a grown man' – which was flattering in a way. I don't think he thought I'd ever tell her – my passivity in the whole thing is really confusing to me. That's why it got so difficult – how could I tell my mother when I'd let it go on for so long? And he knew that.

I didn't ever tell my mother. She found out.

We moved again – he got another job in another city – and we lived in a house with a big yard at the back. One day I had to get

27

something from a trunk in a shed at the end of the garden; he came too, putting me on his shoulders, jogging down the yard, and it was all very jovial. Then as we neared the shed, I thought, Uh, oh, here we go . . ! so I decided to get the stuff as quickly as I could, so I could get out. Often he would start to feel me up and I would try to continue doing whatever I was doing, like listening to the story. So, this time, I was bending over the trunk, and he came up behind me and put his hand in my pants. And my mother walked in. Everything went into total freeze.

Then she told me to go out, and they talked a bit. I don't know what was said – then she came and asked me what he was doing. She asked if it had happened before and I said Yes. So she asked me why I hadn't told her and I told her it was because I thought she'd be angry. And then she just cried – for about three days. And I used to sit around while she cried – just be with her.

We left within a week – right back across the country, to home. I was so sick of that moving around. I don't remember what happened between them – there must have been a shock-horror scene, but I have no memory of it.

I saw him once again, when I was about fifteen. I saw him turn the corner and come down the street and I went utterly hysterical and rushed into my mother and said, 'Johnny's coming! Johnny's coming! Don't let him in. Please, please, don't let him in!' But she didn't, of course. I think she was just as nervous as I was. But we never talked about that, either.

When she cried for three days, I was *relieved*. I was aware that I'd hurt her, and I didn't know what to do about all that . . . but I was so relieved it was over, it was finished, I didn't have to fight it any more, I didn't have to fight, I didn't have to think of reasons why I didn't want him to do it, or excuses to get around it or out of it. I mean, I could go home and it would be easy. That's all I thought.

When we got back to Sydney I spent as much time as I could with my grandmother, whom I loved desperately. My mother was unemployed for several months – that on top of this disastrous relationship with a guy who turned out to be a child molester, made her pretty depressed for quite a long time. So I spent the time with my grandmother, because I wanted to be a kid again; I wanted to be healed myself. I couldn't really cope with the heartbreak I'd caused my mother – that's a lot of responsibility for a kid – so I went for my own healing for a while.

My mother tells me that all through my early teens, if she did get close to a man at all, like him putting his arm around her, I'd find some pretext to slip between them and break it up. I can't recall it at all, but she tells me I was obviously determined that it wasn't going to happen again.

I never went through that heavy boy-crazy stage at eleven, twelve, thirteen. I just didn't want to know about boys. I was sixteen or seventeen before any of that happened for me. I think there was a fear that I had all this sexual knowledge, and when I finally went to bed with a man, he would 'know'.

I once told some girlfriends a story about a 'friend' of mine who was in my situation and they were so shocked, I certainly didn't mention it any more. Only dirty girls did something like that!

It was when I was twenty or so, and in love, I told the man I eventually married – at that stage when you tell your deepest darkest secrets, as part of getting to know each other. And that was certainly mine! So that was eight years and I'd never told anybody. He told mutual stories of being approached by men when he was a boy, so my telling him felt OK – he certainly didn't think I was dirty.

When I was sixteen or so, my mother and I were talking about sex, and she told me it was often better not to talk to other people about what you did in bed, because what two people did together in bed was *never* wrong or dirty, if it's what they both wanted to do. Which I think's quite an amazing piece of information for a mother to impart, especially at that time. I sort of knew it was true because I had experienced the pleasure part of it. I think she was trying to let me know that the pleasure was good in itself.

But at the same time, my mother seemed absolutely terrified of me and my sexuality all during my teens. When I did first fuck, at eighteen or so, I didn't feel a thing. Of course, I was really confused because I had all this knowledge that there is meant to be something more that happens, but I couldn't tell him that because I was meant to be a virgin. He thought I was 'insatiable' because I was trying to find that pleasure again. I loved the lying in bed, naked; the skin-to-skin sensation really turned me on. I totally enjoyed that part of it.

When I first fucked with Patrick, the man I married, it was after weeks and weeks of getting closer and closer – then we did it and it wasn't much at all. Afterwards, we went to a party – and realised we didn't want to be there, we wanted to be in bed – so we went home and made love for weeks. It was fantastic. I remember, after the second or third time, I cried – and it was with relief! Here was someone who was meeting that pleasure need in me and it was all right. It could happen. I cried and cried. It was very healing.

I think I've come out of it all pretty well with very minor scrapes compared with what I could have come out with. And it very obviously is something to do with pleasure – I've been able to hold on to that – pleasure doesn't have to lead to a disastrous situation, or come out of one.

I'd like to know about the parts I can't remember. That's why I talk to people, because I think I might remember a bit more. My mother doesn't want to talk about it at all, whereas I think it helps me sort out stuff that might still be going on in my life. I can't find a way to talk to her that means she doesn't have to take blame.

I see her as a woman with real passion who is game to act on it, but she feels like a fool. Being a divorcee in the 50s, and having this experience, followed later (after I left home) by another marriage that failed, means that she feels a fool, as though the way she lived her life wasn't good for me. Whereas I really admire her ability to love. I think that her strength to say life can be OK, it doesn't have to be terrible, is much of what has helped me be where I am today . . . to feel I'm coping and optimistic about life.

Ann's Story

I was adopted at the age of two. My adoptive parents had three natural sons, who were then about nine, seven and three. My parents adopted another girl after me – she was five or six years younger again. After that, they adopted a boy, so he must be two or three years younger than her.

The youngest of my parents' natural sons, Billy, was the one who raped me. He grew up to be a normal, healthy, strapping young man, whereas I was very small and I stayed small. [As a woman of twenty-three, Ann is about four feet nine inches in height, with an extremely slight figure. Her build is similar to that of a slim ten to twelve-year-old girl.] So my size put me at a physical disadvantage for a start. It could have been either of the other brothers – they were all so much bigger than I was. The second eldest brother did the same to my little sister, and Billy did as well – so she was molested by two of them.

It went on for ages and ages: years, in fact. I think it started when I was about nine – around third grade, going on to fourth grade. That first time was just curious: he showed me his dick and wanted to look at me. I guess I was curious: I had never seen a penis before. I thought it was a great big sore that he had between his legs. It

30

looked to me as though an accident or something really bad had happened to him. Like it was a deformity to me, and I felt really really sick. I can't really remember clearly if he looked at me much or if he touched me – because I just remember this thing he had and feeling sick. I can't remember how it changed from that first time, to the raping. It went on for so long that when things actually happened isn't very clear to me, like exactly what age they happened and so on.

You see, my mother had to look after all of us, do all the caring. My mother had been brought up with that whole attitude that boys are so much better than girls; that women and girls aren't any good . . . and she passed that on, see? My father never did anything: he didn't rape me or bash me, but he didn't defend me, either. He was just there. So somehow, the whole family structure was set up to let Billy get away with screwing me, and with Alec and Billy screwing my sister. They'd already been conditioned at home. They must have learnt about the screwing at school, because they certainly didn't learn that at home. We weren't told anything about sex at home.

So screwing, for him, was a power: it just became something he did to me, just to assert himself over me. It was pure force. When he first showed me his prick, it wasn't all that big, and he mostly used to touch me and kiss me after that. But later on – I think it was about a year or so – I'm not really sure – he showed it to me again and it was much bigger. That was when he started trying to put it into me. Before that he used to kiss me and stuff like that – and he'd touch my breasts. If I didn't let him do it – have a feel or a kiss – he'd go to my mother and make up lies about me or plant money in my room and pretend to 'find' it by accident, and of course I'd get into trouble. My mother never stopped to consider how it was that he always 'found' the money in the right place without even searching for it. When I made that point to her once she just got scornful. And so of course, whenever Billy stole money from our parents it was always I who got the blame.

Well, then he started trying to put his penis into me . . . and that was really painful. I don't know how far he got it into me. It was just intense pain . . . and there was a lot of bleeding. It was always like that . . . always pain and bleeding.

Once, when my mother was out, he tried to get me to suck him off. I started screaming and carrying on. I thought I was going to be ill . . . I didn't want the bloody thing in my mouth. He started to bash into me, but he didn't make me do it. I felt so ill. And it had a smell . . . the sight or smell of it would make me start to feel literally ill. It's strange, but I always associate the smell of a man's penis with death! I always feel really sick and think about dying. I always think about women in the news who have died horrible deaths at the hands of men, you know when they get raped and murdered.

The actual screwing was usually when my mother was out – and he was set to 'look after us': my sister and myself. It would happen in the bedroom or the lounge-room, or even other places. And it was often in the backyard or the cubbyhouse: it didn't matter who was home then.

Even when everyone was in the house, he would be doing things. I used to have to sleep in the hallway – on the floor, with my eiderdown around me – until my sister went to sleep. That was because we weren't allowed to talk to each other. That was when she was about five, and I was about eight, for years. It was because my mother didn't want us to talk. I still don't understand the point of that: she just didn't want us to have contact with each other.

The boys would have to walk past me to get to their room, and they would always kick me. I was kicked in the back like that, for years. And I was fairly accessible to Billy there, in the hallway. He always hassled me and touched me. I'd wake up to someone mauling me. I think now, that that part of me is still scared. I always like to sleep by myself, because part of me is still scared. I always like to sleep by myself, because I hate to wake up and feel someone touching me . . . I'd be sort of moaning and trying to piss him off. And so I tried to stay awake . . . I mean, I gave up trying to sleep at nights. I used to stay awake and just sort of wait . . . wait for him to come, so he couldn't do things when I was asleep.

Both Billy and the second eldest brother used to touch my sister. I never really saw it, but one of them would take her somewhere – the cubbyhouse or the bedroom – and I'd hear her crying and saying, 'No, don't do that. It hurts' . . . things like that. I don't know exactly what either of them did to her, because she and I never really talked about it. My mother sort of set us against each other. And I think we were trying to pretend that it wasn't happening to either of us, because we felt guilty and bad.

Billy used to make me watch him masturbate, too. One time, he made me go into the toilet and lie on the floor, while he pissed and shat all over me, on my stomach . . . [In the interview, which took place on a verandah, we turned the tape off here, and sat for ten minutes in silence, looking at the garden, at Ann's request.] That

32

was what he called 'initiation'. Maybe there was a boys' club at school, where they talked about things like that . . . I know that whenever he used to bring his school-mates home, they would be talking about sex all the time, even at around ten or eleven years old. They would tell each other all sorts of jokes and make all sorts of suggestions about girls and they would be passing dirty books to each other. I know they were bad because I found one of them that he had been hiding in the laundry at home and I read it because I was curious, see? It had all these rape scenes in it and the men were doing all these horrible things to these women, and having a good time doing it too.

I really think that if a male can even start thinking of things like that, when he's ten or eleven, then that just shows . . . how heavy it is . . . how easily they pick up those attitudes towards girls. I think that 'initiation' was part of his whole attitude . . . it was probably inevitable that it would happen.

Once when he was hassling me in the hallway . . . he must have had diarrhoea or something . . . and he wiped it on my eiderdown. All I felt was something wet, and I thought he must have ejaculated. But the next morning, I found what it was, and took it outside to wash it off and clean it. I didn't want my mother to think I'd done it, and I couldn't tell her that he'd done it. But, I mean . . . that's freaky, isn't it. Weird. To do a thing like that.

The same as the scene in the toilet. He was laughing when he did that. Like it was an hysterical joke. I was just sort of there. I was just lying there, letting it happen. I didn't know what to do. It never occurred to me to kick him in the nuts then . . . that just doesn't occur to young girls. I felt more like a *thing*, then, more like I had less to me in terms of feeling, than any other time. Just a *thing*. Then he shoved the loo paper at me, and said, 'Here. Wipe it off.'

There was money involved in all this. I got money from my brother for what he was doing to me. What I can say about that, is that it wouldn't have made any difference if he'd given me money or not. The control was there. I didn't feel like I had any say in it. He had the idea of money. It made him feel like he wasn't forcing me, I suppose. And I guess, later on, when I was taking whatever I could, it was my only way of making him pay for what he was doing to me. I spent the money on chips and stuff like that, at school; and I saved up a whole $2 once, because I was going to run away from home! But I told someone at school, and she told a bloody teacher, so that plan didn't go far!

But I did run away several times. The first time I ran away, was

33

when I was in fourth grade. It was just after he started really hassling me – the screwing part. I walked all the way from our suburb to town – about five miles. It was a really nice walk. I had the time of my life. It was the one time when I was really free. I walked alongside the lake, and it was lovely. No one stopped to ask what a little girl was doing out all alone. Not till I got to town, when this enormous policeman came up to me, and said, 'Hello, little girl. Have you run away from home? Where's your mother?' So they found out that I'd run away. I didn't tell them why. For a start, I wasn't *able* to explain what was going on. I wasn't sure, you see, in terms of morals and things like that, whether it was a really good thing or a bad thing – only that it *felt* bad – as in horrid. There are so many things that don't *feel* right but you're told that they are *good* for you and vice versa. And I didn't even tell the police that the immediate reason I ran away was to do with my mother.

When they took me home, my mother came out, gushing all over me. 'I've been so worried . . . I didn't know where you were . . . ' And before we were even inside the door, the police still only a few yards away, she was saying in my ear, 'Just you wait till you get inside . . . ' So, I got a hiding.

My mother was so concerned about reputation. She put so much energy into getting everyone to think she was a good woman, and a good mother . . . She was consumed by guilt, because she couldn't say, 'I don't like my child.' Not like you can now. I mean, at least that's recognised now – that it does happen. But she was full of guilt about how awful she was to us, me and my sister especially, and she was terribly concerned to cover it up.

I used to believe then, and I thought until recently, that I ran away because of things my mother did. But now I think that what happened was that the things she did tipped off the feelings in me about what he was doing . . . because a lot of my desire to get away was wanting to escape from him. She used to do quite minor things, that weren't of much consequence really, like bawling me out for losing a biro . . . and I sort of took that on, and ran away. I used to focus on these things that she did on the spur of the moment: I didn't focus on the things that he did. I think now that I can see that when I ran away, it was always after I had been really really pressured by my brother.

I ran away five or six times. Those running-away times were really nice, except for the fact that I couldn't get any food, and I didn't have any means of support, or anywhere to go. That was my problem: nowhere to go. Nowhere to go, where people would ask no questions. Adults are really scarey people when you're just a little kid, because they have so much power over you. It's almost as if they were never kids themselves – because they don't relate what's going on with you to anything that might have happened to them when they were kids. So I used to just sort of run away, knowing I'd get caught . . . but it was nice to be away for a while.

I wasn't this 'poor little girl' running away, because I felt really *good* about being by myself. I used to love looking at the lake, and the trees, and walking amongst all that nice grass: it was really good. And I didn't get molested on the streets. All those times I ran away, no strangers picked me up; nobody hassled me. When I should have been my most vulnerable, walking all the way to town that time, no one stopped me. That was all happening at home. It felt really safe out there – out on the streets, or out anywhere, away – but it didn't feel safe at home. My mother would say, 'You could be picked up by strangers! They'll cut you up into little pieces with razor blades . . . ' and she tried to fill me with horror stories. I sort of believed her, but there was this real contradiction about how she was telling me there was all this danger involved in being out there, but at the same time, I was feeling really good about being out there. So I guess that's why I didn't really take much notice of her. The only time I really got scared of that stranger stuff was when the family went away on holiday, and I was left alone in the house. That was when I was fifteen, and starting to work . . . and it was in that house at night that I felt really scared. I was too scared to be out in the street and too scared to be alone in the house. I didn't feel safe anywhere at night.

One time when I ran away, I stayed all night at the school: the primary school. I think it must have happened after the 'initiation' thing . . . because I remember that I didn't plan on running away. I just thought that I'd like to play by myself; I didn't want to go home after school. So I stayed under the trees, and then it got too late to go home because I would have gotten into trouble. So I snuck in a side door and spent ages dodging the cleaners, and when they left, I went to the sickroom where there was a bed and a blanket. I didn't have anything to eat, but there was plenty of water.

My eldest brother and my father came down to the school early the next morning: I tried to sneak out and miss them, but they found me. When they took me home, Billy went ape over me, doing the 'good brother' act. He cooked me eggs for breakfast, and I can remember hating them . . . trying to eat them and feeling absolutely sick.

35

I used to think a lot about going off into the hills . . . the hills you can see from anywhere in the town. I used to think I could start learning to kill my own food, and start finding things to eat in the bush, and things like that. I had it all worked out, except for the fear of things like thunderstorms . . . so I never did get it together to go into the hills. I still wonder what it would be like to do that . . . I used to plan how I'd make bows and arrows, to kill food, and to shoot anyone who came and tried to take me back. I thought all this, when I was a really little kid.

Anyway . . . the whole thing went on till I was in high school when my mother found out. She apparently found Billy and my sister doing something out the back, and she was questioning her when I came home. I saw Margaret making this pulling-off motion – like when guys pull themselves off – and I thought, 'Oh, God, she's telling her.' I was really scared. My mother sent Margaret inside and asked me what I had been doing with Billy – lots of questions. I said that he'd made me do it, and she asked me why I hadn't told her: she asked really angrily. And I just thought, Well, when I come to tell you one of them has bashed me up, I get a hiding for telling tales, so why would I come and tell you this? But I didn't say it. I didn't say anything.

She raved and ranted all night. I could hear her – all night. Finally, in the morning, she got my father up, and he said, 'OK – I'll give them a hiding, if that's what you want.' Up till then he hadn't done anything about it; not said anything; just nothing. I heard her say something about 'two little prostitutes', but she wouldn't let Margaret get punished because she said she was too young to know what it was all about. So Billy and I each got a hiding. As far as my mother was concerned, we were simply engaged in sexual activity, and I was getting paid for it. In her mind, there wasn't any force. She was brought up with the attitude that you don't get raped unless you ask for it; and only bad girls get raped. All that sort of thing.

There was another time when Billy brought home a young girl. He was obviously just using her for his status. Like he was a big man now because he had a girl. Apparently they were kissing on the lounge and so on. Well, mother got very agitated and when she spoke to me about it she kept raving on about this 'little tramp' who was 'using her son' and 'leading him on'. He wasn't at fault in *any* way because he was a boy. When I think about that girl and the look on her face I realise that she was just a frightened kid. I think she knew she was being used and so did I, although at the time I pretended to agree with my mother. But mother just couldn't see that her precious son was using the girl.

Anyway, as I was leaving for school the day after she found out about us, she stopped me by the gate, and said, 'Just as well you haven't started your periods yet, my girl. I don't keep pregnant girls in my house.'

Going to school that day . . . It was all too big. It was too horrid. After being told that . . . I mean, I hadn't been told anything about sex then. I thought if you kissed a guy on the mouth, he'd know you weren't a virgin, and he wouldn't want to marry you . . . crazy stuff. So, going to school that day, I felt ghastly. I felt like a real slut. It was all too big. I was in a daze because part of me couldn't cope with what mum said and what that meant. It was good when I got to school, I suppose, because I could pretend that nothing was wrong. I just blocked it all out and tried to concentrate on school.

After she found out, it stopped for a couple of months, and then it started again. Billy used to say, 'If you don't do what I want, I'll bash the shit out of you.' So, one time, I rushed to tell my mother, really scared and trying to be 'a good girl', like she'd told me to; and he came racing in, saying I was a liar, and she just said, 'Oh, you can't believe either of them. They're both liars.' Billy grabbed my arm while all this was going on: he tried to break it, and started bawling his eyes out, pretending he was all 'innocence', and that I was telling malicious lies about him. My father had to get him off me. So then I thought, 'Well, I'm not going to tell you in future. I just don't care.'

When I was at high school, I hit on the idea of carrying a pair of scissors, and when the boys teased me about being small, or about my feet [a slight deformity], or about not having a boyfriend, I used to try and stab them in the nuts. Looking back at that, it seems that it's how I tried to get my anger out. I never actually got one of them, but there were some close calls. Everyone was scared of me, because of my anger. I used to kick people, and throw things, and yell at teachers. The boys didn't ever tell on me, about the scissors. I think they didn't want anyone to know that a little girl could get the better of them!

I came on the idea because I saw a boy at school who'd been hit in the nuts by one of his friends. He was sitting on the ground screaming and crying and holding himself, in great pain . . . so that probably helped me realise how I could get back at them. I figured it hurt a lot to get them in the nuts.

At school, there was this pressure from the boys . . . about sex and things. I'd hear them call girls 'cunts' and using all that language of how vile they really thought women were. There was still all this crap about opening doors for women and girls and how girls couldn't fight and that they should be treated like china dolls. It only made the boys despise girls more, not that *their* role models were anything to emulate. Even despite what happened to me, I am still glad that I was born female. I wouldn't be a boy for anything. I don't think I could live with myself if I was. When I was a little girl, I was in danger at home – from my brother; and when I went to school, I, with every other girl, learned how much the boys really despised us, and when I got older and went to work I heard then, what men thought of us. They just thought women were shit. Good fucks, maybe – and good for cleaning up their houses – but as for respecting us as human beings, well, they didn't. The worst part about it was that it seemed to come so natural to them. And I never could figure out what we had done to them. We didn't rape them and use their bodies. We didn't use them to clean up our messes. Sometimes, the hatred and contempt was very subtle, and other times, not so subtle. I don't think I could bear letting a man screw me, knowing that he is going to go to the pub or work to his mates and talk about the good screws that they had with so and so. And then coming home to me with a smile on his face and pretending that he loved me – or liked me, even.

I also learned at a fairly young age to be careful of doing anything that might offend men and give them an excuse to rape me. Not that it made any difference, mind you. Girls weren't supposed to swear or wear the 'wrong' clothes. We weren't supposed to walk the streets alone or talk to men or smile at them or get angry at them when they leered at us on the street. I would have to just ignore them and walk with my eyes in front and hope to goodness that it didn't go any further than a leer or an obscenity, as if that wasn't bad enough. And after all that, it didn't make any difference anyway, as I realised afterwards, because it seems that most men have already planned what they are going to do anyway. My brother planned his rapes. He didn't get carried away on the spur of the moment, nor did I encourage him with the 'wrong' clothes or stuff like that. No, he had decided all along what he was going to do to me. And that's how it is with men. The conceptions about where you're safe are really misconceptions: they're not true. You're not safe at home, and you're not safe with a boyfriend.

I started working when I was fifteen. The chance to leave home came when I was sixteen. One of the women I worked with wanted someone to live with her, to help look after her daughter. Since we worked shift hours, it meant that I could usually be home when she wasn't. So I seized the opportunity. There were various scenes and ups and downs with my parents, but I did it the very same day. I moved out! After I'd lived in the new house for a while the daughter told me that she was being molested by her grandfather, who also lived in the house. He was what I call a really smelly, dirty old man. Later, when I went away, and boarded with another family, it was happening again – this time the mother's boyfriend, and the girl was thirteen.

Things didn't work out at the first house. I was too irresponsible and mixed up to look after the girl properly so I moved from there to a hostel, and then to another house. I moved many times that year – people found my anger hard to cope with. After I left, I rang my father once, at work. And that was all. I'd got free of the whole lot of them. I saw my mother in the street once, and she saw me; but we both walked on past as if we'd never met each other. I saw my brothers once or twice too, but I always hid. Once, Billy pulled up in a Volkswagen alongside of me when I was walking home from work and tried to talk to me. Suddenly, it hit me. Here was the horrible stranger that I had always been warned about, sitting in a car, trying to talk to me – and I had been living with him for years! It was just the visual impact of him in a car and me on the street that made me realise how truly horrible he really was. Up till then I had always thought of him as my brother. I hated his guts, yes, but I hadn't really thought or let myself be really terrified of him or seen him in that way. And suddenly there he was – the evil wicked stranger. I just screamed and screamed at him and really got into realising what I had been living with. He just looked at me curiously as if he couldn't possibly know what I was screaming about and then shrugged his shoulders and drove off.

A few months after I left home, I told one of the women at work about what Billy had done to me. She told the supervisor, who came and talked to me about it and she was really wonderful. She was a strict Catholic, and yet she said things like, 'It wasn't your fault. You're not to blame. The money part wasn't either – you had no choice.' Which was the *first* time anyone had said anything like that. I think that her saying that saved me from doing something harmful to myself because I was so screwed up at the time, that if she had said something hurtful to me like I was bad, or something like that, then I think that I would have gone off the deep end sooner or later.

Around that time, my mother rang this supervisor and said that if I didn't come home, she'd have me charged with being exposed to moral danger. And this wonderful woman said to her, 'Look, Mrs Reid, if you cared about your daughter, she wouldn't have left home, and you wouldn't be saying things like this.' And she also pointed out to me that if my mother did carry through with this threat, I could tell people about Billy, and she'd run a mile, because family reputation was so important to her. Anyway . . . I didn't hear from her again. That was seven years ago.

I moved to Brisbane after a while, and lived in different parts of Queensland for five or six years. Then, last year, I came back here because I was told that I could get help for my feet – and arriving back was quite strange.

I went to the Women's Refuge, because I didn't have anywhere to go. The train arrived at four in the morning . . . and the door of the Refuge was opened by one of the women I used to work with! I really freaked out: I hadn't figured on meeting anyone that I used to know! So I just pretended that I didn't know her. I sat around for a day or two (it was the weekend), not talking, figuring I'd soon get out of there.

But all the women were talking to each other, and she finally got talking to me, and she said, 'It was a pity about Billy.' I said, 'What about him? What's happened?' She got all funny and a bit uncomfortable, and she said, 'Don't you know? You should ring your family.' But there was no way I was going to do that, so I got her to tell me. And she told me that he'd died – of a drug overdose.

I was so pleased, I laughed. It felt funny, but I was pleased. I spent about a week waiting to feel guilty about feeling pleased . . . but I didn't. I was glad. I even felt glad when I thought about the pain that junkies go through. And it meant that I started telling more people about the whole thing. His dying really enabled me to work through a lot more of it.

One evening, I was sitting there in the Refuge, and a table-top that was propped up on the mantelpiece fell on my head [laughter] . . . and I honestly thought that someone was trying to do something to me. And I realised that even from 'beyond', I couldn't be got at. I still didn't feel guilty. And I didn't even bother trying. I was still glad. It was like a fierce joy. I'd gotten revenge after all. So I felt stronger . . . I really felt that I was becoming a strong person.

I used to just wish and wish and wish and wish that he'd die. So I felt that I was partly responsible for him dying, because I wished it so hard. I used to feel guilty about that, and feel that it wasn't good to wish him dead . . . but it always came back . . . I still wished he'd die. I think I put pourri-pourri on him, as the aborigines say.

You see, I used to have these really intense killing fantasies where, in my mind, I would mutilate my brother by chopping off his dick; or burning his eyes out and chopping off his hands. Or I'd get a long pole and ram it as far up his bum as possible. Or I'd stake him out and watch him burn slowly to death. You name it, and I'd think of it. I'd imagine him screaming for help and pleading with me not to do it and I would just sit there calmly and smile at him and watch him suffer! I just couldn't kill the bastard enough! I think if he hadn't died when he did, he would probably have ended up raping his daughters when he got older if he ever had any.

I really think that retaliation on the girl's or mother's part is the only answer. Mothers and daughters should be able to kill or cripple or maim in some way these men and boys no matter who these men are, without any interference from the law. We didn't make these laws about rape and we are not covered by them. But we are victimised by the laws. Even if there were changes in the laws I doubt whether it would stop men from raping women and girls either in the family or on the street. The law can't stop something like that. It is only us that can. The women. We need women's vigilante groups who will go out and deal with these men because I don't think that these men understand anything else. I used to plead with my brother not to do those things to me. I used to try and tell him how I was feeling inside and it didn't make any difference with him. Yes, I am all for retaliatory violence. I don't think that men realise the hatred that builds up inside their victim's minds. I think that it's perfectly normal considering the pain and suffering and emotional, mental, and physical horror that we have had to put up with. A lot of women feel the same way as I do. We might hide it, but it is still there, deep down inside all of us.

Something that used to bother me a lot is the fact that I have always had rape fantasies. It was very confusing to me because when I was being raped I *loathed* it. I was sick, I was angry and it gave me nightmares and caused lots of problems inside me. But there were times when my brother would touch me and I enjoyed it. It wasn't that I wanted him to touch me. I wanted him to leave me alone. But I had no control over my own body anyway. He had control of that. I used to feel very bad about enjoying some of what he was doing to me. I felt as if I was worse than he was. Like I could no longer say that I was being raped. The thing is that our bodies are not machines. They can't just switch off because someone is abusing us. If someone is forcing himself on to you, you just can't control your reactions whether you are feeling pain, fear, pleasure or feeling sick. I just wasn't given any choice in the matter. So I don't see why I should feel bad any more. It just wasn't my fault.

Anyway I think that the rape fantasies are about being brought up at home and in the larger world on that whole notion of how women and girls *supposedly* like being treated. When I think about it I have mostly seen only images of women being dominated by men. It's everywhere – TV, books, movies. I never saw/was never shown any images of women fighting back and being strong, and when I was a girl at school I think some of my anger was about that. Not having a strong female role model who supported girls and other women.

Well, whenever I had these rape fantasies I would wonder what was wrong with me and why I was doing this to myself. I think in a way I was punishing myself. I know that when I think that people don't like me or I'm in some sort of trouble, that's when the fantasies become really strong. It's like I think that that's all I'm good for. For someone to use me. When I'm around people who are gentle and affectionate with me, my fantasies become gentle and caring. So rape fantasies are really just a reflection on a woman's conditioning in this society, I feel.

There's one other thing that I really want to talk about. When I left home and started telling people about it, everyone, even that nice supervisor woman, told me that I should go to a psychologist or a psychiatrist because 'you might not want to have anything to do with boys again'. I don't know what it was I was supposed to be cured of. My anger? That really pissed me off, and frightened me. It was really horrible because it meant that no one cared about *me*: about me relating to me. About how I felt about myself. Everyone wanted me to go to these experts – the medicine men – to get my head fixed up so that I'd be right for men again. Like a lamb being led to the slaughter.

I didn't feel safe with men, which wasn't only to do with my brother. It was also to do with how I'd seen men treating women generally. I didn't go anywhere near any experts, because I didn't want my head changed around to suit other people's ideals. My brother had already done that to my body. I didn't want my mind raped as well. They really drummed it home though; over and over: you must get 'cured', so that you can relate to men. People weren't listening to *me*. I didn't want *my* mind reorganised.

Anyone trying to help women get over this sort of stuff should *not* have that sort of attitude. I wanted to get over lots of it for *me* so that I'd feel good about *myself*, not in relation to *anybody* else. It's really ignoring and isolating, to say that you've got to learn to like men because of what happened to you. It's utterly ignoring the fact that the woman has been assaulted and raped. To say you should learn to like men again is ignoring the woman's feelings. It also stops women from feeling and caring for other women. Every single woman who gets raped either as a woman or girl (and I think that we make up a large percentage of the female population), has probably heard the sayings 'Not all men are like that' or 'You've just had a bad "experience" with men'. This sort of crap only helps to isolate us even more and to make us think that we are the only ones that this happened to. But I know that it's happened to lots of women and we should realise that these sayings are deceptions and ignore them and concentrate on looking after each other.

Another thing that pisses me off is the sob-stories about these 'poor' men who rape women or their daughters, or their sisters or whoever. It seems that I was expected to feel sorry for my brother because maybe he was having problems . . . . I think this is a con. It is just to divert me from my anger. My anger which I have every right to feel. I have lots of problems but I don't go around raping little boys, or men. Again, my feelings are being ignored.

People should help a woman in that position to like herself. It's herself that matters.

About a week ago, I rang up my sister after looking all over the place for her. I wanted to see if she was all right. She told me that my father was dying of cancer, and I'm not really affected one way or the other about that. I mean, he just stood or sat around and let these things happen to me. He didn't give a damn.

Anyway, when I asked my sister how she was affected by what the two brothers had done to her, she insisted that she hadn't been affected one bit. She said it in a real funny voice, deathly calm, and I got the shivers. I think that she is dealing with it by pretending not to be affected by it. I don't think that we shall get together to talk about it because there is just too much pain and anger between us. We used to take out on each other what the brothers were doing to us, because we couldn't fight them. So we did horrid things to each other instead. I think that Margaret will deal with her rapes when she finds someone safe to do it with. It certainly won't be me because as I said before we are not very close at all. It would only make matters worse for her.

Anyway, I suppose we each have to live our own lives. She will live hers in whatever way she can and I shall do the same.

Vera's Story

It happens in so many families and no one ever talks about it. I think it's changing now – more people do talk about it – but when it happened to me and in our family, no one talked about it for twenty years.

I'm thirty-eight now. I chose to live with my grandparents, my mother's family that was, from when I was three until I was five. I don't remember why, but I did. My grandfather used to interfere with me and I didn't ever say anything about it, not at that age.

But when I went back to my parents, and my grandparents came up on holiday, he tried to interfere with me again, and I scratched his face.

About four years later I ended up living with them again, because my father had died. From then until I was fifteen, he wouldn't talk to me, he wouldn't have anything to do with me. He was just a cranky old man. I think now that the molestation was what was behind it, but then I couldn't associate the two. I just knew he hated me, and he didn't hate my sister.

He also interfered with her – and she never told anyone. She was more compliant. She didn't scratch him or anything. Just last year she had a very bad breakdown, and she pins it mainly on what happened – what he did. She was disgusted by her husband . . . and couldn't . . . all that, you know.

There was also a very young cousin; when she was four, it was finally detected. My aunt found stains on her clothing, and when she asked the child where they came from, she told her, and the whole thing blew up. He wasn't actually penetrating – well, he didn't to me and I presume he didn't to the others – but I don't really know. I assume they were semen stains, not blood.

So then we tracked it back and there were at least two of my mother's generation, the aunts, at least two that we know of, and there were a further two that we suspect, but we couldn't find out because one was an alcoholic and the other had killed herself, eventually. They were his own children.

These are just the people that we know about – there were probably dozens that we don't know about.

Looking back on it, I was very lucky that I got off so lightly. But it appears that I was the only one, and that was because I stood up for myself. I can't remember that I objected all that much, except that one time I was very young – I just knew that it was something you didn't talk about, so I didn't tell anyone.

I can't remember exactly when it started, but I know I was very young – three or three and a half. The first time was in the toolshed that he had down the back. I was on the stool he used, for sitting at his workbench. It nearly always happened in the toolshed, or when we went out walking.

What he did was to pull my knickers down, to round my knees. He used to position me so that I couldn't see him. I would be doing something at the bench, and he would be standing behind – and he'd put his penis between my legs and he would hold me in that position. When he finally ejaculated, he would just wipe between my legs with his handkerchief, and that was it. I was never ever facing him; he was always behind me.

For a good ten or fifteen years, I blotted it out completely. I wouldn't think about it at all. But in later years, I've tried to remember what I felt. I can't remember anything erotic about it. It was a bloody nuisance.

I don't remember being scared of him – but I'd send my sister if I could, when we lived there later, if there was a message or something. I'd find reasons not to be with him. I think I turned on him when I did because I was a very headstrong, wilful child. If it was something I didn't want to go along with any longer, nobody forced me to do it.

When he was caught interfering with my niece, my aunt came to see me and asked if he'd molested me. I was very upset by that because I hadn't thought about it for years. I started to cry and I said Yes. We sat and talked about it: he had molested her too. I can't understand why she would let her child be alone with him. I never would have. But she did. So we discussed it briefly and that's all there was to it.

I did tell my mother when I left at fifteen, because my sister was still living there. But she didn't believe it. She was the eldest of seven children: there were brothers in between her and the four younger sisters. Maybe it didn't happen to her, only to the younger ones. In later years, when it all came out, I reminded her that I'd told her and asked her why she didn't do anything about it and she said that she thought we'd made it up. I said, 'Why would we make it up?' And she said that she didn't know. She obviously didn't want to think about it – didn't want to know. Her father – who'd want to think that of their parent? . . .

No one told my grandmother, when it all came out. She still

doesn't know. We thought she should be protected. She's a very moral old lady – very high morals – so we kept it from her. We thought it would be her undoing.

I used to have all these revenge thoughts when I was seventeen or eighteen. I used to think: I'll go back there and kill the bastard. I'll kill him with a knife. All that sort of thing . . . When I was nineteen, I did go back, and he was old and ill. I nursed him till he died. And I couldn't feel anything for him, except, You poor old bugger. You poor crazy old bugger. That was all.

After my aunt, I only talked to my husband about it, until I got into a consciousness-raising group. And that was very traumatic . . . because someone asked what he actually did, and I hadn't ever talked about that, so I became very upset, and angry with him, and cried a lot. My sister has had a bad breakdown. I've been overseas to see her recently, because she thought I was the only one she could talk to. And lots of stuff came out: it went on with her till she was thirteen. She told me how she got involved in various love affairs, from sixteen onwards, after she left their place. And how it was never the sexual thing she was interested in; it was simply needing someone to love her for what she was.

She'd obviously brooded about it. It had happened from when she was four, until she was thirteen . . . that's awful, isn't it? That's nine years – and at thirteen you're not a child any more. She didn't ever tell anyone.

She couldn't really bring herself to discuss it, even with me. She could only say it was terrible, and cry and cry and cry. About how terrible it made her feel. She was obviously more deeply affected than I was; it went on so much longer. She couldn't ever bring herself to refuse, or find out how to say No.

With one of the aunts, it went on until she was fourteen, when she began to menstruate. Then he was very kind and told her what was happening and that they couldn't do it any more, because she was old enough to have a baby.

My youngest aunt (his youngest daughter) married when she was seventeen. She was pregnant by her boyfriend. He (grandfather) wouldn't have anything to do with the baby; and he ignored her completely for years afterwards. She used to be the favourite daughter. I can only presume he was still interfering with her, at the time that she got herself a boyfriend, and that he felt let down. I imagine – and it is imagining – that it was sexual jealousy.

The daughter before that (the second youngest) had some falling out with him when she was sixteen, and, in a fit of rage, he cut up her school uniform. She ran away after that. I can't ask her why because she's dead now – she's the one who killed herself.

And the one before that, the third youngest, also ran away. It all fits in. Of all the girls, only my mother, the eldest, escaped. At least, I presume she did.

I didn't ever feel that I was doing it too. Any approach always came from him. I don't think there was any guilt on my part – it was more a matter of feeling dirty, soiled, not being the same as other girls.

When I was about nine, a girlfriend told me about a boy who interfered with her fairly regularly. But I didn't tell her about my grandfather. One day she told me she'd arranged to meet him: I couldn't bear the thought of it, so I raced over and got her parents. They found them in the creek-bed and there was a terrible scene. She wasn't allowed to see him again, and he was sent away to boarding school. It wasn't a moral judgment – it was just something that I thought was horrible. I wish there'd been someone to stop it for me, but there never was.

I was very protective of my daughter: I never let her go alone where a man was. I really *hated* her to be demonstrative, like sitting on a man's lap, or cuddling a man. It used to make me feel sick. I used to tell her not to take lollies from strangers, not to accept lifts . . . just not to go *anywhere* with a man. God, I hope I haven't fouled her up! It was a warning about *any* man. Any man. I just didn't trust *any* of them.

My husband used to have a friend who was homosexual – I really liked him as a person – but I could never leave any of my boys anywhere alone with him. I was just terrified . . . not about homosexuals molesting little boys. It was just any man.

I have a small son now. I've never been in a position of having to leave him with anyone except his father [Vera's second husband]. I presume his father's all right, but I don't really know. If I had another daughter, I'd definitely be on the lookout. The man I live with now is very different from any other man I've ever met – I wouldn't be living with him otherwise. I feel I can trust him because his sexuality is not very strong. But I suppose you can never really know.

I don't like seeing little girls anywhere with men – especially men that fondle them. It's a sad thing when a kid can't be genuinely open and affectionate . . . but I'm always terrified that there's more than that behind it.

I must have trusted my grandfather when I was little. I remember

47

I used to sit on his knee. He wasn't openly affectionate: his sort of affection was horse-bites. He'd grab your knee and squeeze until it hurt, or bend your little finger until it hurt, or give a chinese burn. He was a cold fish.

The real molesting happened once a week, or maybe once a fortnight. It was regular on wet days: my grandmother would send me down to the shed, to get me out of the way.

I'd completely ignore what was happening, if I could. I'd go on hammering nails into a piece of wood. I wouldn't look round. He'd wipe me; then dress himself, although I didn't really know what he was doing; then adjust my clothes; and walk away humming or whistling or something like that. So there was no acknowledgment of it between us . . . until I scratched him. And then he snubbed me for nearly ten years. All through that time I was seen as sly. I survived . . . I just did what I had to do . . . I became hardened. All the time thinking, When I'm old enough . . . when I'm old enough . . . until I can leave. And eventually I did.

I never saw his penis. I remember now: he used to hold his handkerchief in front, over his penis. So the handkerchief served two purposes, I suppose: to catch any stray ejaculate, and also to stop me from seeing what was happening, in case I looked down.

I can see how he came to do it: thrown out of the family bed with the birth of the seventh child. But I can't excuse it. I'd much rather he'd taken up with any lady anywhere, than molested his own . . . children . . . and grandchildren.

There was bribery involved usually: I'll give you this or that, if you let me. Though not as openly as that. If you went along with it, if you didn't protest, and he did what he wanted to, he'd always give you two bob. Or he'd take you to town and give you a pound, which was a lot of money in those days. So there was this tacit bribery, I suppose. My sister always had money – I never connected the two things then. She used to bank a lot of money. He gave her at least a pound a week . . . oh, dear . . . poor thing.

I remember, too, he used to wash his own hankies, and hang them out. My grandmother washed all the rest of his clothes, but he always washed his hankies. I guess she just wouldn't let herself think about it.

It definitely affected my sexual development. Of course it did. I was frigid until I was thirty: I married at twenty. I figured it was my husband's fault. He could do what he had to do, for himself, but I didn't want to feel sexual things. I couldn't bear to be touched sexually. I used to see orgasm as desirable, but not possible for me.

48

When I first had intercourse, I was in total ignorance. Just ignorance. I had *no* idea what was going to happen. I had *no* idea it would be so painful. Maybe it was painful because I was so terrified.

When I had my first orgasm, which was with a lover, I was totally taken by surprise. I didn't know that such a thing existed. Then I became dissatisfied – you know, the search for the elusive orgasm.

When I told my husband about my grandfather, he became very angry: called him an old bastard, and so on. I really don't see why men should get angry about it.

About my mother, though . . . I idolised my mother. To me she was like a queen. She was little and pretty: I adored her. She just wasn't like other people. She explained why I had to go back to my grandparents when my father died, and I understood that. But then she married within a year, and I hated her for that. It seemed wrong to me. Anything to do with sex embarrasses my mother terribly.

For example: I remember once when my sister and I were very little, we had to sleep together because people were staying. I was five or six; my sister was very young: she usually slept in a cot. It was very hot, summer-time, and I undressed us both – we were just lying there. It was lovely . . . you know, skin to skin. Then my sister started crying – my mother came in and grabbed my sister and she walloped me! She said, 'Don't you *ever* do that again!' I wasn't 'doing' anything. We were just lying there. All I'd done was strip us – and I was enjoying that feeling of skin against skin. She gave me a real thing about it. You know . . . disapproval.

So . . . on the incest . . . I think it's one of the 'hidden crimes'. No matter how many books are published, it'll only be the tip of the iceberg.

It's very strange . . . the effect that one man can have on a family. He was strange, with all the girls, even after they were married. He was always very cool and withdrawn as far as the husbands were concerned.

It was the violation that I remember. It's a violation of self. I haven't been raped, but I would take rape to be the same thing. It's a violation; there's no assent. It's not the sexual part – it's the self.

I suppose not to worry – he's dead and we're not . . .

Cathy's Story

[Cathy wrote this herself, provoked by nothing but her own anger. Her parents are separated; she was staying with her father, which she does a couple of times a year. She is sixteen. Her mother gave me a copy, with Cathy's permission.]

I didn't spit back my anger.

I just let him cuddle me, my frustrations bubbled.

Now, physically, he was again holding me down, moulding my image back to a little girl, but then confusing it with a woman's body and treating it how he would treat a woman's body.

So while he called me his little one, I was aware how close I was to his crotch and the little kisses he gave me on the cheek and neck. The little licks that left a wet patch on my skin and I longed to wipe it off. Tear myself away and stand alone, by myself and not fiddled with by this man, my father.

He's very perceptive. Suddenly he says in this contradicting manner, 'Soon you'll be a woman and won't want these cuddles your Daddy gives you.' Too right I won't.

I pull away and go and collect some empty plates from the diners. My father manages a hotel and I am helping him. I come back – it'll be a while before I'm wanted again to serve or clear away. I'm cold, so I go up to him, hoping I will receive an ordinary, no-strings-attached cuddle. But no, this time he says 'are you cold' and starts to scratch – rub me with his fingers. He does it on my arms then tries to move my cardigan and do my sides, 'accidentally' touching my boobs. I push his hands away uncontrollably and answer his question with a 'no, I'm not cold', hard, firm and angry.

Virginia's Story

I find it hard to remember a lot of detail – I'm sure that's because I've blocked it out. It happened over a long period of time. I think it started when I was seven or eight. It was certainly something that happened when I was very young, and it kind of kept going until I was seventeen or so. So it was always there; there was always a fear of it happening, rather than it being something that happened every day. So the incidents become blurred because the *fear* of it happening was the overriding thing that I remember: it was there the whole time.

I've got no memory, for example, of whether it happened once a week or once a month or whatever – do you know what I mean? It was simply *always* there; it was something I was aware of constantly, but I don't know how often it happened.

It started off, as I say, when I was quite young. We lived in a really big house, and my father had a separate room which was like an office, off my mother's bedroom. It was at the other end of the house from where the kitchen and activity things went on.

My first memory of what happened would be that I'd be in summer pyjamas, like shortie pyjamas: I'd be in my father's office with my father and he'd get me sitting on his knee and start feeling my breasts. I know I was very young then. That became a regular kind of thing – it happened quite frequently, quite a lot. I felt really guilty about it happening. And of course it always stopped when anyone approached – so that reinforced the feeling that it shouldn't have been happening, which I kind of knew.

Then, I'm not sure when, it became a thing of when I was going to bed – I suppose he was meant to be doing the good fatherly thing of putting me to bed – and he would come and fondle me in bed. He'd touch my breasts and my vagina. That became an ongoing thing – it happened over a really long period of time. I was in a state of constant fear because I never knew when it was going to happen. It got to be that he'd come after I was in bed: I'd wake up and find him there. He'd just be there. I had no way of knowing when it would happen.

I'm really conscious that I've probably blocked a lot of it out. I think probably what happened was that I started avoiding going to the office; I'd avoid going there in my pyjamas; I'd avoid any situation that would allow it to happen. But him coming to my bed I couldn't avoid. I was asleep. It was just touching that I remember; I don't think he kissed me.

The worst part of that was the guilt; and also the feeling so *powerless*. I'd just lie there, absolutely petrified. I'd be totally unable to move or respond, or whatever. I just felt *totally*, utterly powerless. And it would go on for a few minutes . . . and then I'd kind of find the strength to fight him off . . . and he'd go away.

But the thing was . . . there was always the time interval, the few minutes, where I did submit. I think that's part of the guilt. When I only understood it as a sexual thing, there was the kind of guilt that said that if I let it go on, I must have enjoyed it. But now I understand it as a power thing: I was obviously totally powerless to repulse this person that I was completely reliant on at the same time. It poses such a contradiction: I can see, as an adult looking back, that a child is quite unable to make choices about that contradiction. How can you repulse someone whom you're reliant upon?

Understanding it as a power thing has resolved the guilt for me. I certainly don't remember it as enjoyable: I was literally unable to move or respond, and there was obviously no enjoyment in that. But I have felt guilty that maybe I did enjoy it and that that was why I didn't repulse him.

I was the only daughter; I had four brothers – three of them much younger than me. But I was very much the only girl and there was always this big thing about me being 'Daddy's little girl' . . . that was always promoted and encouraged – to the point that I would invariably be the negotiator to get things out of him that the family wanted. It would be put on to me to go and ask favours of my father for other people in the family. And after dinner at night, for example, he'd give me a bit of a cuddle: not an intimate cuddle (he wasn't that kind of person, I don't remember having any warm affection from him), but the sort of cuddle that made him and everyone else feel better. My mother would ask me to take messages to him. I was meant to keep him approachable . . .

He was in no way an ideal father: he was really wrapped up in his businesses and making money. My mother defended that side of it: he made money and that was OK, she didn't expect him to do much else. His money-making was portrayed very positively. I don't remember him doing family-type activities at all. I've no recollection of him going on picnics. I think there were four family holidays in all my childhood – which is pretty amazing for a well-off middle-class family.

I'm not sure when that business of coming in at night stopped. I think it had stopped for a couple of years – and then when I was about seventeen and had just left school and was hanging around at home, at a bit of a loose end, my father was going to Melbourne on a business trip and it was suggested I go with him. I can't remember who suggested it, but it seemed an all right idea at the time . . .

He'd already booked to go . . . but when it was decided I'd go too, he changed the booking and there was some sort of crude story: the woman who changed the tickets made some sort of sexual joke about his secretary going with him when he said it was his daughter. I remember I thought it was yukky.

When we got to the motel, there was only one room booked. I found the whole thing really uncomfortable – but there was nothing I could do about it. I couldn't fly away or anything – he had the tickets. So, the first – or maybe the second – night, he tried to get into bed with me (I was in the single bed). I responded very vigorously straight away and wouldn't let him. He never tried it

52

again there. But all the fear came back: I had no idea if it would happen again.

I guess I feel that my mother did know what was going on – she seemed to know about everything else that was going on in the house. I don't know how much to accuse her . . . but the way that she treated me was that she didn't trust me at all. If ever I came home with a story or an idea, she'd say it was a load of rubbish, or dismiss it . . . so that was just another aspect of my childhood, I always had very negative receptions from my mother. I remember her classic line was: 'Where did you get that idea? Who have you been talking to?' Nothing would ever be recognised as anything that I had initiated. So part of my fear, why I didn't tell her, was because she was so negative to me, and because she didn't trust me. So she wasn't someone I could go to with this enormous burden that I was carrying, because I thought she'd say that I was making it up, or wipe it in some way. I had nobody else that I could tell. So the way she was with me kind of contributed to all of it.

Apart from being the person that she always pushed towards my father . . . my mother *consciously* pushed me into the role of being a substitute for her. She positively encouraged me to do things with him. Like the trip to Melbourne: she could have gone with him, or come with us. I'm not saying she was pushing me into a sexual role, directly, but she was certainly pushing me into a close relationship with him. They had had a crisis in their relationship for years . . .

My father and I were very close for a while, in my teens . . . when I was about eighteen, he had a lover, another woman – and he *told* me about it. That was the degree of closeness, the confidences . . . He'd talk about his relationship with his lover, and kind of want a response in terms of me talking about the guy I was going out with. He actually asked me if I was having sex with him!

Suddenly something clicked – at least, over about a year: it was the way he told me about having this lover. It all clicked, and I became totally and utterly repulsed by him. At the time I sort of pushed down all the incest thing – it wasn't something I recognised as being part of the repulsion. I was just revolted by him: I thought he was a revolting person! I saw him as incredibly irresponsible in terms of the whole father thing.

He had some really weird twists. He saw it as really important that I was able to be financially independent: he was really supportive of the idea that I should have tertiary education and that it should be something I could make a living at. So it was a peculiar mixture: of encouraging my independence, while at the same time this other stuff was going on. I think he wanted to be proud of me. I did pharmacy mainly for his benefit: because then I'd have to own a pharmacy, probably two, and he wanted that. He felt, I think, a great attraction in having one of his children be a pharmacist.

It was one of the quirks in our family: there was actually pressure on me to be the potential supporter of the family in case he should die – it wasn't put on my elder brother. It was partly because I was brighter, but it wasn't the only reason. (And I'm not altogether sorry about that part – I got some positive things out of it!)

I never saw or felt the sexual stuff as a form of attention, or as getting something special. I saw it, perceived it, as something quite separate from how we related the rest of the time. The ways he related to me were sort of separated into day and night: all this encouragement of me was part of the daytime thing. It was quite separate from the night. It was all very contradictory.

I don't think I carried my rage from the night-times into the next day. I think I cut off. I was certainly submissive – a revoltingly submissive child. Part of that was because of how my mother treated me, that my opinions didn't count – so I kind of got it both ways, being put down by them, but differently. But I don't remember rage in the daytime, about him. But the night-times . . . I just remember being *rigid* – unable to move, powerless. There was nothing like cuddling, nothing sensual or positive or friendly – he just went straight for the heavy stuff, then.

I was a very mopey teenager. I always thought that I was just so put down, so not allowed to be myself, that that was why I was so unhappy! But fear was there, as part of the incest thing. But anger I'm not sure of, not consciously, not till later, and then I found it!

He'd often be late for tea, or have it after us, but when he was there, there was this thing of me going and sitting on his lap after dinner. I felt quite safe; it was quite separate. After all, it was in front of everyone else. But it was all part of me being 'Daddy's little girl' and keeping him happy.

But – I remember some time later, when I was eighteen or nineteen, we had a party at our house and I sat on the knee of this guy that I was quite attracted to at the time: it was just for a while, we had a chat. The next day, my mother gave me this great lecture about sitting on men's knees and how I wasn't ever to do it because there was some Dreadful Reason (which I can't even remember), but how I musn't do it! The absurdity of that didn't hit me till years later: how she'd positively encouraged me to sit on my father's lap and the *only* time she ever saw me sit on another man's knee, she told me never to do it again!

There's also a lot of stuff to do with my brothers. When I was about twelve, my elder brother and I were having a bit of a wrestle – we hadn't had that kind of contact for a while – and he started trying to touch my vagina. He actually put his hand inside my pants . . . [voice very low] . . . they were sort of tight . . . I think that was the only time.

I suppose my father sort of set the pattern by which my brother behaved. This sexual thing was fairly prominent in the family. There were daughters of my parents' friends used to come and stay sometimes: they were my friends too. We'd all be getting changed or whatever in my room . . . A few times, my brother, sometimes with a friend, would burst into the room. And everyone would just sort of *stand there*: no one ever kicked him out or yelled or screamed or told my mother. It was that *power* thing. A couple of times he came in and touched the breasts of one of the girls who used to stay. And that was about it . . . except that the sexual thing was always there, in the family.

None of those people ever talked about it, with each other . . . except years later a mutual friend of many of us commented to me about what happened when the girls came to stay. At the time I was absolutely *mortified*: to think they must have spoken about it. But of course now I'm glad to think they spoke about it and I'd like to think they told their parents or someone they could confide in and get positive feedback from.

The other thing that happened was that one of my younger brothers, when he was six or seven (I was sixteen I guess), started this thing of peeping through keyholes and things like that. I was so on edge about things like that, that I became immediately aware of it. But again I felt totally powerless: it was just something that went on.

So I'd go to the bathroom and hang a towel over the keyhole – so it was little things like that that became a habit, to sort of get around it, to cope with it. And he even . . . [pause] . . . bored a hole through my bedroom wall! There was a sort of playroom next door. It was all kind of unbelievable. So then I'd always open the wardrobe door and hide behind it when I was undressing. I got so I didn't know if I was just being totally paranoid or whether it was real.

He was the only one I did anything about: probably because I was older than he was and the power thing was not as great. I became aware one day when I was having a shower that he was in the ceiling

55

looking down through the exhaust fan. I got really angry and went and told my mother he was there – and nothing was made of it at all. It was just kind of covered up . . . which absolutely confirmed my fears of what would have happened if I'd complained of the others when I was younger. Him doing that went on, I think, till I left home. I just became more and more careful about dressing and things.

I actually told him, that brother, last year, why I didn't go to see my father, why I wouldn't have anything to do with him. I told him about the ongoing molesting; I felt really good about telling him – and he was just speechless when I told him! I'm sure part of that was his own guilt . . . and he just sort of accepted it. He doesn't like my father either, for reasons I agree with – but I've got extra reasons. And it was good that he didn't argue or dismiss it – he just totally accepted that that was what happened to me. That affirmed my position: it was really important for me.

My parents separated after I'd left. From the age of seven, I had this very very strong feeling that my parents were going to get divorced which was very heavy at the time: I didn't know anyone who didn't have two parents. And when I was eighteen or nineteen, there was this business of my father's lover and they separated for a while. My mother went through an enormous effort to bring about a reconciliation. She went away to stay with him and my younger brothers were very distressed: they thought she wasn't going to come back. I don't think very much had been explained to them. They did get back together; they lived together for a few more years . . . and then I moved inter-state, I really left home . . . and they separated for good within a couple of months of me leaving. I always felt my going had something to do with it. I didn't feel guilty: I think I'd always carried that burden, keeping them together somehow. My values in terms of marriage had changed by then anyway, so I saw it as quite a positive thing – that my mother would be released from that horrific bondage. I was very supportive of her then in trying to build a separate life for herself.

I never realised . . . till now . . . it was when I was about seven that I began to feel they might separate: and that was when all the sexual stuff started! It may have been other things as well, but it's interesting that they're connected like that.

I *never* spoke to anyone about it as a child. The first time was when I was twenty-seven: it was with a lover. He'd been molested by an uncle or someone: he was the first person I knew of who'd had it happen too. Then, gradually over the last few years, I've been able to mention it, if it became appropriate in a conversation and so on. That change has come about through reading, and talking with women, I suppose. It's become something very much easier to talk about, over a period of a few years.

Then, last year, a friend who is a counsellor was telling me about a girl she was seeing who had all these behaviour patterns which I recognised straight away! My friend said, 'I'm beginning to think it might be a case of incest,'and I just said, 'Of course. It's obvious.' That was pretty amazing: it was her job, and here was I just seeing it.

My friend was amazed because I'd never talked to her about it and when I did I realised I was still very upset about it. There was still a lot of guilt. So I went to a woman counsellor, just a few sessions, which totally erased the guilt. The counselling made the power part of it clear to me. And I worked out a lot of my anger. And then a week after that I began to talk with a friend [Jude in Jude's Story] who had had very similar things happen – and that was really important! I didn't want to talk about it to people who would find it a burden. With her, it was really good – to talk about it for a long time, several times, over a long period of time. Sharing like that, knowing I wasn't boring the other person, was very important.

I'm not guilty now, but I am still angry and I've made a definite decision to have nothing to do with my father. I stayed with him for one night a few years ago: I thought I should give him a chance, view him again now I was an adult, he might have changed – and I found him just as revolting as ever. He kept telling revolting jokes: I found him quite repulsive. He's been living with a woman younger than me since he separated from my mother. He's exploiting her too: he has other women too. I could see it all.

On this night when I stayed with him and found him, from my adult point of view, totally revolting, I decided, on that basis, not to see him again. My mother *has* changed: she treats me as an adult. I don't feel I should force her to carry the past by telling her. Except that now I know that this might be in a book, I think I'd probably send him a copy, and my mother too – and point it out to them. That's not doing it directly, but it might have more impact.

I don't want to write to him and tell him: I don't want to acknowledge my connection with him in that way because it implies I want a dialogue with him – and I don't!

[After being interviewed, Virginia sent me a copy of a very long letter which she had written to her younger brother and his wife, explaining her decision to have a baby without an 'involved' father. Much of her reasoning came from her own experience of fathering. I quote some pieces here which are relevant to what she said in the interview.]

I have, until last week, put down my fear that our parents would separate, to an enormous quarrel that they had when I was seven. It was the worst, in my memory. Dave and I were through at the other end of the house with Ian who was only a baby and we were really scared because it was the first time anything like that had happened. I never remember it happening again like that but of course that may just be my childhood imagination. So I always thought that my fear that they would separate stemmed to that argument. When I was being interviewed, I realised that that was the same age as I linked to the beginning of the incest.

That in itself was amazing, but talking later with a friend who has done a lot of reading on the subject, she explained that the burden of holding the family together is the role, or at least the perceived role, of the incest victim. If one felt the marriage and the family were secure then a child could take the risk of exposing the incest in the belief that it would be resolved within the family. But if you live in fear that the marriage/family is on the verge of falling apart, you cannot take the risk of introducing something that will clearly either tear the family apart, or, perhaps what would probably be a worse aspect for a child to face, the rejection of both parents and the whole family as they unite against the victim.

I don't as clearly understand the other person's (in this case, the father's) side. I understand that it was power rather than sex. Perhaps it was a sexual turn-on for him – I don't know – but there was nothing 'nice' about it, no kissing or cuddling, for instance. Perhaps in his frustration of not meeting Mum's expectations as a husband/father, he had a need to exert his power over another, and the obvious choice was a younger, weaker person of the same sex as my mother. This is just my guessing: I have not, until writing this, even thought what his motivation was except to understand it in terms of exerting power. I know that he has always groped women – Mum's friends, his friends' wives, my friends. As I grew older, I could only guess that it extended to others, e.g. staff.

. . .

I haven't told Mum. I am getting closer to it. I suppose I still have a fear of being rejected by her. Perhaps it isn't very rational, but it is there; and I accuse her of knowing about it. She knew about everything else in the house so I can't believe she didn't know about that too. So it is not just a matter of me telling her about a very unpleasant childhood experience, but that I hold her responsible for not protecting me. It is the one thing that makes me most sceptical about families. Her offering to 'help' now means little to me. Sure it is nice to have a bundle of baby clothes, but when I needed her most in my life she rejected me, wittingly or unwittingly, so I don't understand what people mean when they talk about families always being there when you 'need' them.

Marge's Story

I was married to Rod, and his son Neil lived with us. He was sixteen when it happened. My daughter Vicki was nine and a half, and then there were the two that I had with Rod: Alice was four and a half, going on for five, and Dean was a year or so younger. Rod and I got together about six years before all this, when Neil was ten or so, and Vicki was three and a half, so Neil and Vicki had been living together as brother and sister for six years.

I didn't know about what was going on, until one day when I went up to my mum's place and she told me that every day when Neil came to pick the kids up, the two girls would scream and yell and put on a turn . . . she wanted to know what was happening, and when she asked the kids, Vicki told her. So when I went to see mum, she told me about it.

My mother said that Neil had been having intercourse with Vicki and Alice. It happened when Rod and I went shopping of a Thursday night. When we got back, the bed would be all mucked up, and the curtain was pulled back. I'd noticed that for a month or so, but I hadn't taken much notice because kids do jump on beds and things like that. I'd shown Rod though, because I wanted the messing-up to stop, but he said that I was lazy, and that I didn't make the bed before I went out. So I said, 'All right – you come home one afternoon and I'll prove to you that the bed was made, and the house was clean and tidy.'

He did. It was a Thursday afternoon, and we went to Moorabin shopping centre afterwards to do the shopping. When we came home, the bed was all mucked up, and I told Rod to come to the bedroom and he saw it was mucked up too, and he said, 'Oh, it's

·only the kids jumping on it,' so we didn't take much notice then.

I'd also had my suspicions when I was bathing Alice – she wasn't old enough to bath herself. I was washing between her legs . . . and the water wasn't hot, it was warm . . . and she started screaming. I lay her on the floor to dry her . . . I was drying between her legs and I noticed her vagina was red, down both sides of it. That's when I got my suspicions that he must have been playing around with her. That was about a month before my mother told me about it. I was suspicious from the bed too – but I couldn't say anything then. Rod wouldn't have believed me. I had to wait . . . I didn't know . . . and when mum told me, everything fell into place.

So I told Rod, and we confronted Neil with it. He said, 'I wouldn't touch my two sisters. I wouldn't do anything like that to them.' So . . . I didn't believe him. I called him everything under the sun. But his father believed him. Rod reckoned that I wanted to get rid of Neil. He thought I didn't want Neil in the house. Rod thought I was making it up, to get rid of Neil. But I wasn't.

Vicki talked to a girlfriend of hers who knows somebody in welfare, and this friend told the welfare and they told the police. That's how the police came into it.

The police were at the school on the Monday – I was picking up the children. I was sitting there waiting with a friend, who was picking up her children too, when the headmaster came and told me there were two detectives waiting to see me.

So I went in, and the police said, 'You know what we're here for, don't you?' I told them I didn't. Then they told me that they wanted to take me and the two girls down to the police station and talk about it. I asked them, 'About what?' They said, 'You know,' and I said that I didn't. So it wasn't till we got to the police station that I found out what it was about.

They spent about three-and-a-half hours at Hawthorn police station, and while the police were questioning the two girls upstairs, the detectives were questioning me downstairs. They were asking me about how the family situation was, and that. And I told them. They said that it sounded as though the son is trying to break you up. And I said he was, but I wouldn't budge. Maybe he'd decided that the only way to get at me was to interfere with the two girls.

I asked them, 'Would the two girls make a story like that up?' And a detective said, 'At nine and a half, and four and a half – no, certainly not.'

The next day, the police took Vicki and Alice to a police surgeon in the city. They examined Alice, but she wasn't touched: there were no signs of it. Then they took Vicki in, but I went in with her . . . when he started to examine Vicki, she wouldn't let them. She started yelling and screaming – she just wouldn't let them examine her internally.

The policewoman told her to cut it out, and to act like a grown woman. I said, 'How would you know? I don't suppose you would know.' And she said that she didn't. So I said, 'You just mind your own business. She's my child. She's only a child. She's only nine and a half; she's not a woman yet. She's got a long way to go. You just keep out of it.'

So the doctor didn't proceed because she wouldn't let him do it. But he did have a look and he said that she was penetrated and she was broken inside . . . so . . . it never got any further than that.

I don't blame Vicki for not letting the doctor examine her – she thought he wanted to do exactly the same thing to her. I was trying to calm her down and explain it to her and tell her he wanted to examine her inside . . . and she just said No. He said there was no use going on with it if she didn't permit it. I knew there was something really wrong then . . . so that was when I made up my mind that the only way I could deal with it was to leave Rod. She was so upset. I started to cry, but I held it back until I got into bed that night and then I couldn't stop. Next thing I knew, she was in bed beside me, saying, 'Don't cry, Mummy. Don't cry.'

When the doctor told me that Alice had not been penetrated, I was so relieved. If she had been like Vicki, I don't think I could have coped. I think the redness I saw came from when Neil tried to put it in, and he couldn't because he was too big and she was too small. She told mum, and she told the police, that he 'wet' her – so he must have been rubbing his penis up and down her legs . . .

When I found out about it, I asked the girls why they didn't tell me, and they said that it was because they were frightened that I would belt them. I said, 'I'd never do that.' I was upset that they felt like that, and I've been upset ever since.

The police told me to tell Neil to see them the next day. That night, I was scared stiff. I had the kids bathed and fed – they were in bed when Rod got home. So I told him what had happened: how the police had had us down there for three-and-a-half hours and about the surgeon the next day. And of course he said that the kids were lying, that they were making it up. So I told him how the policeman had said that girls that age would never make anything like that up. Anyway, Neil said that he wasn't going to the police, and Rod said that he could go if he wanted to. I said, 'If he doesn't go, they'll be here to pick him up, or they'll go to his work and pick him up there . . . '

If Rod had believed the girls and made Neil leave, I would have stayed there. We'd have had a much happier life . . . but he just wouldn't let Neil go. He wanted to hang on to him. I thought, 'Well, if that's what you want, you can have him.'

Rod went to the police with Neil, and he got a copy of Neil's statement. He happened to leave it at home, so I decided to read it through. When he got down to the part where he said that all he knew about sex was a man and woman going to bed to make love . . . that's as far as I got in reading it. I didn't want to finish reading it, because it was all a pack of lies. I was disgusted by it. I knew he was a liar because at high school they pick up everything. And he also had a girlfriend – she spent a lot of time at our house, and he'd have the door of his room locked a lot when they were in there. I knew he was a liar because he knew what he was doing, and he told the police that he didn't. He told them he didn't know anything about sex. So . . . I just put the statement down and that was it.

I told Rod I'd read it and how I felt. He said, 'Are you calling my son a liar?' I said that I was; he said that the two girls were lying too. And I said, 'I believe what those two girls said, more than I believe Neil.' We kept arguing: it was more about Neil than about the two girls. Rod had tracked Neil down in a kids' home where his mother had left him and got him back when he was three years old and they'd been together all that time. There were arguments about Neil for about a month. So I said, 'I'm leaving you.' He said, 'If you leave, you can have Vicki, but you're not taking Alice and Dean.'

The next morning, when he left for work . . . I was shaking. I packed all the things I could for the kids; I didn't pack anything for me . . . and I left while he and Neil were at work. It was 17 October 1978. I haven't seen him since.

The girls were getting raped for four or five months before I knew about it. I was annoyed at that – that it was so long and I didn't know. But once I found out, I decided I had to do something about it: wait for the right time, and go.

We went into the city and went to a Salvation Army home for women and children. We stayed there for three weeks. Then we went to another Salvation Army home for about two weeks. And then I decided to come here, to Adelaide. I waited for the court case, to try and get maintenance from Rod for the kids, but he'd left. He didn't turn up in court: he was nowhere to be found. I heard he and Neil went to Tasmania.

When I came here, I went to a Women's Refuge because I didn't have anywhere else to go, while I got housing. My brother lives here; he'd told welfare what had happened with the girls, and they'd said I should come here and start a new life. I don't want Rod back now. We're contented to be without him.

I feel that Vicki needs to talk about it. I'd like somebody else to talk with her and find out how she feels about it. I know I'd only break down and go berserk; I know I couldn't do it. Barbara tried, and Susan tried [two Women's Refuge workers] – she likes them, but she didn't really talk. I don't know about Revesby [a child psychiatrist] . . . I don't know if he tried to get around the subject. I'd like to know if he was successful or not. Vicki always saw him alone, so I don't know what happened.

He put Vicki in hospital because of her behaviour and her dirtying [at age twelve]. They were studying her behaviour for nearly six months. She came home for weekends and school holidays. I don't know what it was about her behaviour that they were studying. I was a bit frightened of him at first; I've never felt comfortable with him . . . so I don't know what went on or what he was looking for.

When I brought her home, I found that the six months in hospital had changed her. She wasn't dirtying so often, and now she doesn't at all. And she helps me round the house more – she loves cooking, so she likes to get tea, cook it herself, for all of us.

I don't bring the subject up with the girls myself, because I know what their reaction would be. They'd just back off. I think Alice could talk about it: she talked with Revesby about it last year. He gave her a tape of their sessions, so I know she talked about it. If Vicki and I decide to talk about it, one of us will break down in front of each other, and I don't want to be the first one to break down. I find it's very hard to control myself.

I think it would scare her to find out what happened to me. I think she'd have a different opinion of me altogether. She doesn't know that I was raped by her father: that's how I came to be pregnant. I told him and he didn't want anything to do with her. I went to an unmarried mothers' home and stayed there till I had the baby. I could have put her up for adoption and no one would have known . . . but I just didn't want to. So I kept her. It was very hard. I had to work, plus pay someone to look after her, plus pay board and buy food at the same time. Vicki used to get sick a lot, so I kept having to give up jobs to look after her. It was very hard.

Vicki and I identified with each other right from the start. From when she was six days old, she could sense when something was wrong for me. I know what's going through her mind now: she thinks that she's unclean since all this happened; that she's just filthy. I still feel like that from when I was raped. But I was twenty-three; Vicki was only nine and a half – that's a big difference. It's not so hard for me now. I know she feels unclean: I've noticed that she has three or four showers a day.

My own feeling about being dirty is gradually going because I don't think about it so much. I tried to put it as far from my mind as possible. When the time comes, I'll tell Vicki about it . . . in about another four or five years, I'll end up telling her. She might be mature enough to take it then. I fear she'll hear about it from someone else first and come and ask me. I want to be the first to tell her, but I feel she's not ready to be told about my past yet.

When I was raped, I felt dirty; I felt my life was ruined; and I felt I'd never find a man who'd accept my child. Her own father didn't want anything to do with her. I didn't want that to happen again; I wanted a proper father-figure for her. I found one – Rod – but I didn't know at the time that he had a seven-year-old son, and what that was going to mean.

I just can't talk to her about it. I was never taught anything about sex. My mother never told us anything: we had to learn from a book that she gave us – me and my brother. If I did have to talk about it, I wouldn't know where to begin.

Vicki is learning about sex education through the school. I think she knows what sex is all about. But I worry that when she gets to the age when she wants to go out with boys, that she's going to back off, because I don't think she'll trust a boy – any boy, whatsoever. And that worries me because I want to see her happily married, with a family. In my mind, I don't think she'll be able to have any children; in my mind, I know that she won't be a mother. That disappoints me because I know she's good with kids – she loves children. It's a feeling in me about what happened to her when she was nine years old . . . I don't think she'll want a boy to touch her.

She used to think I was paying more attention to Alice and Dean than to her. Maybe that's what Dr Revesby was trying to find out about. I wasn't: I was trying to equalise it, share it around, because I thought I should give the others more attention. Vicki needed a lot of my attention: she was being very demanding.

I've found that since we left, the children have been quite contented to stay with me; they're quite happy. Also, they're not frightened; they're not scared; and they're not fidgety, like they were when we first left. Rod reckoned I'd never make it on my own with the three children. I had to prove to myself I could do it . . . without anyone interfering. So I feel proud.

I would like to have a man about the house again – but he'd have to accept the children as well as me, not just me for myself. I'd want him to like the children and for them to accept him as their father. But I haven't found one yet . . . I think that's a long way off. I can go without sex . . . I've been without it for nearly three years. I'd say it'll be another couple of years' time . . . then I might start looking around. But he's got to accept my children . . .

If anything like what happened before, happened again, I don't know what I'd do . . . go berserk . . . I'd kill somebody, I suppose. So I'd rather struggle on how I am now, being mother and father to all three of them.

Rod didn't drink a lot or anything like that. He was a very reasonable man and I still love him. I wasn't unhappy with him . . . it was just that I had to get away for the girls' sanity.

Dean was brought into it too. I didn't know that till a long while after we left. We were staying with my mum, and she and I were talking about the rumour that Rod was back in town . . . Dean was awake and listening. I didn't know he was awake until he sat up and said, 'Goody, goody gumdrops – we don't have to live with Daddy any more.' He told us that Neil used to make him keep a lookout through the window, while he was interfering with the two girls. He was very upset when he told us; he was almost crying. His job was to let Neil know if we were coming . . . he wasn't quite four then. I told him not to worry; that he wasn't going to have to live with them again.

Hearing about that made me angry all over again. I didn't think he'd been brought into it. I think he was too young to know about sex . . . I think he thought it was odd . . . what Neil was doing to the two girls.

The more I find out, the less I like Rod. I just hope I don't ever meet him again. I don't like him now. If ever I did meet him, I think I'd end up killing him. The same with Neil. I just hope I don't ever meet either of them again.

I didn't really want to do this interview . . . but I thought I would if it could help anyone else, who's in the situation I was. I want to say that they should just leave the chap, or the person, that's interfering with their children. Get well away – you'll be much happier on your own, bringing the children up. I know it's a struggle, but it's worth it in the long run. I've proved that to myself. Rod said that I'd never make it . . . and I have; I've made it. And I think other women can make it too, with their children, on their own.

Lynette's Story

My father was killed in 1958 when I was only four: in an accident. Mum couldn't cope with my brother and me for a while so we went into a home for eighteen months, but she kept my older sister. That wasn't too bad, although we didn't see her very much.

A couple of months after we got out, she was remarried . . . and from the time that I first knew him, I just didn't like him. I just never felt comfortable with him, even at that age. We just had to do what we were told or we'd get a beating. He was a pretty strict stepfather, but nothing had started then . . . How can I explain it? It was just a gut feeling: I don't like this person. I do that now: if I don't like someone, I don't like them. That may be judgmental, but it's how I am.

After they got married, we left our family house and moved into another one. Moving into the new house took me so far away from anything I'd ever been with.

He started the sex stuff with me when I was about nine and a half. I know he must have been doing the same thing with my sister, but I had no indication at the time – because my sister and I weren't close. She and I slept in the same room at first, but he had another room built on, so my brother and sister and I each had our own room. I know why that was done now, but at the time it was just put down to the fact that Sue and I couldn't get on with each other. That was done about a year after mum had the operation: her hysterectomy.

It started when I was going to guides or brownies or something, and it used to be when he'd pick me up after I'd been there, and it'd be in the garage, where he'd start on me in the car. We'd be sitting in the car in the garage – he'd fondle me to start off with, and then he'd take my clothes off. That happened a few times – a few nights. I told mum about it and she just didn't believe me. There was no way she'd accept that that was going on.

He'd fondle my breasts, body, thighs – he'd rub his hands all over me. When he took my clothes off, he started kissing me all over, and then he . . . He hadn't taken his clothes off at this stage, but he'd be feeling himself through his clothes. I don't know whether he just worked himself up enough . . . or whether the time factor . . . he didn't have that much time because mum knew we were home. We'd go inside . . . and I'd go straight to bed [voice very quiet].

Even before this, if I was having a shower, he'd come in and take his clothes off and have a shower with me. He never believed in any locks on any doors . . . I mean, he'd just walk in where he wanted to. Like, if I was undressing or anything, he'd come into the room. When I was younger, it didn't matter that much to me, but when I was older it did – I wanted my privacy.

After the garage part, it'd mainly be on Saturday mornings. Mum would go shopping, and we'd be in the house by ourselves. Sue would go with mum, and my brother would be playing down the street with friends, and he'd lock all the house up and take the phone off the hook . . . just to make sure no one would disturb him – that's the way I see it now. He made everything secure.

I used to worry about it, and say, 'I don't want to. I'll tell mum.' And he used to say, 'OK, you tell your mother, and I'll just deny it' – which is what happened a few times.

He kissed me on the lips, on the breasts, on the vagina . . . everywhere . . . [crying] . . . that's not the worst of it. When he used to lock all the house up, he'd take all his clothes off and he'd sit on a chair, and he'd take my clothes off, and he'd make me kneel in front of him. And then he'd start pulling himself off . . . and then he'd make me lick him. He'd force my head down to his penis . . . and that went on for *so* long [crying]. Once he ejaculated into my mouth, and I just . . . couldn't stand it. I ran out of the room . . . I just couldn't. He'd pull himself off in front of me . . . and then he'd get me on the bed and lay on top of me. He never went all the way, because I think he knew that if he did, he'd be . . . you know. But I think that what he did is worse than that – that's the way I feel. Much worse. When he was hard, he used to rub his penis all over me . . . I hated it, I hated myself, I hated everything.

He'd touch me and kiss me in the shower – everywhere. I couldn't handle it – I didn't want him anywhere near me – but there was no getting away from it. That was when I first realised . . . my mother . . . I just despised her because she wouldn't help me get out of it. Over the years I told her half a dozen times. I gave up in the end. I got to the stage where I knew what was wrong, and I knew I didn't want to do it, but there was nothing much I could do about it.

And mum just kept at me, wanting to know why I didn't like him. But how do you tell her when she won't believe you? It was just so . . . it went on for so long. That's what I can't understand – why I didn't stop it before I did.

What happened was that one night when I was twelve and a half or thirteen, I was sort of half asleep (it was late) and I saw him in the doorway. I must have gone to sleep because the next thing I knew he was on top of me and mum was screaming because he was on top of me. He tried to rape me that night, he really did. I still get nightmares about that now. That's the only time that mum accepted it – but she blamed me!

They were sleeping in separate beds at the time, and I think she just felt he didn't want her, that he was getting his sex elsewhere. I can't remember exactly what she said but it was like that: he didn't want her, he wanted me. But she *had* to believe it, she had no choice, because I was screaming . . . That was the first time he'd ever really tried anything like that. There was no foreplay or anything like he'd done before, it was just straight into it, and I just screamed. He'd lain on top of me before, but not with as much intention as this time.

After that he went for volunteer treatment to a psychiatric hospital. That went on for eight or nine months, and during that time he didn't touch me. Then, as soon as he stopped, it started again – but he never laid on top of me again. He used to come in during the night – I'd be asleep and I'd wake up – and he'd be standing over me, with a full erection, with all his clothes off – but he never tried it again.

That went on for years . . . I don't know why I haven't been locked up in a loony bin! . . . because that just went on and on. He'd walk in when I was showering – everywhere, all the time. He still touched me for a while, but he never tried complete rape again.

I don't know if you'd call it incest or molestation or what . . . it was the mental side . . . It would happen every night for a few weeks, then it wouldn't happen for a few weeks, and then he'd be there, standing over the bed with no clothes on, and it'd start again. When he stood there . . . I still get nightmares over it . . . it's as if he sort of possessed me. Yes, that's it: I was sort of his, I was there for him. That's the way I feel. There was no way I could get out of it . . . I'd just try and turn over, and . . . when I turned back, he'd still be there! It's just . . . . I can't explain.

68

All this was going on, and him getting into the shower with me and holding me, and I was fourteen and fifteen.

About then we moved to Brisbane, and I made things so difficult about then – as far as I could, I just wouldn't have anything to do with him. And he started telling me I was a cheap little tramp and a slut and that's all I'd ever be. That's what he drummed into me – all the time – and I started believing it! I wouldn't do anything he wanted – he'd ask me to do something and I'd say No, and he'd slap me over the face. I just wouldn't co-operate in any way. And I demanded to have a lock put on my door, and I got it – I got mum to get a neighbour to do it, by saying it was to keep my brother out of my room.

Things were so bad, mum couldn't cope with the situation, so we went back to Melbourne for a few months – without him. But then we went back again because mum didn't seem to be able to go on without him. My sister wouldn't go back with us – she'd got a job in Melbourne and she wouldn't go back to Brisbane – she said she wouldn't live in the same house with him. I understand why now, but at the time I couldn't see why – I should have, because I wanted to do the same thing. I begged and pleaded with mum, but she said I had to come with her. I left school in all that moving around – I couldn't cope with going back.

I was a few days off sixteen when we went back, and the first night there, he came into the shower, and then he came into my room that night . . . and I said, 'You come near me and I'll tell the cops.' And he knew I would. It was the strength of not being around him, those few months away, that allowed me to stand up to him.

The next weekend I wanted to go out – just sixteen – and there was a huge row. He never let me go out – but that time I said he couldn't stop me, and he said, 'If you go out, you don't come back!' When I came back, my cases were on the doorstep. That was it – I went. And mum just stood by and let him do it. He took over the running of the family and she let him, which is what we couldn't understand. Because there was no love from him – and she didn't show us any love either, which was the hardest to take. There was no love anywhere.

I went to live in a hostel for young people: I grew up overnight there. The first time a guy touched me, I just freaked out: I couldn't stop screaming . . . I just felt so dirty, it was wrong – it was unbelievable, how I reacted.

I had to work out everything about sex for myself – mum didn't tell me anything. He told me some of it – when he actually told me what was what and I realised what he had been doing, I felt so cheap . . . and so used. That was before he went for treatment, when I was about thirteen. It was after that, that I got stronger. And that was when he started telling me I was a bitch and a slut and a cheap tramp. When I left home, that was what I thought I was, because I felt as though I'd let it all happen!

I haven't seen him for eleven years, and I feel as though if I were to see him again, I don't know if I could handle it. It's a gut thing.

I had no one all that time that I could talk to. Just no one. Only myself to rely on.

Everyone else thought he was the most wonderful person, but he gave me and my sister and brother the hardest time you could believe . . . He worked in the personnel section of the Health Department; he often worked at nights, but he didn't stay out and drink or anything like that. He didn't have many friends.

The only way I coped was to throw myself into my schoolwork – I was fairly good at school. I blocked it out that way, I think. I made friends like myself at school – girls who were into sport and schoolwork. We didn't talk about boys – all that sex stuff didn't come up between me and my friends. I was a loner a lot of the time, I was dux in primary school and I got a bursary for all of high school, but moving around for his job, and all the things he was doing to me, just mucked that all up. I wanted to be a librarian, but as it was I didn't even finish school. I went to night-school for a while after I left home, and at least I got my school certificate. When my kids get a bit older [Lynette has three daughters], I really want to go to college and do something – keep myself active.

My mum eventually split up with him – I wasn't there then, so I'm not sure what happened, except that I know my brother started giving him a hard time and he became very violent. My brother saw him throw mum on the floor and things like that. It was getting so he was going to throw my brother out, and my mother wouldn't have that, because her son was her favourite. So she protected him. And they split up. I've hardly ever seen my mother since I left.

Both my sister and I got married the same way: we each ended up living with a boyfriend in his mother's house. I guess it was the only way we could sort of have a home, but get away from him too.

When I got married, I really tried to be a proper wife. The worst part of all that he'd done to me was when he made me kneel down and forced my head down. My husband used to get me to do it too – he'd say, 'If you love me, you'll do it.' And I did love him, so I did it. But when I realised I didn't love him, I just couldn't do it. I put a

70

lot into my marriage because it was all I had, but that's over now. My husband gave no love either – I've never really been shown love. That's why my children are so important to me – I want to give them what I didn't have.

It happened to one of my kids too. When Monica was five or so, this friend of ours took her and Roberta (who was two and a half), for a drive to the shops – there was a barbecue going on or something. We knew him pretty well – he'd been a friend for years.

When they got back, Roberta said, 'He took us to his house, and he took Monica's clothes off, and he had his clothes off.' And I jumped! 'Right!' I said. It had happened about six months before – Monica had said it when she was only four, but I thought she'd got it wrong . . . But this time, because Roberta said it – even though she was so little! – I knew it was true. I asked Monica and she said that he took her clothes off and started kissing her on her chest and on her tummy and then he was licking her with his tongue – and I knew then that she just wasn't making up stories. And then she told me that he'd starting licking her between her legs . . . and I got really upset by that. And she said that he was playing with his 'thing' (I think that's the word she used) and that he was laying on top of her . . . Well . . . I rang the cops, and we went down there and saw them and they said that she'd have to have an examination. I was shaking enough – I didn't want them to do that to her . . . But it happened, and they said there was no semen, but there was saliva on her vulva and in her vagina – so he had licked around.

So the police looked things up and found that he had a criminal record, and my husband sort of got scared and he wouldn't go and face him. The police saw him and he denied the whole thing. There was nothing we could do. From that day to this, we've never had anything to do with the whole family – except, years later, I saw his cousin, whom I trusted, and I told him all about it, and I convinced him, and he said he'd keep an eye on the little girls in that family. So at least someone knows.

I never got close enough to my husband to tell him what happened to me – he freaked out about Monica – I'm sure that he couldn't accept it from me. Anyway, I never got close enough.

I was raped really brutally recently. I'd gone to a social thing for single parents with a girlfriend, and we went to a disco with two men we met there, and I got taken to a country road and raped. He didn't even take his clothes off – it was horrible. Brutal. Through my mind, while it was happening, it all came back . . . I was going all through it again . . . over and over. I feel so cheap and

71

used . . . I don't know if I'm going to come out of it, if I'm going to be normal, or what . . . [crying].

When I was seventeen, I was raped by two guys. I was kind of set up for it. I went to a party with people from the hostel . . . it had taken me all that time to work up to being able to go to a party. And I went to the shops with a girlfriend and two men, and she jumped out and they drove off with me in the back. They went to the river. And they both raped me . . . and I went through all of it again . . . through my mind.

One of them, Paul, was really upset when he realised I was a virgin, and he sort of looked after me after that. He became protective. I could talk to him. He was a friend while I lived in the hostel, and made sure things like that didn't happen again.

My sister and I did talk about it once, in a kind of way. I mentioned him, and I was talking about not being loved, and she said, 'You weren't the only one, you know.' That's all she ever said.

I think he went further with her. There was an incident when she was about fourteen: she'd run away, and then about a month later she was taken to hospital, and she was there for about five days. I don't know if it was a miscarriage or what – it was never explained. I know she was bleeding when she left the house. It was in the middle of the night. Only my mother visited her in hospital – my brother and I weren't allowed to.

My sister is just the opposite from me now. She goes from one guy to the other – she thinks it's love! She's really promiscuous. She's told me she just can't make it with her husband, but she can with other men. Her husband really loves her – she's got it all there if she wanted it.

My mother has let me down – so many times – so I despise her. There's nothing I can do to change it – she's not the sort of person you can talk openly with.

I want my kids to know that whatever happens to them, I'll be there, and I'll back them. I was a weak person when I was younger, but I'm a strong person now – I must be! After what I've been through . . . I'm going to make something out of my life.

The way you feel after that sort of thing has been done to you – you don't feel a person, you feel like a thing. You just don't feel a human being, you feel like an object that they've done what they liked with, and that you haven't got any feelings. With me it's an emotional need more than a physical one. I've got no physical feelings about sex which has really got me . . . Why? I don't feel as though I've got any sex drive at all. I guess it's because I've been given such a bad impression of sex.

It takes away all dignity from your body, and from your soul. It is the ultimate invasion of privacy. There is nothing private left. Your whole body – and all your feelings too – have been displayed against your will.

II · BRIDGE PASSAGE

Theory

What chance has the female storyteller had, making her way
through closed gates to an alien city to an inhospitable
audience in the town square of the patriarchy?

LOUISE BERNIKOW, Among Women

1 It Could Have Been Me

one famous surrealist painter painted his pictures
over his wife's pictures.
he tried to convince her she had never really
painted at all.
when she went mad,
he painted a very
convincing picture
of insanity.
why is it my worst dreams
are never as bad as reality?

Alta, *The Shameless Hussy*

The rape of girl-children by a Father is an integral
product of our society, based as it is on male supremacist attitudes
and organisation, reinforced by the fundamental social structure of
the family.

'Child sexual abuse' is the new catch-cry phrase, attracting
interest from diverse groups within the community. Many of those
who begin to focus their attention here deduce that 'incest' is what it
is all about, since most child sexual abuse occurs within the family.
Clinicians have used the term 'incest' for decades, except when they
sought to minimise the impact of their findings, in which case they
tend to talk of 'sexual contact' or 'sex experiences'.

Most writers exploring 'child sexual abuse' write about what they
call 'father–daughter incest' because the father is the most frequent
offender. Operating within this linguistic term of reference, two
feminist psychologists conclude:

Like prostitution and rape, father–daughter incest will disappear
only when male supremacy is ended.[1]

While agreeing with this sentiment, I eschew the term 'father–

77

daughter incest' because it blurs reality, leading patriarchal thinkers to considerations of 'appropriateness', 'family dysfunction' and 'deviation', rather than the simple fact that a girl-child has been sexually abused/carnally known/raped by an adult man.

Psychological, sociological and theological concerns about the blood or kindred relationship between the victim and the offender, which are contained within the usage of the word 'incest', also blur reality, by focussing attention upon *who* is involved, rather than upon *what is happening*. What is happening is that a child is being victimised and that she and the offender usually belong to, and live in, the same family. The particularities of this rape dynamic mean that the offender has almost unlimited access to the victim, in space, and over a long time, as well as the access of a parent/adult/male over a girl-child.

In the last forty years or so dozens of articles and a handful of books have been written on 'incest' – predominantly father–daughter 'unions' – as an aberrant 'phenomenon' within 'advanced' western-style societies. This literature, most of which comes from the United States, approaches the subject via the scientific method favoured by social scientists (in this case psychoanalysts, psychiatrists, medical practitioners, sociologists and criminologists): here is some 'material' which is 'interesting' because it does not fit the 'norm'. In this academic mode they tabulate 'facts' and attempt to draw conclusions about causality and possible 'outcomes' for the various 'participants'. No attempt is made to probe the background: to examine the values of a society within which the rape of girl-children by the Fathers happens frequently. Everything is examined *within* the mores of the system which caused it: patriarchal society.

Thus, what other writers refer to as 'father–daughter incest', I shall refer to as 'Father–Daughter rape'. My first reason for doing this is, as outlined above, that 'incest' focusses attention upon who is involved in 'sexual activity', rather than on what is happening for the girl-child. 'Incest' is a label applied to sexual unions which have the particular characteristic of violating the prohibition on sexual contacts among related persons. As such, it is used to refer to mutually consenting unions such as those between adult siblings, as well as to the non-consenting unions between a girl-child and an adult male. Thus, a welfare worker might say, 'Oh, that's a case of incest', thereby denying in linguistic and affective terms the fact that a form of abuse is taking place.

Secondly, 'incest' is widely understood and used as an anthropological term. This is a usage which grows out of the evidence amassed by (mainly male) anthropologists that all societies have a special taboo pattern concerning sexual relationships amongst people who are related by blood, kinship or marriage. Anthropologists go to other societies to examine the patterning of allowed sexual relationships, thereby drawing comparisons and conclusions about differing cultural taboos of sexual partner choice. In this sense, the word 'incest' has a specific application, within a precise academic discipline. (What the anthropologists will make of their methods when they realise that the incest 'taboo' of western society is, at best, a one-sided sham, may well provide the raw material for some PhD topics in the 1980s.)

Thirdly, the term 'incest' carries within it the pejorative weight of the term 'incest taboo'. As such, its usage in the context of child sexual abuse serves to imply that incestual unions between girl-children and adult males within the family are extremely rare, and automatically attract widespread disapproval. In actual practice, most rapists of children (and of women) get away with it: rape is the most under-reported and under-prosecuted crime, in spite of the fact that the vast majority of rapists are known to their victims. The apparent moral sanction on incest does not mesh with the sanctions applied by the law or by social networks. Imagine the sanctions did mesh: then a father who sexually abused his daughter would be automatically cast out of the family, ostracised by friends and work colleagues, and punished severely under the law.[2]

Fourthly, having rejected the term 'incest' I had to create a term which would accurately convey the dynamics of the situation. I use 'rape' because I believe that the sexual use of a child's body/being is the *same* as the phenomenon of adult rape. Terms like 'sexual abuse', 'molestation' and 'interference' are diminutions of 'rape': they imply that something *less* than rape occurred. In the process of counselling hundreds of victims of Father-rape, the Sydney Rape Crisis Centre found that the women (of all ages) universally described the experience as 'feeling like rape', no matter what specific form the abuse took.[3] The same is true of the victims with whom I talked.

I also use the term 'girl-child' because the raped children with whom this book is concerned are children who are female. The sexism built into our language would hold that the term 'child' is non-gender-specific. While this can be so, the term is usually used in texts about children in which the 'non-gender-specific' pronouns 'he', 'him' and 'his' are also used. For this reason, the term 'child' is weighted with the load of male privilege that is usually accorded to words which are meant to apply across gender, such as 'mankind'. So although I will be using 'she' and 'her', I feel it necessary to make 'child' quite sex-specific, so that its every use in the text would bring home to the reader that it is girl-children who are the vast majority of raped children.

The sex-specific use of 'child' also helps us perceive and understand that the ontological experience of being female or male starts at birth: it is not merely a mantle donned along with the age-appropriate characteristics of 'woman' or 'man'. The difference between life as a boy-child and as a girl-child is nowhere more clearly demonstrated than in exploring rape. The known statistics indicate that boy-children are victims in five to fifteen percent of cases. It is obvious from the clinical readings that many of these victims are abused/raped by a father, or father-figure, who is taking advantage of the child-status (powerlessness) of whatever children happen to come under his authority, so that it is the fact that the boy is a child that makes him a rape victim. Many boy-child victims are raped by a Father who also rapes girl-children; the statistical information shows an overwhelmingly heterosexual orientation in men who rape children.[4] Some Canadian clinicians who have studied 'father–son incest' claim that 'many of the dynamics occurring in homosexual incest are similar to those apparent in father–daughter incest'.[5] Some boy-children are raped because they are male: most homosexual rape of boy-children which is motivated by the sexual orientation of the rapist does not appear to occur within the family.

The experiences and reactions of both these types of boy-child victims fall outside the scope of this study. The rape ideology of male supremacist society means that girl-children and adult women live, always, with the fear of rape: it is central to the experience of being female. This is not true for males, even those boy-children who may have been victims of rape at a young age.

> In the clinical situation the father who makes sexual approaches to his son symbolically castrates him by making a woman of him.[6]

Like rape in goals, boy-rape is an expression of power, whereby the rapist 'feminises' the victim, reducing him to the passive, receptive state of being that women are seen to hold by virtue of rape ideology. A male rape victim, therefore, has a quite different set of dynamics to cope with: because he is male, he has an inability to identify with the Other-ness of females who are raped.

The ideology of rape is so entwined in the way we live that, for many people, it seems 'natural'. By 'rape ideology' I refer to the underpinning of male supremacist society: the set of beliefs and practices which causes females to actually live in fear of males, or maleness. The ideology of rape creates limitation as a way of life for females: we take a risk in walking down the street, going out at night, being alone at home, hiking alone, drinking in a bar, going to get our own vehicle in a car-park, waiting for a cab or a bus at night. The ideology of rape says that male sexuality is innately active, aggressive and insatiable; that female sexuality is innately passive, receptive and inhibited. The ideology of rape creates needs in men which support a billion-dollar porn industry, in which females are always and immutably Other. The ideology of rape sees war and sexuality as one and the same battleground:

> Here is my cock,
> here is my gun:
> this is for fighting,
> this is for fun.[7]

The ideology of rape creates a social structure in which men set out to conquer, invade and plunder women's bodies: the 'armchair rapist'[8] who reads soft porn may wish he was the leader of the rape-pack. The ideology of rape is discernible when the judge (and/or jury) in a court case treats the victim as the guilty party. The ideology of rape is discernible when men make jokes in which sex and rape are interchangeable, and women smile uneasily and turn away to pick up the plate and pass the olives/cheese/buns/canapés. And the ideology of rape is discernible in Father–Daughter rape situations, where the Fathers are forgiven, the Daughters and Mothers blamed.

The law manifests an attempt to establish a graduated scale of *types* of rape, such as 'sexual assault', 'attempted rape' and 'forcible rape'. Legal distinctions about the age or type of consent, vaginal penetration, or measurement of the amount and type of coercion used, have nothing to do with rape as it is *experienced* by the victim. To be raped, as a woman or girl-child, is to experience

. . . an act of aggression in which the victim is denied her self-determination. It is an act of violence which, if not actually

81

followed by beatings and murder, nevertheless always carries with it the threat of death.[9]

Rape always 'carries with it the threat of death' because rape is a complete taking over, a taking away, of the girl-child's or woman's process of being in the world. To be quite taken over is to be in a state of complete powerlessness over your own existence. It is to be no-thing; the raped woman becomes pure matter; in the act of rape her spirit ceases to be experienced, even by herself.

Each of the women who told her story for this book *felt* raped. Jude was not penetrated by her father: she was 'fondled', used as a voyeuristic object, and 'courted' by her father. Yet she felt defiled; she felt powerless; she wanted to kill him. Jude's case is not unique:

> Many men station themselves around corners with mirrors or outside of slightly open doors to watch their daughters undress. They are content that this has no impact on their daughters because they are sure their daughters are not aware of it. The girls report otherwise, usually with a strong sense of disillusionment and distress.[10]

A daughter who is visually raped by her father in this way will indeed have her illusions shattered. If her father behaves like this in her own home, then where can she be safe? Another clinician also uses the word 'disillusion':

> . . . even though violence by a stranger is surely terrifying, at least it can be dealt with directly. Everyone can express rage at the offence and support the child. However, seduction or forcible rape by a respected authority figure is more disillusioning.[11]

If such things happen at the hands of a respected (or socially accepted) 'authority figure' (her father), then what illusions about safety for herself can be left? The shattering of illusion for a girl-child rape victim causes 'distress', as quoted above. 'Distress' is a word of wide application; it can be used to describe a variety of reactions in many different situations. Here it has been used in the 'clinical' sense, presumably referring to crying and agitation. The real cause of rape-victim distress is inexpressible rage: rage at the lack of space and safety within which the girl-child may express her anger and her being-in-the-world (self-determination). As we shall see, the girl-child victim of rape by a Father has been rendered invisible: unseen, unheard, unacknowledged, her rage has been denied and misnamed distress.

From the beginning of this chapter, I have used the capitalised form of 'father' to refer to the offenders as a group, or in conceptual form. Many of the clinical writers use the term 'father' when speaking of all incestuous offenders. One study begins:

> We cannot detect from our material any apparent difference in the psychopathology of the participants regardless of whether the girl had relations with her father or with a father substitute.[12]

This study was based on 'incestuous relationships with either father, stepfather, grandfather, foster father or brother'. Another writer states:

> Incestuous sexual acts between parents and foster and/or adoptive children are observed frequently, and the effects of the incestuous acts in these children do not seem to differ from the effects in natural children.[13]

Since about '80% of sex crimes committed against children occur within what we traditionally refer to as affinity systems (immediate family, relatives, close friends and neighbours)',[14] the social relationship existing between the girl-child victim and the offender has the 'father' connotations of a trusted, 'protective' male within the family group. I shall call these offending men 'the Fathers'. Where I am referring to a specific instance of Father–Daughter rape which involves the biological father, the lower case letter will indicate this.

I shall likewise use the capitalised forms 'Daughter', 'Mother', 'Stranger' and 'Son' to indicate the conceptualised roles described and maintained by patriarchal culture within the meaning of these words, and within the particular context of the dynamics involved in Father–Daughter rape. Thus, for example, the term 'girl-children' may appear in the same sentence as 'the Daughters', in which case the former will indicate the common-noun naming I have selected for these people, while the latter will indicate the girl-children who are raped by the Fathers. In the same way, 'the Mothers' may refer to mothers, aunts, grandmothers, adult female friends of the families in which Father–Daughter rape occurs.

A further breakdown of the '80 percent' figure from the statistics that are available (police reports, welfare agency records, rape crisis centre files) indicates that up to 50 percent, or more, of offenders are the actual father; 25 percent or more are other men from the 'affinity system' in which the child lives, i.e. grandfather, uncle, older brother, de facto father, stepfather, foster father, neighbour, babysitter, family friend. Sexual contact with a stranger is usually a once-only event, whereas an integral part of rape by a Father is that access is unlimited – so it most often continues for a lengthy period, often for years.

The only other source of statistics on the proportion of Fathers as opposed to Strangers who rape girl-children is the very notional one which emerges from the writings of psychiatrists.

Of a 250-case sample [from the Centre for Rape Concern, Philadelphia General Hospital] studied from the last quarter of 1970 and 1972, approximately 58 percent of those under 18 were allegedly raped by men they knew. This percentage of just over one half is in striking contrast to my private practice where 90 percent of the victims knew the offender, but the reason is obvious. Who would report a loved one to the police?[15]

Not only has the 'loved one' committed rape on a child, but also the horrendous social solecism of breaking the so-called incest taboo. How many people do you know who could cope with the kind of reactions that such a revelation to public authorities would cause? And yet, since this study in the early seventies, more and more reports are being made all the time. The suffocating fog of silence that has enshrouded the victims for untold decades (centuries? millennia?) is at last lifting – very slowly.

The picture of the total number of cases which might be occurring at any given time is sketchy at best. Virtually every writer in the field states that whatever we know is only 'the tip of the iceberg'. In 1955, Weinberg, who did an extensive study in five countries, estimated the number of cases to be between 1 and 2 per million population.[16] By 1968, De Francis of the American Humane Association estimated a yearly incidence of around 40 per million population.[17] Giaretto, the founding director of the Child Sexual Abuse Treatment Program in Santa Clara County in California (established in 1970, this programme was the first of its kind), wrote in 1976 that the findings of their programme 'indicate that Weinberg's one-in-a-million statistic is wrong by a factor of at least 180'.[18] Each year since its inception, this programme, which operates in a demographically 'professional' white-collar population of over one million people, has had an increased referral rate. Giaretto believes that this is due to 'increased public awareness and confidence in the program', but he continues:

Nonetheless, even the change from one to about 200 cases per million inhabitants does not reflect the true prevalence of incest in Santa Clara County or throughout the nation.[19]

The *Australian Women's Weekly*, in an open survey in 1980, invited women to respond to a wide range of personal, social and political questions, including a battery of questions about 'incest'. Three percent of respondents wrote of 'incestuous' experiences as children: that is, 30,000 females per million of the population are victims if we take this survey as any sort of basis from which to make estimates.[20] In a recent book, *The Broken Taboo*, the survey of statistical evidence concludes with the statement that some researchers claim that 'incest implicates at least 5 percent of the population and perhaps up to 15 percent'.[21] Several writers have attested to the belief that the incidence of 'sexual abuse' of children is far greater than that of physical abuse.[22] All that is really clear at this stage is that as more avenues are opened offering help to raped Daughters (and their families), the more the reported figures rise. The iceberg is gradually being revealed, but there is still a long way to go.

Weinberg discerned only one significant factor in terms of 'fluctuations' in the reported figures, but it is a very telling factor:

In the five English-speaking countries and in the various states of the United States, the rates of incest were not sensitive to the rise of urbanization, to the density or increase of population or to the business cycle. The main discernible pattern was that *incest behaviour declined during the war and increased in the postwar years.*[23] [My italics.]

The reason for this fluctuation is obvious: the Fathers were away. Most of the problem had been removed – removed, that is, from their families and access to the Daughters. As soldiers, the Fathers have (semi-)official permission to rape: rape of women is part of warfare. World-wide, therefore, raping of females did not decline: it merely shifted location from the family to the war zones.

Weinberg's finding that the state of the 'business cycle' did not affect Father–Daughter rape is disputed by the simple observation of an acquaintance of mine who has been a teacher of disadvantaged and retarded children for nearly thirty years in Australia. She 'dreads' rising unemployment because her lengthy experience of being close to such children has taught her that a father at home all day means his girl-children are far more likely to be raped.

Along with the uncovering of the iceberg in terms of figures, the myth that Father–Daughter rape only occurred in low-income families or amongst isolated rural communities has been revealed as a denial mechanism of middle-class researchers. As with most other crimes and sins of omission, those with least means at their disposal have least power to maintain privacy over their own affairs. Thus, up until the seventies, most 'studies of offenders' were based on men imprisoned for 'incest' offences; and most studies of victims were based on children who had come under the care of welfare agencies. The conclusions drawn from these simplistic analyses were class-bound: mainstream middle-class minds tut-tutting about 'provocative' girls, 'brutish' fathers and 'inadequate' mothers in *other* class groups. Such analyses

> . . . cannot hold up in the face of the growing number of aggressors whose singular characteristic in common is that they sexually assault their own children . . . By our [sic] insistence that it is only 'those people' who assault their children, we can avoid facing the abuse that is going on around us.[24]

The need to avoid looking at 'the abuse that is going on around us' can even lead to the concept of Other which concludes that 'they suffer less pain', as in the following convoluted attempt to deny the reality of horror for the victims of Father–Daughter rape:

> Since most of the cases we studied were initially identified by the police and other public agencies, they represent an economically deprived segment of the community. It is possible that victims in our study group, compared with victims from higher socio-economic strata, *hypothetically have fewer and less abrasive long-range effects, because prior conditions of social and economic deprivation have made personal mistrust, hostility, and humiliation a normal part of childhood expectations.*[25] [My italics.]

This is tantamount to saying that working-class girl-children suffer

86

less from being raped than do their middle-class sisters; and as well paints a 'coincidental' picture of working-class life as being riven with 'personal mistrust, hostility, and humiliation'. In putting this negative attention on working-class life and working-class Daughters, the plight of the Daughters from the 'higher socio-economic strata' is actually rendered invisible by not being discussed at all. Much apparently 'liberal', 'honest' discussion along class lines, when applied by male supremacist (middle-class) social scientists to the question of rape in any form, often, as here, merely serves the dual purpose of separating women along class lines, and at the same time denying the horror of rape victimisation for women and girl-children of all classes.

In the case histories I have read, and from women I have talked to, it is obvious that the Fathers come from every class in society. A judge, a barrister, a diplomat, an eminent doctor, a university lecturer, a teacher, a university student, a businessman, a film-star, a labourer, a tradesman, a public servant, a farmer, a counsellor, a minister of religion, a soldier, a politician, unemployed, handicapped, very old, very young: Everyman. All have raped girl-children.

The problem of ascertaining the true incidence of Father–Daughter rape derives from a male supremacist social structure which creates a silence on the subject: most of the Daughters are unable to find someone who will 'hear' them. Most of the Daughters try to tell someone about what is happening to them. They try to get someone to hear them. In all of the stories in this book the Daughter wanted to tell someone; some tried – in most cases they were not heard. They want to share their pain; they need to know that they are not guilty; most of all, they simply want it to end. Where do the Daughters turn for help?

For most, there is/has been no one to turn to except people within the same family unit, where the raping is happening. It is not only the girl-child but also everyone else in her family who believes and/or behaves as though it were the 'safe' place in their lives. Family members look to their relationship with each other to determine their place in the world, their roots in the human race; the family is culturally and structurally presented as each person's haven from the 'other' worlds of school or work or unemployment, of 'other people' and potentially dangerous situations.

The family-as-haven is an ideological construct, obscuring the fact that for the Daughters (at least) the family is a prison. The atavistic desire to maintain the psychic identity of the family keeps people (women and children specifically) isolated from one another, and therefore powerless. The myth that raping of girl-children only occurs Out There is integral to the perpetuation of the necessity, and therefore the notional inviolability, of the family. Susan Griffin writes of the process of learning this myth which, significantly, always occurs within the family:

> From a very early age I, like most women, have thought of rape as part of my natural environment – something to be feared or prayed against like fire or lightning. I never asked why men raped; I simply thought of it as one of the many mysteries of human nature . . . I observed that my grandmother was meticulous about locks, and quick to draw the shades before anyone removed so much as a shoe. I sensed that danger lurked outside.
>
> At the age of eight, my suspicions were confirmed. My grandmother took me to the back of the house where the men wouldn't hear, and told me that strange men wanted to do harm to little girls.[26]

This is what most of us are told: that the danger is outside, out there in the rest of the world. The corollary of this is that we also 'learn' that inside, in the home, among the family, is not dangerous. By default, girl-children learn that some men are to be trusted, and the rest are not. The myth that rape is committed by strangers is integrally linked to the subliminal myth that rape is an adult phenomenon. Feminist research has established that most adult rape victims are raped by a man they know; now it is also established that children are almost solely raped by someone they know, and know especially well.

Thus it is that the Daughter who tries to tell someone in the family, usually her mother, finds that the person she is telling cannot 'hear'. The mother has no cultural permission on which to base the consideration of such a possibility: she was taught that rape-danger was Out There too. (The large body of literature which holds that the Mothers 'know' at some level, or even that the Mothers cause Father–Daughter rape, is analysed and discussed in Chapter 5, The Mothers.) What we, the Daughters and Mothers, are told as girl-children is reinforced by the media in the 'news' and 'drama' alike: child-rapists are presented as psychopaths, completely deranged individuals; never as members of families, as some you probably know. The mass media is a powerful weapon for the propagation of rape ideology: news and drama are the same in that they present no models of Mothers and Daughters seeing the truth about the Fathers. Father–Daughter rape has been invisible in our culture.

Since the Mothers cannot hear, some Daughters try to tell their peers, as Kim did, in telling them her story in terms of a 'friend'. Her peers were shocked: she felt abnormal and dirty, and determined not to speak of it again.

Another avenue for being 'heard' is the professional helpers that most girl-children have some access to, such as the family doctor or the school counsellor. Suzanne Sgroi, a doctor, has written of the frequent occurrence of VD in children (vaginal, anal and oral) and the fact that many doctors do not follow symptoms which would automatically be checked if found in an adult. They have even been known to resort to ludicrous denial mechanisms, mumbling about infected sheets and contagion through toilet seats, when a VD test turns out to be positive. Sgroi understands the cultural base for such unmedical behaviour:

> Recognition of sexual molestation in a child is *entirely dependent* on the individual's inherent willingness to entertain the possibility that the condition may exist.[27] [My italics.]

If tangible physical evidence can be ignored by medical professionals in this way, then very many more cases are obviously being 'screened out' by welfare officers, school counsellors, teachers, doctors, nurses and priests who do not 'hear' the evidence in cues such as running away, school phobia, aggressive acting out, withdrawnness, tension, fear of men, and even straightforward accusations.

Thus, for most victims, there is no one to 'see' or 'hear'. The Daughters cannot (have not) been heard because they do not fit into the image that male supremacist society has created for itself. In the image, the Daughter is sweet, enticing, cute and at all times 'innocent', so that the Father may delight in her naïveté at the same time as he protects her from 'harsh reality'. No, the story of a girl-child raped by a Father does not match the constructed image. No one wants to know.

There are more tangible reasons for keeping silent in many cases. The Father frequently threatens to kill the girl-child if she tells, or he says, 'You'll be sent away', and even more coercively, 'I'll be sent to jail if you tell'. As well, or instead, the Father often mindbinds her with seductive talk of 'sharing secrets', 'being grown-up now' and – very commonly – 'sex education', [28] or he tells her he does this because he loves her. Most frightening of all is the belief that many of the 'inexplicable' family murders that adorn the front page of afternoon tabloid newspapers from time to time are a response to 'incest' being revealed by the Daughter to the Mother. The 'family murders' I am speaking of are those where the father apparently kills his wife and all their children, then shoots himself. When this causal theory was originally suggested to me, I found it a bit 'way-out'; I felt sceptical. In 1979, I asked the then most senior female police officer in the NSW police department if she had heard of this theory. Her reply rocked me: 'Oh, yes. We know that. There's nothing we can do about it.' If this is true then it means that the 'silencing' of some victims is absolute: the Father in his desperation will kill everyone who may ever 'tell'.

As if all these reasons are not enough to explain the silence or not-being-heard of many victims, there is also an accumulation of evidence which shows that many who do speak out are not believed: they are accused of lying or fantasising. 'You're making it up!' has been the response many victims received: which is colloquial phraseology for both lying and fantasising. (In Chapter 2: Freud and the Legacy of Mindbinding, I outline Freud's particular contribution to the notion of sexual 'fantasising' in girl-children.) When this is the response, the case will most likely not be recorded at all, even if the report has come to a doctor or welfare officer. The concept of 'fantasy' has played an insidious role in the further oppression of raped girl-children, because once it has been introduced, lurid extrapolations become possible. For example, Drs Bender and Blau, the first 'experts' in the modern period (1937) to write about children who had sexual 'experience' with adults, made a (personal) observation which became part of the clinical folklore on 'father–daughter incest' for nearly forty years:

> . . . a most striking feature was that these children were distinguished as unusually charming and attractive in their outward personalities. Thus, it is not remarkable that frequently we considered the possibility that the child might have been the actual seducer rather than the one innocently seduced . . . The experience offers an opportunity for the child to test out in reality, an infantile fantasy; it probably finds the consequences less severe, and in fact actually gratifying to a pleasure sense. The emotional balance is thus in favour of contentment.[29]

Even when the girl-child is not implicitly blamed in this manner, there are always the 'helpers' who refuse/cannot recognise the reality of the (rape) situation for the Daughter – as in Jude's case, where the family doctor condoned her father's actions and encouraged her to stay.

While all of these factors have kept, and still do keep, untold numbers of girl-children silent, the surrounding silence within the social fabric is, gradually, being broken. The fact that girl-children are often raped has come to light through the activities of rape crisis centres throughout the world. Rape crisis centres came into existence as a result of women beginning to speak to each other, and most importantly of all, to *hear* each other. We found that rape, and the fear of rape, was a condition of life for all women. We heard individual rape stories, worse by far than the lurid voyeurism of the mass media and male jokes, which never talked about the ensuing humiliation at the hands of police, hospitals, family, co-workers, neighbours, and the courts. We heard these stories and we cried together. And women became angry. Women started self-defence classes for women only. Women wrote articles, gave talks about rape. And women opened rape crisis centres where women could come and talk about past rapes, or rapes that had just occurred. And in these self-same rape crisis centres, women began to hear of the girl-child rapes. Mothers rang in, crying, scared, to ask for help because their husbands were raping their daughters. Girl-children rang in, whispering, scared: how to even say what was happening, when all around, except for this number, the only thing offered was silence. And women rang in, in vast numbers, telling of the rapes they had endured as Daughters. The rape crisis centres were tapping a *need to talk* that was as old as the oldest rape victim alive today.

Although there have always been a few doctors or therapists or teachers who heard and cared and helped in a few individual cases, the recognition of a *mass* phenomenon of Father–Daughter rape has only come about through the international network of feminist caring embodied in rape crisis centres. These centres have a commitment to mass education on rape issues, as well as a commitment to individual women in need of help. 'Education' in this sense means making a lot of noise: writing, talking, arguing, interrupting meetings if necessary – so that the issue becomes one of public concern. As Susan Griffin puts it:

> When we confront rape, suddenly a whole system becomes visible, a system which includes invisibility and silence, which

had covered the crime of rape in silence, and of which silencing and the ignorance of our history of protesting our condition has been an active part. So it follows that rape does not end with the changing of laws; that the causes go deeper and belong to the whole fabric.[30]

I am not going to discuss the 'changing of laws' in this book: other women are ably struggling on that front, forcing through reforms of the law which ease our burden as rape victims and also 'educate' many sectors of the population through their passage of legislation and implementation. The factor here which 'goes deeper and belongs to the whole fabric' is that girl-children, like adult women, are the object of rape fantasy and rape aggression by the Fathers.

The fact that a girl-child rape victim will most often be raped by a Father or Father-figure means, as we have seen above, that she is truly isolated. The 'ordinary' rape victim finds that friends and lovers turn away from her. The myth that she must have asked for it, the sense that she is the contaminated one, is confirmed all too often by the behaviour of the people she turns to for support. The girl-child raped by a Father experiences all the violation, loss of self, powerlessness, that raped adult women describe. As well, for her to speak and seek support is to threaten the family, both the individual family and the social concept of the family; for her to speak is also, in most cases, to risk not being heard, thus compounding and confirming her isolation, and sense of being a freak. It is the 'incest' factor which especially militates against her being heard. A typical expression of the 'normal' social attitudes towards incest is expressed by the sociologist Weinberg, in the opening paragraph of his book:

Incest, the universal crime, violates a taboo that is as forceful among primitives as among sophisticated moderns. It is behaviour that disrupts or destroys the social intimacy and sexual distance upon which family unity depends. It is the recourse of very disturbed and very perverse persons.[31]

Society (people) turn away from the girl-child rape victim to an extra degree precisely *because* the rapist is her father, uncle, brother, grandfather, rather than The Stranger. She, often more than the Father, is tainted as 'disturbed and very perverse'. If any 'special' response is called for, it must be that the rapist was such a trusted person: that society, the rest of the family, and probably the girl-child herself, believed that the Father cared about her/loved her, at least tolerated her. But raped her . . .

There are two 'patterns' that emerge from a study of the actual practice of the rape of the Daughters. The first, like Vera's, starts when the child is very young: anywhere from one or two up to eight or nine. Victims at these ages may be penetrated vaginally or anally or orally; if so, there will usually be severe physical damage and a great deal of pain. More usually, the raping will take the form of ejaculation for the rapist by somehow using the girl-child's body: rubbing the penis up and down her legs, thrusting towards her vagina (as in Alice's case); or between her legs (as in Vera's case); or using her visual support for his masturbation (as in Kim's case); or making her stimulate his penis with her hand or mouth (as in Lynette's case) – one or more of these methods will be instituted as 'what happens' when he initiates a 'session'. For Daughters caught in this pattern, the breaking of it *may* come if she herself can change her responding behaviour – as Vera did when she scratched her grandfather, Vicki did by telling her grandmother, and Lynette did by threatening to tell the police. More usually, the form of raping will continue until the victim reaches puberty: then the Father-rapist will either stop, or escalate, insisting on full intercourse. In the latter and more common event, the Daughter herself may resist at that point, as Lynette did, thus changing the pattern; if this does not happen, the raping continues in its new form.

The second common pattern that emerges from the literature and the Daughters is when vaginal-penetration-type rape begins at puberty or during adolescence, unpreceded by any of the other activities described above. There are endless combinations and permutations of these two patterns. There are also the sickening embellishments encountered in 'ordinary' rape: penetration of vagina and anus with objects; being forced to eat faeces; being urinated and defecated upon; being beaten with whips; being forced to parade in sex-shop garments; having photographs taken; having to consent to intercourse as a condition of being allowed to go out with peers; having a knife held at her throat. Whatever happens in Father–Daughter rape virtually always happens *more than once*.

In Chapter 3, The Fathers, I present the determined efforts by theorists from many disciplines to pin down the precise characteristics common to 'incestuous fathers'. The findings and theories have changed over the years, and are still changing. The approach, however, is always the same: a search for the elusive 'something' that delineates these men from other men. No sooner is 'something' found, than it slides away in the next recounting of case histories. Anne Deveson, a member of the Australian Royal Commission into Human Relationships, 1974-7, writing of child abuse, including sexual abuse, points out that:

> The problem is so complex that it is a mistake to look for a common cause, or *to concentrate too much on the individual characteristics of the parents*.[32] [My italics.]

Deveson, in correctly eschewing the 'aberrant individual' attitude, stresses that child abuse in general is a social problem, but in doing so gets lost in the sea of liberal sociology which pours more money into more outreach programmes for individual families 'having problems', instead of perceiving that there is indeed a 'common cause'. For such well-meaning social reformers, 'a common cause' perception must be avoided because it is too large, too threatening. Rape ideology is the attitude and practice which keeps women in a state of fear and isolated dependence on men, both at home and outside the home. There is 'common cause' in the rape of the Daughters by the Fathers in that each Daughter is alone in her female body, and each Father has the sanction of male supremacist attitudes to use sex as power over females wherever and whenever he can.

The fact that some Fathers rape Daughters in their care and others do not is the factor which lends credence to the overwhelming blindness of society which shies away from even considering a 'common cause'. The fact that some Fathers rape Daughters means that every Daughter, theoretically, is a potential victim of rape by one of her Fathers, just as all women are potential victims of rape by any man. And the fact that girl-children are raped at home means we must question the social structure of the family.

The most recent body of 'theory' about 'father–daughter incest' is that the families in which this occurs are 'dysfunctional'. In sounding clinical, this label implies some sort of profound meaning. All it in fact does is name a self-evident truth: these families are not functioning according to the 'normal' notion of family life. The clinical overtone in this term is appropriate however, because it is part of the language of the socio-medical model of society, which holds that 'dysfunctional' families can be 'fixed up' by a little intervention here, and a little therapy there. Pushed back into shape, made 'proper', so that it becomes a 'good' family, just like all the others.

Why is there so much fear about considering the possibility that it is the very structure of the family which is part of the problem? The current perpetuation of the family is based on the concept of romantic love, which, we are taught, ignites a man and woman with such fervour that they unite to form a couple, undertaking to live together until death (or the unthinkable: falling out of love) separates them. 'Romantic love' is known to be a cultural construct – in many societies it is unknown, inconceivable. Why is it that in our society we not only experience it, but also have it rammed down our throats in films, in songs, in opera, on television, in literature, even in advertisements?

Because it is the salve to our angst. Capitalist patriarchy is based on competition and distrust; it uses violence and sex to promote our susceptibility to competition and distrust; it places us on a life-long rollercoaster of business 'cycles', and of war which is punctuated by 'peace'. The only respite offered us, from this over-arching nightmare, is 'good parenting' as children (Happy Families), and Romantic Love as adults. The crucial flaw in the promise of the Happy Family is that even those few who believe that they experienced it, seek Romantic Love as adults: which means that *no one*, not even those who receive most love as children, is free from the angst of wanting/needing more love/closeness/caring in their lives. (Romantic Love is sought after in 'alternative' communities as well as the majority-world of suburbia; it is sought after in lesbian and homosexual circles, as well as in the majority-world of heterosexuality.) Romantic Love is like a syrup that greases the cogs and keeps the whole machine ticking over.

And the whole machine is made up of families. Families conceived in Romantic Love then settle down with the Happy Families deck of cards; in far too many of them, the Father–Daughter rapist (Joker) turns up. The shortage of more Romantic Love syrup and the fact that there seems to be nowhere else to go, is why people cling to the 'family' and recoil in outraged horror from any attempt to look dispassionately at it.

The girl-children raped by a Father are the ultimate victims of this passionate blindness. Victims of the family structure, they are also victims of the utter dependency of children, economically, physically, socially, legally; and of the violent nexus between power and sex, the instrument of rape, by which women and girl-children are controlled in male supremacist society.

Many attempts to help a girl-child raped by a Father have collapsed under the overriding need of the 'helper' to keep the family together. In several parts of the United States, specialist sexual abuse clinics of various types have 'worked through' this attitude and its concomitant failure, and come reluctantly to the conclusion that at least sometimes the family cannot be 'saved'.[33]

Often Daughter-victims find other places to go – of a sort. Sometimes relatives (more of the same?), more often foster-families (the same in another form?), most often Girls' Homes where they arrive numbered and labelled after running away or otherwise 'acting out' by manifesting 'unacceptable' behaviour. Undocumented speculation around the 'helping' community, in Australia at least, indicates that many or most inmates of these Homes have become 'wayward' as a response to rape by a Father. Then there is the widespread belief among many social welfare workers who are concerned with young people, that many or most of the teenage girl runaways who inhabit the red-light districts of our big cities, living off their wits and their bodies, are there 'because of incest', as Lt John Bond of the Salvation Army maintained in an interview about the 'Street Urchins of St Kilda' in 1980.[34] And they are there, living off their wits and their bodies, because *there is nowhere else to go*. Thus it would appear that society has had 'places' for the Daughter-victims for a long time, but the true function of these places has been camouflaged by the silence surrounding Father–Daughter rape. By focussing on the 'acting out' (self-assertive) behaviour of the Daughters, the victims appear to be the problem. We need, instead, to pay a great deal of attention to the *cause* of the desperation exhibited by 'acting out' girl-children.

The Single Womens' Refuge, situated very close to King's Cross in Sydney, open only for four months at the time of writing, has found that most of those requiring shelter are teenage girls and young women. The experience so far at this refuge has been that 95 percent of adolescent girls have run away from 'incest'. Their life consists of surviving through prostitution and/or the drug trade. They are mostly extremely angry and violent young women. The Refuge workers allow them to express and focus some of their rage, but find that when they explain that two months is as long as they can be sheltered there, new depths of rage are unleashed because this one place has been the first time they have felt safe, cared about, listened to, understood. As new places are being made available to these Daughters, the desperate need for more complex care and *places to live* becomes apparent.

These Daughters, in escaping very courageously from Father-rape, are also giving up, through no fault of their own, a place to live: the security of home and family which most people take for granted. The girl-child, like the mother, is the property of the father (Fathers). The boy-child is too, but briefly, for, unlike the girl-child, he will grow into a man, become a member of the man's world and become an owner of women in his own right. The history of rape laws bears testimony that women have been/are the property of their fathers or husbands (who become fathers). Fathers still 'give' their daughter to a bridegroom. Mothers 'bear' children; fathers 'have' children. Marriage and the family keep surviving as social structures because women feel the need of protection – against rape by The Stranger. In the role of father and husband, the Father 'protects' his wife, sister, girl-children: which, in the case of the rapist-Father means that *he* (not other men) has unlimited sexual access to the socially helpless girl-child, since she 'belongs' to him.

On the notion of 'protection', Griffin writes:

> In the system of chivalry, men protect women against men. This is not unlike the protection relationship which the mafia established with small business in the early part of this century. Indeed, chivalry is an age-old protection racket which depends for its existence on rape.[35]

When the Father is seen as central to this 'protection racket', the power that he has over access to the Daughter's body becomes plain.

When we stop blinding ourselves, we remember the sexual come-ons we experienced in childhood. For most of us it was not rape; for many of us it was not our fathers, or even one of the Fathers; but for virtually every woman there was at least one man about whom we *knew*. For a woman not blinded by the myths, this knowledge is visible in the faces of quite small girl-children when a Father (trusted man) takes her on his knee or speaks to her in a certain way. She *knows*. She knows that he is getting off on her somehow. She knows that he doesn't really love her: she knows that his appearance of loving her is all bound up in his own needs and getting some sort of satisfaction which has absolutely nothing to do with her as a person. The difference between those of us who were raped by a Father, and those who were not, 'Is in degree, not kind'.[36]

Take my own case: I loved my father deeply, dependently,

trustfully. *If* he had approached me sexually, especially when being physically affectionate (a practice which was an integral part of my upbringing), I would have been a passive victim. I was quite assertive about my body/being with other people, usually managing to determine how and when I used it for myself and my own pleasure, but my father . . . he was the centre of my life. He had enormous power over me: because he provided our livelihood; because he was confident and forceful in his opinions; and because he loved me very much.

Once, when I was about thirteen, he put his arm around my shoulders, and his hand came to rest on my breast. I froze. I felt paralysed. I could not *act*. It was a few seconds (I guess). It seemed like five minutes. Then he started, and said, 'Oh. I'm sorry. I thought it was your shoulder.' And that is all that happened. What has come back to me out of that incident in doing the research for this book, in cinemascope and technicolor, is how I *felt*. *I discovered the passive victim in myself*: the Daughter who is raped by her Father. It could have happened to me *because* of the dynamics of that relationship. He could have done anything *because* he was my father. Many victims attest to this split: feeling the powerlessness, hating their own passiveness, but having absolutely no means of doing or saying anything to the very person who normally teaches you/tells you the difference between what is right and what is wrong. If the person who tells you what is right, does something that feels wrong – especially in relation to *your own body* – then it must be *you* who is out of phase. Hence the paralysis: it's *waiting*: waiting for that microsecond of paralytic confusion to pass, for the world to fall back into place where what is right and what is wrong is once again comfortably clear.

For most children, the world that is 'comfortably clear' is the world of the family in contrast to the world outside the family. Safe in here: unsafe Out There. For the victims of Father–Daughter rape, the 'practice' usually continues for years. For them, my microsecond becomes protracted periods – days, weeks, months, years, sometimes their whole childhood and adolescence. Bearing in mind the appalling isolation of such a victim, the surrounding social milieu which is almost always blind to what is happening to her, the apparent passivity of most victims is perfectly understandable. The Father has become split, in her mind and her experience: Daddy has become The Stranger who is still Daddy (or Grandpa or Uncle or Jim). Giaretto describes the girl-child's bewilderment like this:

> . . . the familiar father has suddenly put on the strange mask of lover and his daughter never knows which role he will play at any given time.[37]

The 'familiar father' and the 'lover' (rapist/Stranger) are, separately and together, an authority figure. As such, he has the authority that parents and adults have over children generally: in this case, he also has the 'authority' that a man has over a female in a rape situation. To the dynamics of 'ordinary' rape, in which a man 'seduces', cajoles, threatens or forces a woman to have sexual intercourse, we have to add the dynamics operating between a father-as-parent and his girl-child, in order to understand the powerlessness (which is read as passivity) of the girl-child victims.

All of the stories in this book either refer to, or attest to, the fact that the victim was not taught to say No to a man – meaning any man. Some had been taught to say No to a Stranger, but none was taught to say No to a Father. None of the women who told these stories, none of us, were told that we were in most danger from the men in our own families. None of us knew that the rape of girl-children is based in the home. And yet the No is apparent in the stories in this book. Each of the women was thinking No. They were behaving No, by trying to avoid the Father; by trying to tell someone; by running away. They were fantasising an absolute No, in that most of them desired to kill their Father, some even thought of how and when they might do it.

The family scenario is the pivot of Father–Daughter rape. This type of rape with its utterly dependent child-victim and the resulting prognosis that it will continue, in most cases, for years, means that, for many girl-children, *her family is the least safe place for her to be*. This means that we must radically alter the information that is given to girl-children. We must tell girl-children that it is not only strangers who *might* be dangerous; it is also any man she knows, including her own father, who *might* want to use her body sexually, who might rape her.

The girl-child victim of Father–Daughter rape has been raped in an exceedingly complex and horrendous set of circumstances:

> The victim is more traumatized the less closely her experience coincides with the myth of rape as an encounter among strangers.[38]

Here is one measure of the suffering of the Daughters and the true nature of Father–Daughter rape. Nothing can be less like 'an encounter among strangers' than rape by a Father.

2 Freud and the Legacy of Mindbinding

> For many of [Freud's] pupils the gulf which splits the world is
> formed like a female genital, and the signposts on the way to
> recovery have a phallic shape. Like overgrown schoolboys,
> they notice only the crude sex-urge in the relationship between
> the sexes. They must know that there are other problems;
> otherwise they could not turn so consistently away from them.
> Like children who draw a person's profile, they place both eyes
> on one side of the face.
>
> Theodore Reik, *Psychology of Sex Relations*

The learned men (psychiatrists, psychoanalysts, criminologists, sociologists) who have made pronouncements about
'father–daughter incest' have almost all done so within the context
of Freudianism: thus I was led to examine the writings of Freud to
see why this was so.

Father–Daughter rape was the foundation stone of the inter-
related theories about sexuality which Sigmund Freud developed.
In this chapter I outline the process by which Freud moved from an
initial awareness of Father–Daughter rape, to create an entire
superstructure of metaphysical concepts in order to protect himself
(the Fathers) from having to face the truth about the rape of
girl-children by the Fathers.

The distortion which Freud made of his initial discovery of
Father–Daughter rape was conceived within the framework of male
supremacy and ultimately functioned to reinforce rape ideology. As
such, 'Freudianism' permeates every form of 'therapy' in the
western world. Freud is by no means alone as a theorist who viewed
the world through male supremacist spectacles, thereby causing
untold suffering to women and girl-children – but his name, and the
term Freudianism, still stand as the signpost and place-name of a

way of thinking, a way of practising therapy, which demands thorough analytical criticism and debunking for the sake of all raped women, especially the very young who have been most *dis*believed.

The popularisation of Freudianism functions as subliminal 'psycho-scientific' ideology, reinforcing male desire to believe that women want to be raped. Freudianism holds that girl-children unconsciously desire intercourse with their fathers: thus we have the sexualisation of girl-children as a *reason* for their being raped by the Father. By this and several other means, Freud managed to blame the victim.

To read the original writings of Freud, as one who has been part of the movement uncovering the apparently 'invisible' phenomenon of Father–Daughter rape in recent years, is both affirming and depressing. On the one hand, our knowledge is 'proven' by the evidence of Freud's women patients of over eighty years ago; on the other, there is the intricately woven fabric of phallocratic ideology which Freud constructed out of the information he was amassing. As Florence Rush says of Freud:

> He lived in an age in which logic, reason and science supposedly supplanted religious mysticism – an era which required scientific rather than religious authority to justify brutal social injustice and inequities. Freud filled the bill. His theories, surrounded by scientific aura, allowed for the suppression and concealment of the sexual exploitation of the female child.[1]

That Freud was and is regarded as a hero by the keepers of male supremacist attitudes is thoroughly documented. For example, Galdston, who resoundingly criticises Freud as a purveyor of 'Romantic medicine', also says:

> It is my profound conviction that long after all that is sound and valid in his system of psychoanalysis has been absorbed and incorporated in psychiatry, Freud will be prized and celebrated above all else for the heroic dimensions of his being, for the valiance of his character, and for his Promethean spirit.[2]

He has been claimed as a scientist, a genius, a martyr, a satyr, a pervert, an artist, a revolutionary, a philosopher and a demi-god, as well as a hero. A Man for other other men to measure themselves by.

Freudian*ism* is the school of thought and psychoanalytic practice based more or less loosely on his ideas: 'Freudianism' encompasses the popularisation of Freud's ideas; which have become an integral part of our daily culture. Freud 'named' the unconscious; he 'discovered' the Oedipus Complex; and he 'realised' that children have sexual feelings. Freudianism combines these 'insights' to support rape ideology by forgiving the Fathers and blaming the Daughters – increasingly, the Mothers have been blamed as well. Many of Freud's individual ideas are important and useful in themselves; however, the manner in which Freud and his followers have combined and applied these ideas has been part of our oppression as women, and especially of raped girl-children.

As Mary Daly, writing on Freud's contribution to 'the theme of blaming the victim', puts it:

By the very fact of misnaming and misdefining her [the patient's] reactions, he obscures his own active role in the repetition of her violation.[3]

What follows is an examination of the process of 'misnaming' and 'misdefining' which Freud perpetrated.

In his initial work with adult patients manifesting 'hysteria' or 'obsessional neurosis', Freud reached the conclusion that 'sexual shock' or 'trauma' in early childhood was the actual cause of the adult conditions he was treating. He reached this decision because he found that nearly all (if not all: he suppressed some of the evidence) of his female patients reported having been the victims of rape by a Father as children, and that their physical 'symptoms' eased or vanished after this piece of their past had been 're-lived' through verbalising the experience to another person. Summing up these ideas, as he presented them in a lecture in 1896, (the only time he publicly put forward this idea), he observed that he had received:

. . . reports in some detail on *infantile sexual experiences which have proved responsible for the causation of psychoneuroses.* Their contents are to be described as 'perversions'; *those concerned are usually to be found among the patient's nearest relatives* . . . The presence of infantile sexual experience is an indispensable condition if the efforts at defence . . . are to succeed in producing pathogenic results . . . [4] [My italics.]

Freud used the word 'perversions' because most of his patients reported oral or anal rape. From misnaming these encounters 'infantile sexual *experience*' he went on to further misname these events in his patients' lives by calling them 'seductions'. He was, up to this period and for a year thereafter, working on the assumption that the 'sexual shock' was real, and that the offender was usually the father. He wrote, 'My confidence was strengthened by a few cases in which relations of this kind with a father, uncle or elder brother had continued up to an age at which memory was to be trusted.'[5] The following example is illustrative of just how firmly, at this stage, Freud believed the evidence of his own ears. A woman patient, in telling Freud about what had happened to her, had trouble naming the offender. Freud's report of their conversation reads:

'When I consider that the most excellent and high-principled men are guilty of these things, I'm compelled to think it's an illness, a kind of madness, and I have to excuse them.' 'Then let us speak plainly. In my analyses I find it's the closest relatives, fathers or brothers, who are the guilty men.' 'It has nothing to do with my brother.' 'So it was your father then.'

Then it came out that when she was between the ages of eight and twelve her allegedly otherwise admirable and high-principled father used regularly to take her into his bed and practice external ejaculation (making wet) with her. Even at the time she felt anxiety . . . Naturally she did not find it incredible when I told her that similar and worse things must have happened to her in infancy. In other respects hers is a quite ordinary hysteria with usual systems.[6]

The 'clinical' tone of 'a quite ordinary hysteria' successfully disguises the savage reality of 'hysteria' for late-nineteenth-century middle-class women who had no other outlet for the 'secret' of their rape. Hysteria could include deafness, blindness, compulsive vomiting, anorexia, difficulty in breathing, paralysis, epilepsy, delusions and 'irrational' fears. However, the significant fact is that Freud brought to light a hidden horror: that girl-children could be the victims of sexual exploitation, up to and including forcible rape (to use the legal distinction), by their fathers or other male members of their family. Given the contemporary background, this means that respectable (middle- and upper-class) families in late-nineteenth-century Vienna and associated areas, harboured an outwardly puritanical lifestyle within which rape of girl-children by a Father could and did occur.

Freud was rightly appalled by his findings. In his famous lecture of 1896 he pushed his audience to consider deeply the effect on 'the child' of such an experience, notwithstanding the use of phraseology which we today find quite misleading:

All the singular conditions under which the ill-matched pair conduct their love-relations – on the one hand the adult, who cannot escape his share in the mutual dependence necessarily entailed by a sexual relationship, and who is yet armed with complete authority and the right to punish, and can exchange the one role for the other to the uninhibited satisfaction of his moods, and on the other hand the child, who in his helplessness is at the mercy of this arbitrary will, who is prematurely aroused to every kind of sensibility and exposed to every sort of disappointment, and whose performance of the sexual activities assigned to him is often interrupted by his imperfect control of his natural needs – all these grotesque and yet tragic incongruities reveal themselves as stamped upon the later development of the individual and of his neurosis, in countless permanent effects which deserve to be traced in the greatest detail.[7]

I have quoted this at length because Freud, at this point, showed considerable empathy for the raped 'child'. However, his audience did not share his empathy; indeed, they rejected out of hand his general causal theory linking 'sexual shock' with hysteria. Within a year, he too had abandoned the theory.

Within that following year, Freud himself had a dream which he interpreted as an expression of sexual desire towards his eldest daughter (then nine).[8] Not surprisingly, very few Freudian writers make much, if anything, of this event. One recent writer, a psychiatrist, is an exception, although he does not specifically mention the dream:

Even Freud . . . was having difficulty accepting the full impact of the discoveries concerning childhood sexual trauma, particularly when it was a question of incest. In 1925 Freud admitted to suppressing the fact of a father as molester in two cases reported in 1895. These disturbing revelations, which Freud discovered as he went deeper into the childhood revelations of his patients, must have been difficult for him, as a father, to face.[9]

Freud himself, in a letter explicating another of his own dreams to his friend Fliess, expostulates, 'Where do all patients derive the horrible perverse details which are often as alien to their experience as to their knowledge?'[10] – thereby turning his own 'perverse details' into those of 'all patients' and at the same time moving towards the concept of fantasy (repressed desires).

Before we examine how he did deny the existence of all 'perverse details' by (mis-)defining them as fantasies, it is instructive to look at one of his earlier periods of doubt. In 1895, before his lecture, he wrote to his friend Fliess:

> Note that among other things I suspect the following: that hysteria is conditioned by a primary sexual experience (before puberty) *accompanied by revulsion and fright*; and that obsessional neurosis is conditioned by the same *accompanied by pleasure*.
>
> But the *mechanical explanation* is not coming off, and I am inclined to listen to the still, small voice which tells me that my explanation will not do.[11] [My italics.]

The 'still, small voice' was the precursor, presumably, of the later resonance with which he dismissed 'primary sexual experiences accompanied by revulsion and fright' (or 'pleasure') and consigned them to fantasyland.

However, the distinction that Freud makes here between 'revulsion and fright' and 'pleasure' is another piece of misnaming. While it is true that girl-child victims may experience no sexual pleasure (like Vera) or that they may experience a lot (like Kim), the 'sexual shock' is the same in that the element of *power* and the concomitant powerlessness of the victim is central to the experience of being raped. Freud leaves this element out entirely when he looks for mechanistic clarity of cause and effect in terms of pleasure or unpleasure.

A girl-child who has been subjected to 'sexual shock' is *in shock*: i.e. pain, fear, confusion, anger, unpleasure and/or shame. The nature of this sexual shock is known to all women who live under the rape ideology; either as a trauma she has experienced, or as a trauma she could experience any day, because she is female. Repression in various forms *can* be brought to bear on experience which provokes a distressing effect, and for women, the reality of being raped imprints in their bodies and their minds that they have no power – which evokes an intensely distressing effect. Since part of *being alive*, for females, is to carry the fear of this particular shock to our beings, Freud's qualitative word 'sexual' is super-fluous: we know the potential for this shock, which is about power transmitted through violence and sex, as part of our condition of existence.

It was his utter inabilty to come to grips with the nature of 'sexual shock' that led Freud down his mythological path to the Oedipus Complex. This device enabled him to turn the concrete reality of 'sexual shock' into the theory of a fantasy wish for sexual pleasure with the father (i.e. men). We still see the effects every day: 'You're making it up!' – an especially common response to girl-children who complain of sexual assault. The most abiding myth about rape, 'You must have asked for it . . . ' (meaning every woman really wants to be fucked, all the time, by any man at all), was undoubtedly alive and well before Freud. However, he gave scientific credibility to this myth too, through the theory of Oedipal fantasy (which women could not refute since it resided in the 'unconscious'), thereby 'proving' the aptness of the street mythology of rape ideology.

Freud's use of the term 'fantasy' signifies an inward expression of desired behaviour which has been repressed, i.e. removed from experience into the unconscious. The 'unconscious' is a repository of repressed memories and wishes. These repressed memories and wishes can be expressed outwardly by slips of the tongue, dreams, fantasies and so on – and sometimes by behaviour which we do not recognise as being motivated by unconscious factors. The problem that feminist theorists face is not the theory of the unconscious but how it has been applied within male supremacist social structure: because we find that the *specifics* of what women or men, girls or boys, might fantasise about or act upon have been predetermined *by the tenets of male supremacy*. Thus, psychoanalysis *expects* that girl-children, at a certain age, will be experiencing (and repressing) a desire to be possessed by their fathers.

While this *may* be true, it is the specific content of this particular expectation which has been turned by Freudian practitioners into a mechanistic device to explain (away) Father–Daughter rape. The Daughter who cries rape must have desired her Father and therefore, say the Freudians, *she imagines* (turns the desire into a fantasy reality) that she has had sexual relations with him – i.e. she has not satisfactorily repressed her desire into the realm of the unconscious. This is what Freud himself did: from believing his patients' stories he moved to a position of disbelief, based on the specificity of this one pre-named fantasy in girl-children.

107

Feminist explorations of Freud's description and interpretation of male and female content in the unconscious have established a concrete explanation of how patriarchal culture is internalised.[12] Thus we can see how masochistic and sadistic behaviours are manifestations of female oppression and male dominance. Thus, the female fantasy-wish for a penis/her father is a wish for the phallus, the symbol of power, of the weapons by which she has been and is being oppressed. Feminist theorist Stern elaborates:

> . . . women do not want to be raped, but the idea of rape (not consciously formulated) functions as an injunction to women to submit to the male symbolic order – the psychical adjustments that have to be made in order to live 'normally' are reinforced by state mechanisms – police, legal, hospital procedures – that a rape victim has to endure, all of which rationalize the role of woman as 'natural' victim, as guilty and deserving of humiliation.[13]

While Freudianism is useful, indeed enlightening, at this symbolic level, the fact is that many Freudian-trained or influenced practitioners have used these insights at a *literal* rather than symbolic level. In doing so, they deny the *conscious reality* of their patients: the rapes they have experienced are declared non-existent.

The 'revelation' that the accounts he had been hearing were 'fantasies' is recorded in a letter to Fliess, dated 21 September 1897 (four months after Freud's dream about his own daughter):

> Let me tell you straight away the great secret that has been dawning on me in recent months . . . I no longer believe in my *neurotica*. That is hardly intelligible without an explanation . . . The first group of factors were the continual disappointment of my attempts to bring my analyses to a real conclusion . . . Then there was the astonishing thing that in every case . . . blame was laid on perverse acts by the fathers, and realization of the unexpected frequency of hysteria, in every case of which the same thing applied, though it was hardly credible that perverted acts against children were so general . . . Thirdly, there was the definite realization that there is no 'indication of reality' in the unconscious, so that it is impossible to distinguish between truth and emotionally charged fiction.[14]

Rather than focus on the first and second reasons, asking *why* 'perverse acts by the father' occurred so often and *why* he himself had so much trouble bringing [his] analyses to a real conclusion', Freud chose the third factor wherein there is 'no indication of reality in the unconscious'. Thus he was able to declare that Father–Daughter rape, the frequency of which was an 'astonishing thing' and 'hardly credible', was in fact 'emotionally charged fiction'.

This 'breakthrough' has usually been perceived as, literally, a stroke of genius. It can just as well be read as the repressions of a Father's mind which is frantically trying to see *around* what is staring him in the face. From this point on, he managed to do just that. A typical accolade for this visual feat of Freud's, written over seventy years later, goes like this:

> Early in the development of the psychoanalytic theory, Freud's clinical experiences led him to believe that neuroses were the result of actual childhood seductions. Later the frequency of reports of childhood seductions were so high that *he was forced* to modify his theoretical formulations in terms of sexual fantasy in childhood. This approach led to cognizance of the ubiquitous nature of infantile sexuality and to the *recognition* of incestuous wishes.[15] [My italics.]

The subliminal message conveyed by the use of language such as 'was forced' and 'recognition' is typical of the demi-god, priest-being-called-to-his-true-vocation ambience that pervades most descriptions of Freud's Big Breakthrough into Fantasyland. Another worshipper has written of this step:

> In a major sense this conversion of the patients' reports from actual events into universal fantasies served to broaden and extend the scope of the theory and to give it greater generality since *the adult disorder no longer depended upon the presence or absence of a specific seduction*. From the specific instance of an adult seduction of a child Freud *was led* to the larger formulation of the Oedipus Complex.[16] [My italics.]

The practice of psychoanalysis could now proceed comfortably (for the analyst) since any nasty sexual events from childhood had joined the realm of 'universal fantasies'.

Feminist theorist Juliet Mitchell, in her generally excellently argued book *Psychoanalysis and Feminism*, overstates her case

109

when she deals with this step in Freud's process:

> Freud found that the incest and seduction that was being claimed never in fact took place. The fact that, as Freud himself was well aware, *actual* paternal seduction or rape occurs not infrequently, has nothing to do with the essential concepts of psychoanalysis.[17] [Original italics.]

In her anxiety to re-state the value of Freud's ideas and explain the 'essential concepts of psychoanalysis', Mitchell repeats the grave disservice done to the Daughter-victims by many Freudians, when she both *denies* their reality and then admits, but belittles, the fact that girl-children are 'not infrequently' raped. The contradiction implicit in her explanation in fact highlights the substance of this chapter: in *theoretical terms*, Father–Daughter rape was irrelevant to the pure form of psychoanalytic ideas, but in *practical terms* psychoanalysis has denied the very real existence of Father–Daughter rape.

By consigning girl-child rape to unconscious fantasy on the part of the raped Daughter, Freud was free to arrive at the two propositions that are generally held to be the keys to his whole theory – infantile sexuality and the Oedipus Complex. Freud's Eureka! of insight about the Oedipal theory came not only from his disbelief of the reality of 'sexual shock', but also from his own 'self-analysis' (undertaken from about 1897 to 1900) in which he 'realised' that *he*, as a young boy, had wanted *more love* from his mother than she gave him. The sexual element of this is spelt out in another letter to Fliess:

> . . . [between the ages of two and two and a half] libido towards *matrem* was aroused; the occasion must have been the journey with her from Leipzig to Vienna, during which we spent a night together and I must have had the opportunity of seeing her *nudam* . . . [18]

In his next letter, the personal has become universal:

> I have found love of the mother and jealousy of the father in my own case too, and now believe it to be a general phenomenon of early childhood . . . If that is the case, the gripping power of *Oedipus Rex*, in spite of all the rational objections to the inexorable fate that the story presupposes, becomes intelligible . . .[19]

From here on, Freud's ideas gradually gained acceptance, although there was resistance to his emphasis on sexual content (even in fantasy) for many more years. The tide had been turned, however, because the about-face had not simply been a rejection of the existence of Father–Daughter rape (which would have left the notion dangling round in people's minds), it had obviated it by turning it into something else: sexual fantasy on the part of the Daughter. The ensuing acceptance was even more thoroughly assured because (1) his new theorising was presented in terms of the double standard by which the same generality was *apparently* applied to boy-children and to girl-children, whereas the male analysis was actually the central one; and (2) his theory of sexuality, as it continued to evolve over many years, became increasingly phallocentric.

The shift of focus from girl-child to boy-child and back again was accomplished instantly and virtually imperceptibly through the use of so-called non-gender-specific terms such as 'he' and 'child' as applying to male and female equally.[20] This use of language disguises at a very deep level the fact that female experience is *essentially* different from male experience; it places the male version of reality centre-stage, *implying* a 'human' universality. This can be clearly seen in the language Freud used to describe his own reaction to the story of Oedipus:

His destiny moves us only because it might have been ours – because the oracle laid the same curse upon us before our births as upon him. It is the fate of all of us, perhaps, to direct our first sexual impulse towards our mother and our first hatred and our first murderous wish against our father . . . King Oedipus, who slew his father Laius and married his mother Jocasta, merely shows us the fulfillment of our own childhood wishes. But, more fortunate than he, we have meanwhile succeeded, in so far as we have not become psychoneurotics, in detaching our sexual impulses from our mothers and in forgetting our jealousy of our fathers. Here is one in whom these primeval wishes of our childhood have been fulfilled, and we shrink back from him with the whole force of the repression by which those wishes have since that time been held down within us.[21]

This is apparently a precise expression of the power of the Oedipus story – for men. In spite of occasional expressions of confusion about the appropriateness of a simple reversal of the theory for girl-children, the written works of Freud and his followers show that this is what usually did happen. Or rather, they tried to make it happen that way – but because the power dynamic inherent in a sexist society had been left out, it never quite fits. Thus the Oedipal theory holds that girl-children desire their fathers, behaving seductively towards them, and hate their mothers, behaving competitively towards them; while boy-children desire their mothers, engage in 'heroic' competitive battle with their fathers over the right to become a Man, and ultimately evolve as sane men only if they are lucky enough to have a mother who loves them according to an unidentified mythical ideal which must not be too much, nor too little.[22] If 'too much', then the male child is 'dominated', 'smothered', arrested in his heroic effort to become a Man; if 'too little', then he spends the rest of his life struggling with the unfulfilled Oedipal love for his mother which she denied him. The Mother is set up to take the blame whatever happens; the Father, noticeably, does not play a similar role for the girl-child.

Later, after 'recognition' of the concept of 'fear of castration' (for males) and 'penis envy' (for girls), Freud added to his observations of the play, *Oedipus Rex*, that 'the blinding in the legend of Oedipus . . . stands for castration'.[23] So the theory to which he had been 'led' by his disbelief in Father–Daughter rape, ends in a phallocentric view of the world in which a grown man who had sexual intercourse with a woman, not knowing she was his mother, must symbolically castrate himself in a very real and painful fashion – gouging out his own eyes with long pins. The 'sexual shock' of girl-children (like the fate of Jocasta) has by this stage been quite forgotten as Freud reels under the existential agonies of his (the Father's) frustrated desire for his mother.

Fliess accused Freud, the last time they met, in 1900, of 'reading his own thoughts into his patients';[24] an accusation which seems so apt, on examining the 'development' of the Oedipal theory, that its very simplicity takes the breath away – which is presumably why Freud did not speak again with Fliess. Freud wrote to his fiancée, Martha Bernays, in 1882: 'I always find it uncanny when I can't understand someone in terms of myself': that he still felt his own measure to be the centre of the human world fifteen years later, is clear from his god-like presumption in applying the results of his *self*-analysis to his theories about the *human* condition.

His friend and biographer, Ernest Jones, regarded Freud's three to four years of self-analysis as another Herculean feat:

The end of all that labour and suffering was the last and final phase in the evolution of Freud's personality. There emerged the serene and benign Freud, henceforth free to pursue his work in imperturbable composure.[25]

That his 'imperturbable composure' may have resulted from having created a psycho-scientific 'theory' which exonerated himself (and all the Fathers) from responsibility for rape ideology, could not, of course, occur to Jones, who is also one of the Fathers.

The final part of the theory was that 'sexual impulses operated normally in the youngest children without any need for outside stimulation'.[26] This insight was a truly liberating one at the turn of the century and was largely responsible for the high regard Freud was held in by 'progressive' people of all stamps: 'he made it possible to discuss sex – out in the open, at long last'.[27] However, this theory, like the Oedipus Complex, fitted boy-children straightforwardly enough, but had to be twisted and bent to match the prevailing beliefs about female sexuality. This is a distortion we are still struggling to unknot today – the clitoris (female sensory organ) versus the vagina (female organ preferred by men for sensory purposes) debate.

As early as 1897, Freud wrote, '. . . I am baffled by the feminine side, and that makes me mistrust the whole thing!'[28] While he continued to have moments of 'mistrust', it did not stem his determination to *somehow* construct a theory which would explain female sexuality to his (the Fathers') satisfaction. Indeed, his moments of 'mistrust' read like petulant outbursts from a schoolboy who feels he has missed a lesson in which there was an essential element presented about how to work the sum out. But he persevered, and the 'final pieces of the puzzle' were put together in 1925 in what Strachey (the editor of the *Standard Edition of Freud's Complete Works*) calls a 'short paper'.[29]

In this 'short paper', we find that the use of fantasy for girls has become a very frequent psychological mechanism, transferring its object-focus several times, since to 'fit' the Oedipus theory, the girl-child had to transfer her primary affection from her mother to her father, and her sexual centre from her clitoris to her vagina. His first 'problem' was that

In both cases the mother is the original object; and there is no cause for surprise that boys retain that object in the Oedipus

Complex. But how does it happen that girls abandon it and instead take their father as an object?[30]

His answer lay in 'a momentous discovery which little girls are destined to make':

> They notice the penis of a brother or playmate, strikingly visible and of large proportions, at once recognize it as the superior counterpart of their own small and inconspicuous organ, and from that time forward fall victim to envy for the penis . . . She makes her judgement and her decision in a flash. She has seen it and knows that she is without it and wants to have it.[31]

From this 'recognition' of desire for a penis flows (1) hatred for her mother 'who sent her into the world so insufficiently equipped'; (2) hatred of herself, because 'after a woman has become aware of the wound to her narcissism, she develops, like a scar, a sense of inferiority'; and (3) desire for her father, because 'she gives up her wish for a penis and puts in place of it a wish for a child: and *with that purpose in view* she takes her father as a love-object'.[original italics.][32]

In thus charting a process by which male supremacy creates femininity (i.e. females who are misogynistic, passive and directed towards men), Freud performed a useful task. The fact, however, that Freud forgot the point he had started from (sexual trauma experienced by girl-children) meant that the manifest everyday interaction of male power over females was not confronted, so his theory of sexuality appears to exist in an abstract world of symbolic interactions wherein male supremacy and its agents (men) are not named/blamed. Furthermore, the 'science' of psychoanalysis holds within itself the power weapons with which to silence critics. Freud, in 1920:

> None, but physicians who practise psychoanalysis can have any access whatever to this sphere of knowledge or any possibility of forming a judgment that is uninfluenced by their own dislikes and prejudices.[33]

In other words, only those initiated into and practising the tenets of psychoanalysis are in a position to judge the theories on which it is based.

There have always been significant Freudians who differed in

114

their emphases within the original theory, but the primacy of phallocentricity and the consequent inability to *hear* girl-children have remained. For example, Abraham, one of Freud's earliest followers, argued that the rape of girl-children was most often real, but extrapolated from this position the theory that the girl-child who is a victim is 'preinclined towards her own violation'.[34] So although he initially appears to be on the right track, Abraham is in fact only tightening the screws on the blame-the-victim response, inviting research of the victims rather than of the whole structure which creates and condones Father–Daughter rape.

Horney, also a member of the early psychoanalytic group which gathered around Freud, confronted the prevailing school of thought when she argued that the Freudian view of women was inadequate because it was conceived through male eyes and out of male experience.

> Psychoanalysis is the creation of a male genius, and almost all those who have developed his ideas have been men. It is only right and reasonable that they should evolve more easily a masculine psychology and understand more of the development of men than of women.[35]

She went on to speculate that male depreciation of women arises from the enormity of male envy in relation to the ability to reproduce, and that much of female 'masochism' is actually enforced passivity through the cultural imperative that demands that a woman's place is in the home, playing wife-mother.

Similarly, Adler, who withdrew from the Freudian group in 1911, wrote that women were 'conditioned' into inferiority and had to find ways of allowing the expression of their creative energy within this restricted framework, and that this effort was productive of most female neurosis and psychosis, since its fulfilment was so difficult. As Adler saw it, the girl-child comes into

> . . . the world with a prejudice sounding in her ears which is designed only to rob her of her belief in her own value, to shatter her self-confidence and destroy her hope of ever doing anything worthwhile. If this prejudice is constantly being strengthened, if a girl sees again and again how women are given servile roles to play, it is not hard to understand how she loses courage, fails to face her obligations, and sinks back from the solution of life's problems.[36]

The victims of Father–Daughter rape, who are subject to the most direct 'conditioning' of all, experience the 'prejudice' of females being seen as passive objects in a constant, privatised form.

Given such neo-feminist deviations from the Freudian line within the original psychoanalytic group, it is extraordinary to contemplate the monolithic success of Freud's pure male supremacist vision. Horney and Adler were only two (and there were others) whose insights into the oppressed status of women have been lost in the cultural popularisation of Freud's ideas. This legacy is particularly obvious in the chapters on the Daughters and the Mothers, where we see that many of the specific theories developed by US psychoanalysts that have been advanced as the cause of 'father–daughter incest', are actually ingenious permutations of Freud's original Oedipus Complex theory. The Mothers (mostly) and the Daughters (often) are said to be acting out 'unconscious Oedipal motivations' of various kinds.

A few contemporary practitioners of psychoanalysis have been moved, through their contact with victims of Father–Daughter rape, to doubt the primacy of (Oedipal) fantasy on the part of the girl-child. Dr Joseph Peters, Director of Philadelphia Sex Offender and Rape Victim Centre since 1970, is one of the most outspoken critics:

> It is my thesis . . . that both cultural and personal factors combined to cause everyone, including Freud himself at times, to welcome the idea that reports of childhood sexual victimization could be regarded as fantasies. *This position relieved the guilt of adults*. In my opinion, both Freud and his followers over-subscribed to the theory of childhood fantasy and overlooked incidents of the actual sexual victimization in childhood.[37] [My italics.]

Peters is refreshingly candid about his own awakening in the process of treating girl-child rape victims. In discussing a particular case, he says: 'I abandoned hypnosis because I erroneously concluded that unresolved oedipal fantasies were the primary problem.' He and the patient settled down into weekly sessions of analysis in which 'we aired oedipal fantasies for years'. Eventually, dream analysis revealed that the woman had, at the age of four, been raped by a male adult friend of the family; Peters concludes '. . . it took eighteen years of weekly sessions before there was a complete remission of symptoms . . . Would not an earlier recognition of the actual childhood rape have saved us many hours of analysis? . . . Was this not a prolonged oedipal goosechase?'[38]

Indeed. And what damage has been done to all those victims who were similarly disbelieved: told by the 'expert' that reality was fantasy? How many casualties of this 'over-interpretation' have lived out their lives in madness? When reality is denied, there is nowhere to go except into a reality of one's own which, by definition, cannot be shared and is called madness. Some psychoanalysts concur:

> She revealed the experience to her mother, who believed her statements rather than assuming that they were childish fantasies. Had the mother refused to believe the girl, a more serious psychiatric illness undoubtedly would have developed . . . *We need to consider carefully the statements of those patients who can hardly believe their own senses: we thus give them a better means of assessing reality.* Incest between father and daughter is far more common than we formerly believed. *We can see now in years past patients were lost or driven into psychosis by our failure to believe them because of our conviction that much of their accounts must be fantasy.[39]* [My italics.]

Whether Freud's own use of the concept of fantasy was intended to be actual or symbolic becomes irrelevant in the face of the concrete mechanistic device for determining 'truth' which Freud himself, and many of his followers, turned it into. As such, Freudianism is an integral element of the ideology of medico-therapeutic practice which has been used against us for the whole of the twentieth century.

In a male supremacist social structure, any 'idea' about violent and/or sexual practices against women is going to be automatically based on, and serve to reinforce, sexist principles. Any research within the male supremacist mode must, by definition, *begin* by seeing women as objects, as The Other, as suitable subjects for investigation.[40]

> The test of strength of any ideology is the extent to which its basic presuppositions remain not merely unquestioned but literally unrecognized. The more such assumptions appear to be simply a part of the fabric of fact, the stronger the hold of the ideology they support, and the greater the difficulty of changing the practices arising out of it.[41]

It is only our own experiences, shared and re-told by people (women) who can identify with them, that can form the basis of theories about the existential experience of being female within a male supremacist social structure. Rape is about power, not sexuality *per se*. 'Sexual activity' implies a mutuality between the two people concerned: rape is the experience of powerlessness, of being conquered. The conquered territory is our own bodies.

In spite of the enormous deadweight of male supremacy, the Daughters will be heard. Freud and his followers have had a large hand in closing all ears to the cries of the Daughters, by presuming to deal in 'the dark continent'[41] of women's sexuality, and by assuming that they produce 'truths' from *our* unconscious. Madness, non-orgastic sexual life, distrust of each other, and silencing the truth about girl-child rape: these have been the legacy of the machinations of the doctor from Vienna.

3 The Fathers –
Forgiven and Forgotten

Oh Daddy,
If I can make you see,
If there's been a fool around,
It's got to be me,
Yes, it's got to be me.

Why are you so right when I'm so wrong,
I'm so weak but you're so strong,
Everything you do is just all right,
And I can't walk away from you, baby,
If I tried.

From 'Oh Daddy' by Christine McVie,
sung by Fleetwood Mac on *Rumours*

The main source of literature about the Fathers is the American clinical accounts, in article form, of psychiatrists who report cases of 'father–daughter incest' – the number of cases per article may range from one to a couple of dozen, most often being three to six. Some of these articles approach the subject generally; others do so via the offenders or via the victims; but nearly all belong to the same network of ideas. They quote each other frequently and usually present the same set of theories about the offenders and the victims (*and* the mothers), no matter what emphasis they indicate in their titles. Another source is the 'sex offender' literature which attempts to study the whole range of (convicted) sex offenders, determining similarities and differences in types of personality and possible causality of the offence. Such studies cover the range of sex offences from violent rape through incest, paederasty, sodomy, etc., to 'minor' offences such as exhibitionism. A third source is the 'sexual abuse' component within the general child abuse literature which has appeared in recent years. In terms of information about offenders, this source mostly reiterates the theorising developed by the specialist clinical authors.

In all this literature little attempt is made to distinguish between 'consanguinal' (blood-tie or genetic) relations and 'affinal' or 'contractual' (kinship through marriage or understanding) relations, even though most researchers are purporting to explore incest *per se*. The Fathers (my term) are 'the fathers' to most of the researchers because the single largest group of offenders are the fathers of the victims.

A fourth source is the evidence of our own senses. The memories, the hidden secrets, the knowledge, the awareness of our Fathers' sexual feelings towards us in our own girlhoods, are beginning to be shared. The women whom I interviewed for this book; Armstrong's book, *Kiss Daddy Goodnight*;[1] some short films that have been made; women's movement 'speak-outs' in many countries: all are giving new evidence on the Fathers and what Father–Daughter rape really is.

Sagarin (1977), a sociologist, in an article which is an earnest attempt to suggest that Daughter-rape by a natural father might be very different from (worse? not as bad as?) rape by a stepfather, writes:

> It is entirely possible that more would be learned if a distinction were made, treating as two separate phenomena true incest and statutory incest [Sagarin's term for non-consanguinal 'incest']. Frequency, etiology, and consequences may be found to differ when this distinction is made.[2]

The fact that even the most conservative researchers have not come across evidence to lead them in this direction presumably supports my thesis that the Fathers who rape girl-children do so from the same motivation, which has nothing to do with hair-splitting definitions over types of relatedness, but much to do with accessibility to powerless females. Sagarin argues that 'probably' a higher proportion of stepfathers are Daughter-rapists than are natural fathers. While this *may* be so (there are no studies to support this claim), his hypothesis has to be set beside his own belief that 'incest' with a natural father instills 'in a considerable portion of the population a sense of such complete horror that one recoils as if it were an instinctive repugnance',[3] by which he implies that 'incest'

120

with a stepfather is not nearly so 'distasteful'.

I beg to differ. Being centrally concerned for the Daughters, I find no consolation in differentiating the horrors of 'incest' along these lines: I have an 'instinctive repugnance' at the contemplation of girl-child rape victims trapped in a family with the offender, no matter how he is socially or genetically connected to her.

Historically, the literature has undergone significant changes. Due to the Freudian influence, the clinical studies for a long time focussed on the Daughters because of the abiding psychoanalytic preoccupation with childhood sexuality and the role of fantasy. Much of this literature 'investigated' the pathology of the girl-child victims and tried to ascertain whether or not they were 'really' harmed by the experience. Often these writers concluded that the Daughters had been active participants and even the initiators. Then the broader sociological spectrum examined by Kinsey *et al.* (1950s) caused attention to shift to facts and figures concerning the offenders, as well as the victims. This shift, in throwing some light on the offenders, gave rise to a bundle of theories, each attempting to explain the individual pathology of the Fathers (and the Mothers) in 'incest' situations. From there it was a short step to the more recent period of seeing the problem as one of 'family process' – thereby fitting neatly into the general therapeutic practice of the western world in the last twenty years or so, with its increasing emphasis on 'family therapy' and 'family psychiatry'.

This chapter is an analysis of the information and theories about the Fathers contained in the professional literature. What we can find through this avenue says more about methods of research and (unconscious) male supremacist perception than it does about the causality of Father–Daughter rape. It does, however, remove some of the cobwebs from the subject: by dismantling the theoretical superstructure which has been created to protect the Fathers, we can see more clearly who they are. We will see that the psychologists, psychiatrists, sociologists and criminologists have mostly been concerned to excuse the Fathers by establishing that they are not to blame for having raped their Daughters. The role of the clinicians has been to forgive the Fathers, and thereby forget that they are rapists of dependent girl-children.

Weinberg (1955), a sociologist, was the first to attempt a classification of the Fathers into types: (1) the 'endogamic' (endo: within; literally endogamy means 'marrying within the tribe or group') man who turns inward to the family, seeking no outside contacts; (2) the 'psychopathic' man who is highly sexually oriented, but cannot form tender relationships with anybody, so sees his wife and children as sexual possessions; and (3) the paedophile who is 'immature' and can only obtain sexual satisfaction with children.[4] There have been refinements on these categories by other researchers, but generally this classification of three types appears throughout the literature.

It is believed that the paedophile will rarely marry or have children. He is The Stranger: the man who goes to parks and hangs around schools at the end of the day, because for him children (female or male or both) are his sexual turn-on. The paedophile who marries and has children will still be attracted to children in general. If he rapes his own daughter, he will probably also try to rape other children. Weinberg cites two such Fathers who 'went to the extreme of forcing their daughters to bring home their friends for sexual purposes'.[5] Weinberg writes of the paedophile: 'though sometimes promiscuous, he is shy of or averse to adult women'.[6]

Most of the Fathers who rape their Daughters are not paedophiles, but fall in Weinberg's first two categories. The 'endogamic' Father 'does not crave social or sexual contacts with women outside the family'.[7] Many researchers have attested to the shy, withdrawn, 'ineffective' characteristics of these Fathers. Tormes (1972) found that these family-centred, affection-seeking, 'passive' fathers ruled the household by keeping hold of all the money, by being 'ill-tempered' and 'over-protective'. In one such case:

> The father went with her to and from school. She was not allowed to have friends of either sex. In three families, the mother was not allowed to send the victim unaccompanied on an ordinary family errand . . . The methods the affectionate father used to dominate were even more thorough-going and effective than those of the brutal father. His constant preoccupation with family cares seemed to have reduced his wife to a state of willing cooperativeness to such an extent that she personally counted for nothing in the family.[8]

The 'endogamic' Father often appears to be the best possible 'family man'. From the outside, this family would appear to be the ideal 'intact' family: nuclear perfection.

The 'psychopathic' Father in Weinberg's classification is, in contradistinction to the endogamic Father, 'indiscriminately promiscuous', a man who:

. . . desires and pursues adult women and perhaps children before and after his incest experience. He may seduce [sic] his daughter and, in contrast to the endogamic type, he does not develop a progressive emotional attachment for his incest partner. His initial sexual desire for a family sex partner is precipitated by the absence, refusal or declining attraction of his wife and by the inaccessibility of other women.[9]

This last sentence means that he will take whatever sexual 'partner' (object) he can get, even a girl-child. The implicit message conveyed in the reporting of such research is that the Father was 'precipitated' (almost pushed) into raping a daughter because of actions on the part of his wife, including her 'declining attraction' which is surely an act on his part, not hers. The 'refusal of sexual access' on the part of the wife is a repetitive theme in the literature. Never have I come across any tentative theorising, let alone analysis, of *why* a wife may have refused to have any further sexual contact with a man who had already become, or later became, one of the Fathers.

The 'psychopathic' type has been found by later researchers to often be physically abusive: a classic 'patriarchal tyrant'. Raphling *et al.*, psychiatrists, found that 'he tends to maintain a façade of competent patriarchal strength'.[10] Tormes found that the Fathers 'appear to be as "ineffectual" outside the home as they are grandiose within it'.[11] She cites examples of excessively brutal behaviour on the part of several Fathers, including locking his wife and perhaps other children in a cupboard while he rapes the Daughter, or of forcing his wife to watch the same activity.[12]

The family dynamics instituted by the 'endogamic' and 'psychopathic' Fathers are actually very similar, in that both utterly dominate the family group. Thus the two types of offenders, as discerned by the researchers, are generally failures as men in the public world, and dictators of one sort or another within the private world of the family. So the two types in fact become one: a man who is shy and ineffective except at home, where he rules his castle by either passivity or aggression. Meiselman (1978) writes of the Fathers in this light, where all the fathers become 'endogamic', and identifies typical 'incestuous fathers' as both passive and aggressive:

. . . he often did not respect or esteem the women in his family, 'forsaw' that his daughter would become promiscuous anyway, and considered it his paternal prerogative to initiate her sexually.

Although he was very dependent on his wife and children, he was at the same time arrogant and domineering in his relations with them, and he tended to be suspicious of their extrafamilial relationships, attempting to control their social lives. This odd combination of dependence, seclusiveness, and domination of family members led to incest when the wife became sexually unavailable and when the husband's self-control was weakened, often through the use of alcohol.[13]

(More on alcohol as a causative agent in Father–Daughter rape later in this chapter.)

Two psychologists, Rita and Blair Justice (1978), in indulging in a more descriptive classification scheme, give a conveniently summarised list of the common rationalisations used by the Fathers. Having established that the typical Father 'hungers for a closeness, a sense of belonging and intimacy that he seldom can verbalise and never has experienced',[14] they catalogue the Fathers in terms of the method utilised in attempting to have these needs met via rape of a Daughter.

First, there are the 'introverts' who are outwardly successful, but inwardly depressed and lonely:

They remain indoors virtually shut off from contact with other people. The father is often the most introverted and sets the style for the family. He leaves the house only to go to work . . . The introvert does not go outside the family to have sex with other women – he may even consider that to be a 'sin' – but turns to his daughter, whom he regards as belonging to him. Since she belongs to him, she is a 'permissible alternative' to his wife.[15]

In all the other categories listed by the Justices, the notion of 'ownership' of the Daughter by the Father is also present. Cormier *et al.* found that when

. . . asked why he did not seek outside affairs as the solution, he will quite often explain that 'it is a sin to go with other women'. The daughter is thus placed in the special role: she is not a woman outside the family with whom it is a sin to commit adultery, *but someone who belongs to him*, a permissible alternative to the wife.[16] [My italics.]

The second type is the 'rationaliser' who 'uses lofty words and

124

sentiments or plausible-sounding, but specious, reasons for establishing an incestuous affair [sic] with his daughter', such as showing her what 'love' is; or who justifies his actions in terms of 'sex education'; or who 'protects' his daughter from 'the corrupt minds and manners of men in the world outside' by 'initiating' her sexually himself; or who feels he 'owns' his daughter as his 'exclusive property' and has a right to use her to satisfy his own needs; or who attempts to 'liberate' his daughters by extending the sexual liberation demand to children.[17]

Thirdly, the Justices name the 'tyrant' type:

> *Some of the qualities of the tyrant can be found in several types of incestuous fathers,* but we reserve the label for those whose typical mode of family behaviour is designed to inspire fear and obedience . . . They believe that one mark of being a 'real man' is to be sexually active and powerful, so to them sex is not for closeness but for expressing manly virility . . . Outside the home their bullying tactics seldom work, so they usually confine themselves to sexual activity with the daughter.[18] [My italics.]

Next, the Justices list the 'alcoholic' type whom they found to be few in number (10 percent to 15 percent). They cite the evidence that alcoholics generally have a 'strong need to be dependent', and so:

> An incestuous father who drinks is trying to blot out his dependency needs at the same time he is turning to his daughter to satisfy them.[19]

They finally discuss the 'psychopathic' types who 'seek stimulation, novelty and excitement'. These men are found to be, according to the Justices, either heterosexually extremely promiscuous or pan-sexual. This type of offender may seek sexual stimulation from men, women, sons, daughters. If he is pan-sexual, he gets turned on 'by everything and anything . . . the cat, the telephone pole, the mailman, or his children'.[20]

In a recent case in Australia where a man, who was a member of an international paedophiliac club, was sentenced to nine years' gaol, it was revealed that he made tape-recordings and took photographs of his rapings of girl- and boy-children, and that in the previous ten years or so he had also 'committed incest with both his daughters, had interfered with a cousin's child and with his wife's sister, aged nine'.[21] Whether such a man could be classified as a 'pan-sexual', a straightforward 'psychopath', a 'paedophile' or a 'tyrant' type seems rather beside the point. The labels of 'types' shudder and blur into irrelevance.

The Justices point out that the 'psychopathic' (including pan-sexual) type is rare. In fact:

> The typical person who commits incest is not oversexed, is not a psychopath and does not have psychotic tendencies. Sex is not the issue in most incest cases. The basic problem is using sex to fill other needs.[22]

Here the 'typical person who commits incest' sounds like a vast majority of males within the population of any western country.

Since most researchers are looking only at fathers (as opposed to grandfathers, brothers, uncles, friends) the statistical information that has been collected on 'incest offenders' tends to present a fairly uniform picture:

> The fathers tend to be middle-aged, or in their late 30's or 40's and are beginning to realize that they are growing older without, perhaps, having accomplished everything they wanted to. They are more often than not of normal or above-average intelligence, tend to be good workers and are usually not involved with other criminal activities. The marital relationship is usually poor and sexual relationships tend to be either non-existent or very unsatisfying.[23]

This could be a picture of Mr Average. Mr Nextdoor. The Father could be almost any man, especially since the evidence also indicates that:

> . . . most sexually abusive fathers and stepfathers are fairly well respected by their peers *before* it becomes known in the community that they were sexually involved with their daughters.[24] [Original italics.]

Thus the offending Fathers appear quite normal – until disclosure of the fact that they have been raping their daughter(s). *Covering up* their middle-aged 'identity crisis' and deep-seated dependency needs is a necessary part of creating the image of a successfully functioning male: since such behaviour is normal in our society,

Daughter-rapists are indistinguishable from those men who do not rape their Daughters.

Even in very specific studies, such as one which compared 'alcoholic' and 'non-alcoholic' offenders:

> . . . significant differences *were not arrived at* as to depression, psychotic disturbances, intellectual defects, problems of jealousy, psychiatric hospitalization, and earlier sexual behaviour.[25] [My italics.]

On all of these psychological criteria, one 'incest offender' is much like another – and none is significantly different from Mr Average except in that he is known to have raped his daughter(s).

In the most thorough recent analysis of all the extant clinical evidence, Meiselman concludes with this extraordinarily open-ended explanation of the Fathers' behaviour:

> The typical incestuous father is not mentally retarded, psychotic, or pedophilic but is *characterized by some sort of personal disturbance* that interferes with his ability to control his impulses in a situation where the temptation to commit incest exists.[26] [My italics.]

This tautological attempt to find a characteristic common to 'incestuous fathers' is the clinician's way of stating the obvious: men who rape their daughters have not been able to control their 'impulse' to rape an accessible girl-child. The corollary of Meiselman's argument, of course, is that men who do not rape their daughters have merely controlled their 'impulse'. Throughout the literature, the phrase 'poor impulse control' recurs: the researchers who use it really appear to think that it explains something about Father–Daughter rape, as though 'poor impulse control' in the matter of raping a girl-child were an identifiable condition, like 'manic behaviour' for example. The Complete Oxford English Dictionary definition for 'impulse' is 'impelling; push; sudden tendency to act without reflection'. It is presumably 'a sudden tendency to act without reflection' that is intended by those who use this term to excuse the Fathers; however, a 'sudden tendency to act without reflection' is a poor palliative for the Daughters who have been given no power to act at all, when the Father approaches them sexually.

The role of the Fathers who are brothers (and half-brothers, step-brothers, foster-brothers) is completely overlooked in the body of literature about the offenders. Most writers aver that 'brother–sister incest' is believed to be more common than father–daughter, but that it is usually not damaging to the participants. Superficially, this easy statement is quite acceptable, giving rise as it does to memories of sibling genital exploration and childhood sex-play. These kinds of experiences are usually not damaging, in fact they are often the reverse, forming an important base for knowledge of hidden parts of the human body for many of us. However, many older brothers rape their sisters (the Daughters) within much the same authoritarian rape/power framework as adult Fathers – the stories of Ann and Marge in this book bear testimony to such rape by brothers.

It is convenient for researchers to confuse sibling sex-play and real rape in this fashion, since it frees them to examine therapeutic theories of husband–wife relations, and the interplay of Oedipal connections as the cause of Daughter-rape, rather than recognise that larger/older males within the family have power over girl-children. The power dimension is the nexus of the reality of male supremacy operating within the microcosm of the family: this reality can be ignored within clinical wordgames about father–daughter 'affairs'.[27] The rapist being a brother does not turn rape into innocent sex–play. The fact that *some* similar-age brother–sister sexual arrangements are truly mutual, and satisfying for the female as well as the male, does not mean that all sibling sexual activity is non-damaging. Brothers can be among the Fathers: those who rape their sisters (Daughters) repetitively with the unspoken sanction of rape ideology. And brothers are even more likely to be completely exonerated: as we have seen, they are invisible in the literature. (One exception, a British study, indicates that when brothers are prosecuted for 'incest' they are more likely to be convicted than fathers – apparently because the brothers who are reported and then 'caught' tend to have a high rate of conviction for other crimes as well.[28] It may well be that these brothers are reported for 'incest' by parents who are in fact disapproving of the other behaviours in which their son is indulging.)

Apart from the attempted categorising process and the hunt for 'common characteristics' which is focussed on the Father-offenders, there is also a body of Freudian theory about the Fathers which originated with Ernest Jones, Freud's friend and biographer. He wrote:

A man who displays an abnormally strong affection for his daughter also has a strong fixation on his mother. He begets his mother [fathers a female child] and becomes her father and so arrives at the latter identification of his real daughter with his mother.[29]

Jones' theorising shifts the focus of concern from what transpires between the father and his daughter, to what transpired between him and his mother. This, of course, opens the way for an analysis of his mother's actions in an endeavour to construct a causal connection between her behaviour and the fact that her son has raped his daughter.

Kaufman *et al.* (1954) used Jones' argument in suggesting a complicated three-generational theory about the web of interpersonal family relationships as the cause of 'incest'. The maternal grandmothers were found to be 'stern, demanding, controlling, cold, and extremely hostile women, who rejected their daughters and pampered their sons' – most of these women had been deserted by their husbands and were bringing the children up alone (before the days of welfare benefits). Kaufman and his observers found that these women reacted to the desertion 'by selecting a daughter whom they would describe as being like the maternal grandmother, and on whom they would displace their feelings of hostility and hurt at having been rejected'.[30] The theory then goes that the second-generation mothers chose one of their daughters to be a 'little mother', so that they themselves could be daughters again; and that they also chose 'deserting' men or else they themselves 'deserted' their husbands sexually. As a result of all this psychopathology on the parts of the grandmothers and the mothers, the fathers 'then became involved in the incestuous activity with the daughters'.[31]

While any of these observations *may* be true of some (or many) 'incest' families, I am left with the familiar sense of having read only half, or less, of the story. The authors write that 'all the family members appeared to be searching for a mother figure'.[32] The Eternal Mother: the all-understanding ever-nurturant figure who gives unconditional love. We all want it, especially women, who get least of it. When looking at these 'incest' families, why do the researchers not talk of fathering: often both grandfathers had deserted their families, the current father raped his daughter(s) – so why the unilateral emphasis on the 'shortcomings' of the female (Mother) figure in the family group?

Kaufman's 'family constellation' theory was a godsend to the theoreticians of 'father–daughter incest' in that it finally confronted its incidence as a reality, but exonerated the Fathers by focussing on the inadequacies of the Mothers, thereby moving away from the prevailing primacy of the slightly discomforting conclusions of the Bender and Blau (1937) study which unequivocally blamed the victims who were, after all, children.

The 'rejecting mother' theory became very popular, especially among the qualitative researchers. Cavallin (1965) is typical. Here he writes on the evidence 'found' in a study of twelve offenders:

> In six cases their mothers were physically absent either because of *death* or abandonment. In two others the mother *had to work* and spent most of the time away from home. Of the other four cases, in one the mother was described as indifferent, in another as very critical and narrow-minded, in a third as very religious and strict, and in only one case did the patient describe himself as his mother's favourite.[33] [My italics.]

Even though this blame-the-female-principle attitude generally prevails in the studies, there is paradoxical material in some of the sociological studies which are basically concerned with facts and statistics. Gebhard's study of all types of sex offenders found that:

> . . . the incest offenders vs. children [victims under 12] got along better with their mothers than with their fathers. The number who preferred the mother is much greater than the number who got along equally well with both parents . . . [These] are the only group of heterosexual offenders who exhibit this maternal preference.[34]

We can only conclude that the researchers dislike mothers in general and (unconsciously) bias the evidence accordingly, while the offenders actually like their mothers; or that the evidence is inconclusive. The relevance of a Daughter-rapist's attitude to his own mother is, for our purposes, highly problematical and suspiciously specious. The desire of most researchers to fit the Freudian mould in terms of Oedipal considerations sometimes seems overwhelming: even Gebhard, following his factual statement above, writes:

> The combination of incest with a young person and the youthful partiality for the mother suggests an Oedipal phenomenon that we are not equipped to analyze.[35]

130

The 'youthful partiality for the mother' in fact puts these offenders closer to the 'normal' man, again, than other kinds of sex offenders.

The motivation of many researchers seems to be, understandably, to establish that the Fathers had 'unhappy childhoods': as we all know, an 'unhappy childhood' can lead to all sorts of acting out in adult life. The statistical evidence (slewed to low-socio-economic strata) does indicate that the Fathers had, generally speaking, unhappy childhoods. However, as we also all know only too well, this is a not uncommon experience. If unhappy children become unhappy adults, then there are a lot around. Armstrong, in considering causation of 'incest' in these terms, concludes:

I think the difference between millions of unhappy family units where sexual abuse takes place and millions of unhappy family units where sexual abuse does not take place is that in the former families the father commits abuse.[36]

This tautology leads us, again, to Anyman.

There is other evidence however. Another widely held belief is that most of the Fathers are alcoholics. Gebhard found a high alchohol rate among the offenders he studied (and that teetotalism was the lowest among groups of sex offenders);[37] the Minnesota Program for Victims of Sexual Assault manual for professionals (1979) gives a figure of 65-percent rate of alcohol abuse among incest offenders.[38] Neither of these studies explain their criteria for determining what constitutes 'alcohol abuse'; and several other researchers found either a normal or low rate of alcohol consumption in their samples. McCaghy (1968), in a paper entitled 'Drinking and Deviance Disavowal', found that:

For child molesters, reference to drinking in connection with their offences plays an important role in deviance disavowal. It permits them to admit their deviant behaviour without accepting responsibility for it . . . Thus insulated from the offending behaviour the molester can present to his audience the image of a person who possesses socially approved attributes . . . He drinks too much and does not condone it. But child molesting is simply an unhappy side effect of his 'real' problem . . .[39]

which is drinking. The use of alcohol, which is widely available and socially acceptable, can be and is used as 'deviance disavowal' not only for girl-child rape, but also for wife-beating, 'ordinary' rape of adult women, robbery and murder, as well as many other things.

The actual use to which alcohol is presumably often put by a Father wishing to rape a Daughter is ably expressed by Meiselman:

> If paternal dominance gives the incestuous father the intrafamilial power to effect a sexual relationship with his daughter, alcohol very frequently deadens his moral constraints and allows the first act of incest to occur.[40]

Thus we are again left with inconclusive evidence. We get the impression that the Fathers as a group use alcohol in a fairly average manner: as a de-inhibitor of social restraints, which in this case includes the rape of his daughter or another girl-child.

Another common assumption is that the Fathers are 'highly sexed': that they need or want more sex than most men. This notion mirrors the general rape-myth that rapists are sexually motivated, overwhelmed by an uncontrollable sexual urge. As has already been pointed out, the evidence seems to indicate that most of these men have few social relationships, let alone sexual ones, outside the family, and that they are generally shy and ineffective about sexual matters. But on this point, there is, as on so many others, contradictory evidence. Gebhard found that 'incest offenders vs. children' had an extraordinarily high interest in 'mouth-genital contact', as well as being 'highly tolerant' of non-conventional coital positions, and that 26 percent of them (the highest proportion for any group of sex offenders) had had anal intercourse with their wives.[41] However, *they did not show a preference for young women* in their sexual history or in their sexual fantasies.[42] Gebhard postulates from the fact that these offenders had a high tolerance for 'unusual' sexual practices, that the breaking of the taboo on sexual contact (rape) with a Daughter could therefore be virtually understood as merely another, more 'unusual sexual practice'. Another writer maintains that incest offenders do not have the neurotic reactions of other sex criminals, but seem to consider incest to be essentially normal and not reprehensible.[43]

Contrary to rape mythology the sexual 'practice' of the Fathers shows that they are not 'overwhelmed' by sexual passion:

> The great majority of offences were premeditated; most incest offences are repetitious, rather than one lone event, and therefore all but perhaps the first are premeditated.[44]

We have already seen that many of the Fathers claim non-responsibility for the first incident, claiming impaired awareness through the use of alcohol: but Father–Daughter rape *normally* continues for years. There can be no 'impairment of awareness' in such a situation. Nor can there be claims of uncontrollable sexual urges, of being 'overwhelmed' by sexual passion.

An ingenious twist to the prevalent rape-myth of uncontrollable sexual passion in the male, whereby the Father's role is rendered quite invisible, occurs when his actions are described as the giving of affection. The rape-as-affection theory argues that the Father is simply fulfilling affection needs in the Daughter, because her mother is not; and even if it is undesirable that this be done sexually, it is better than nothing, isn't it? The unstated assumption behind this argument is that it is natural, or at least understandable, for an adult male to express affection towards a girl-child in a sexual form because men are so strongly sexually motivated that sometimes they cannot tell the difference between a girl-child's desire for a cuddle and their own desire for sexual excitation. Hersko *et al.* point out:

> . . . these men, in fact, took advantage of their daughters' craving for love by making sexual activity the price for gratification of affectional needs . . .[45]

The reading of this sentence has, however, to be seen in context. It is preceded by these observations:

> It would appear that the process starts during the child's early years. All of the mothers *were unable* to meet their daughters' needs for dependency gratification. The girls, therefore, *sought* such gratifications from their fathers. The fathers, *because of personal inadequacies*, which were further aggravated by the wives' rejections, *tended* to sexualize the relationships with their daughters.[46] [My italics.]

In this, as in much of the clinical literature, we find stunning testimony to what feminist theorists Stanley and Daly have named 'agent deletion'.[47] The Fathers come across as peculiarly passive: they are like helpless dolls being manipulated by their wives, their daughters, their mothers. In the above example, the wife and daughter are given transitive verbs, strong in their meaning, to describe their actions: thus the wives are 'unable' to satisfy their daughters' needs, and they 'rejected' their husbands; the daughters 'craved' love and 'sought' gratification. The Fathers, on the other hand, are forgiven in advance: they do things 'because of personal inadequacies' which seem to be somehow hanging around, with no verb to make their ownership or evolution plain; and they 'tended' (only) to sexualise their relationships with their daughters. The almost invisible language of do-ing, act-ing, be-ing used in this way *subliminally* establishes the wives and daughters as the active parties, and the Fathers as passive puppets.

Sarles (1975) goes even further in his use of verbs, managing to make it sound as though the Fathers are doing the Daughters a favour: in this case the Fathers are given strong active verbs as well as the Daughters, but the content of the verbs ascribed to the Fathers is concerned with reaction to the Daughters, who are therefore attributed power over the Father – again by subliminal use of language.

> . . . psychologically in the case of incestuous relationships, the child *gratifies* her unconscious desires for the father who *condones the act* and *suppresses* the prohibition.[48] [My italics.]

The word 'condone' means to 'forgive' or 'overlook' as of 'an offence, especially matrimonial infidelity' (Oxford English Dictionary). That any clinician can write, within any context, that the Father-rapists 'condone the act' (i.e. forgive the Daughter) is a measure of the power of rape ideology. Most reasonable people would expect that clinical reports of Father–Daughter rape would be informed, at least in part, by disapproval of the Fathers; instead we mostly find the pseudo-objectivity of psycho-scientific research which is in fact informed by a desire to forgive the Fathers by blaming the female principle in whatever form can be found.

In the wake of the naming of sex-role stereotypes and the consequent widespread awareness of sex-role 'problems', some very recent researchers have found evidence of sex-role anxiety about masculinity among rapists.[49] The need to be a 'man', the need to be seen to be a 'man' is central to the act of rape. As Brownmiller (1978) has noted:

> Not much force is needed to molest a young child, and for this reason, I think, older men prove quite successful at it, whereas young men use rape as a test of male prowess and male solidarity [as in group rape].[50]

The Fathers do not, according to the evidence, usually *appear* to feel inadequate as men before disclosure of rape of the Daughter: but if we assume, for the moment, that some of them do feel this way, then Father–Daughter rape is a perfect solution, *for them*. In being a rapist, he is asserting his maleness; in taking his daughter (who has no choice), he attempts to build a lover-relationship into his life. Thus he asserts himself as a man, and at the same time tries to combine the love of a child for a parent with the love of a woman for a man – all fused into one, with himself as the subject. This rapist wants everything – and uses girl-children to try to get it.

The Fathers have an extraordinarily developed capacity to deny and rationalise what they are doing/have done: maybe that is an understandable component of being the perpetrator of long-term, institutionalised, I-want-everything, Daughter-rape. Gebhard found that incest offenders deny their actions more, both quantitatively and qualitatively, than any other type of sex offender. (All this, of course, means also that many victims have been disbelieved in the face of the Father's lies). After 'disclosure', many Fathers continue to deny their actions for as long as possible: when they are finally 'helped' to admit what they have done, they typically feel sadness and depression, rather than guilt about their actions. They also feel the loss of the Daughter, as well as the family group:

> There is a great need to be forgiven, as if he were a child who must be reconciled to his mother. In some cases, *a state of depression can only be alleviated when there is forgiveness* and a satisfactory relationship can again be achieved.[51] [My italics.]

Such touching concern for the Daughter-rapists' state of depression is actually manifest anxiety to forgive the Fathers by (pseudo-liberal) understanding which takes the approach that the Fathers are 'sick' but can probably be 'cured' by a little more caring.

The Father will also attempt to rationalise what he has done, and shift the blame to others at the same time. He may eventually

> . . . admit the fact but find many excuses, such as the frigidity of the wife. There is also the need to implicate the daughter and make her equally responsible. The father thus accuses her of being provocative and seductive, or he says that she was a willing accomplice . . . The father may, on the other hand, accuse both wife and daughter of laying false charges against him in order to put him in prison. All these manoeuvres serve to preserve a

self-image, to deny the reality of the fact, and to avoid guilt by placing responsibility outside himself.[52]

Such rationalisations on the part of Daughter-rapists are to be expected; their litanous repetition throughout the clinical literature I find far more frightening. I use the word 'litanous' (from the word 'litany', which refers to a form of church service in which the congregation respond in set formulas to incantations by a clergyman) to stress the complementarity of the patterning of the content and intonation between the claims of the Fathers and the responses of the clinicians.

The Fathers' denial mechanisms are, of course, to be expected. They know that they have committed a crime. They do not spontaneously confess, or seek intervention. Nor, it should be noted, do the perpetrators of most other crimes. In the process of writing this book, it was put to me that 'the men who do, won't read it' and I replied that I didn't expect them to. I agree with Tormes that

Considering the father-offender as a possible source of control of incest behaviour seems . . . like considering the fox for a position as guard of the henhouse.[53]

The Fathers who rape Daughters are indeed foxes in disguise: the outside world sees them as Daddies, Protectors, of the women in their care. Many Fathers who have been 'named' as foxes, then questioned, therapied, or even charged and gaoled, have been in the past (and probably are in the present), allowed back to guard the henhouse again – and many of them rape the Daughter again, and again.[54]

This brings up the question of recidivism. The evidence, once again, is contradictory. Some researchers maintain that recidivism is low; others that it is high. Since very few real follow-up studies have been done, and could only be done on the small percentage of known cases that are dealt with by public authorities, it may be some time before there is any real knowledge in this area. What is clear, is that the Father will continue to rape *until* disclosure; or, as in the case of many of the women I talked with, until they themselves can leave the situation (like Jude and Ann), or are protected by their mothers (like Alice and Kim). This does not auger well for cessation on the part of the Father, either spontaneously, or after disclosure when he immerses his pysche in denial and rationalisations which shift any acknowledgment of responsibility from himself.

The Santa Clara programme which has, as far as I am aware, by far the most experience of dealing with the whole family in cases of Father–Daughter rape, has found that very swift intervention followed by immediate removal of the Father is the most effective way to begin treatment. Using an illness/treatment/cure model, and with the assistance of the local judicial system, they tell the Father he must stay away until he has been judged 'cured'. If the family dynamics or legal situation are such that the Father can insist on staying in the family home, then the Santa Clara programme workers endeavour to remove the Daughter(s).[55] They have found that if either the Father or the Daughter(s) are not removed in this way, the raping nearly always continues. Often, too, the family 'closes down' and everyone denies the original accusation. In this event, the Daughter will feel unsupported, disbelieved, and abandoned to the same situation she has tried to stop.

It is the continuing aspect of Father–Daughter rape – the fact that it usually occurs over years – that lends credence, within male supremacist attitudes, to talk of 'seduction' and 'affairs', rather than rape. In a paper entitled 'Seduction is a Four Letter Word', Greer observes that:

> . . . we must insist that only evidence of positive desire dignifies sexual intercourse and makes it joyful. From a proud and passionate woman's point of view, anything less is rape.[56]

In most of the stories told by women in the Exposition of this book, we can see that they tried to resist in some way: only Vera was effective immediately when as a five-year-old she scratched her grandfather's face. Many would say that a girl-child cannot possibly have the 'pride and passion' of an integrated female being in the world. I suspect that while some girl-children approximate this state of being, insofar as they are spirited in defence of their own integrity, no girl-children have the means to express an *equal* 'positive desire' with an adult male, while both are living in and created by a male supremacist society. Tormes mentions that within the family setting, a girl-child's '*normal* position is subordinate' [Original italics.][57] Subordinate people *cannot* contract equal social and/or sexual relations with anyone except their peers – and even then, in the case of girl-children, there are 'normal' inequalities operating between boy- and girl-children in terms of self-esteem and (learned) attitudes to sexuality – their own and that of the opposite gender.

The Fathers, in raping these most subordinate of people, girl-children, have been exonerated by the sexist myth of the female-as-temptress. They have themselves named their raping 'passive seduction', and been supported by the professional 'namers' in this. From the cultural stereotype of horrendous psychopaths, the Fathers have been redefined by the experts as unfortunate men with weak impulse-control: a more understanding wife or mother (or both) would have 'saved' them.

The clinicians forgive the Daughter-rapists by shifting the blame to the female principle. A psychologist, Chesler, writing of therapists, opines that:

> . . . men of science cannot, except momentarily and romantically, and therefore safely, identify strongly with their female subjects. Their own sanity can remain firmly moored between their legs.[58]

The phallic centre of sanity named by Chesler is the real nexus of identification between the Fathers and clinicians. The phallus, symbolic of patriarchal power, is, for these two groups of men, both symbol and reality of their interconnection about rape of a Daughter. The therapists, mind-doctors of male supremacist society, exonerate the Fathers' use of sexual phallic power with the use of their own specific phallic power, that of being the agents of social control in the interests of maintaining a male supremacist society.

Rape is rape: rape is about power. Each single time a Father approaches a Daughter sexually, it is rape. The Father's need for forgiveness, his desire for reassurance that he is not irredeemably deviant, will no longer be heard through the cries of the most vulnerable members of society, those whom he has raped – the Daughters.

4 The Daughters –
Labelled and Libelled

One day my eyes will grow
Too tired for crying.
I long for it.

I want them lizardy,
Dry hard and nimble,
Seeing everything.

I want to put
One foot after the other
Through this city,

Through my days,
Through my children's days,
Seeing everything dry.

I want the next juice
Anywhere near to spring
Flowers in my sockets.

> Tina Reid, 'Dear Sophie: Letter to an Ill Child',
> from *Smile Smile Smile Smile*,
> by Fell, Pixner, Reid, Roberts and Oosthuizen

Popular mythology would suggest that the Daughters are nearly always precocious adolescents: there is widespread belief in the 'Lolita Syndrome'. This myth is so deeply entrenched in our culture that it conjures a (seemingly) automatic image: a twelve-year-old with ragged blonde hair, lips like Brigitte Bardot, a seductive walk and fluttering eyelashes. Nabokov's Lolita, Tennessee Williams' Baby Doll, Georgette Heyer's girl-child love-object-heroine in *These Old Shades*, adolescent film-stars posed in attitudes of seductive innuendo: the 'little minx' is a cultural construct designed to show that girls are born as temptresses,[1] and that it's no wonder that some men are led astray. Male supremacist society may *wish* that all girl-children fulfilled this stereotype, but in reality girl-children are not Lolitas, nor little minxes.

Daughters of any age are raped. Daughters across the whole spectrum of possible behaviours and types of appearances are raped. The reality of the rape of girl-children demonstrates that the stereotypical Lolita exists only in the minds of men (and women who still accept male supremacist cultural myths). The Daughters, as children, are expected to be seen but not heard. The Daughters, as females, are expected to be passive and tractable in the face of a Father's 'needs' or demands. Most of the Daughters carry the crippling effects of their childhood rape experience throughout their lives. Some, and hopefully many more in the near future, manage to transform the scars of their experience into symbols of awareness, through clear womanvision (rejection) of their victim status. These women can not only acknowledge, but also use, their righteous anger.

The median age of Daughters who are victims of rape by a Father, as determined in several group studies, appears to be around ten years old. This means that there are very many victims who are less than ten years old. Here are some examples of rape by a Father involving very young Daughters:

> A Florida newspaper tersely reported to its readers early in 1975 that the city's youngest rape victim to date was only two months old at the time of the sexual assault. No other comment was offered.[2]

> In 1979, in an Australian city, a young mother of two daughters had reason to go away. Her mother came to stay, to help with the children. She was awoken by cries from the three-year-old, saying, 'Stop, Daddy. You're hurting my bottom . . .' She found her university-educated son-in-law in bed with his daughter.[3]

> Stephanie, at age 17 months, was brought to a hospital emergency room by her mother who had noticed blood in the baby's diaper after she returned home from work. On examination, the child was found to have a small anal fissure that bled freely when touched. There was no previous history of abnormality or trauma and the mother was reassured that the fissure could be easily corrected surgically if it did not heal by itself.

Several weeks later, Stephanie was found dead in her crib – a victim of asphyxiation. An autopsy revealed the presence of semen in her mouth and throat. When apprehended, the babysitter, a 19-year-old boy, freely admitted to sexual abuse of the child but protested 'I didn't mean to kill her!'[4]

A clinician's report on a four-year-old girl-child whose father had been raping her and her sisters, aged eight and ten: 'It was the youngest of the three children who concerned the social workers most. She seemed possibly retarded and was without affect except when she was around a man. At these times she would become coy, smile at the man, and then rub her genitals against the man's knee and reach out to touch his genitals . . . Her attempts to make contact were conditioned by her previous experiences that offering sexual overtures was the bridge to affection. This suggested ultimately a sadomasochistic substructure to her character. She was not retarded but rather was preoccupied with prematurely stimulated sexual impulses.'[5]

A typical clinical finding is that the age of girl-child rape victims ranges from six to seventeen or so, and that the frequency of incidence is fairly evenly distributed throughout the age range.[6] One clinician comments on such a finding:

This suggests that the sexual maturity of the daughters, apart from gross physiological capacity, does not contribute significantly to the occurrence of incest.[7]

As we can see from the stories above, even 'gross physiological' characteristics determined by age and development do not deter some of the Fathers from raping Daughters who are younger than six. In Israel, recent court figures on child sexual abuse showed that 60 percent of those raped were under ten, the remaining 40 percent ranging in age from ten to fourteen.[8] In the stories in the Exposition of this book, there are three examples of Daughters raped before school age: Alice was three and a half, Vera was aged three to five, and Susan was aged four to five. In all of these cases the Father-offenders were using these little girl-children's bodies to create the stimulation needed for ejaculation.

The child is regarded at times as some*thing* other than a child, or as a surrogate of someone else. The child *becomes an object for* *the needs of the adult* without adequate recognition of the inappropriateness or inadequacy of the child to meet these needs.[9] [My italics.]

The 'something' or 'object' that the girl-child becomes in the eyes of the Father is a sexual 'aid' to his own expression of sexual power. The stimulus, in the being of the girl-child, consists of her powerlessness and her femaleness.

In the clinical literature, however, one finds no consideration of male-to-female power dynamics, and very little consideration of power as a factor at all. Indeed, there is an implicit assumption in much of the clinical literature that the Daughters actually wield considerable power of their own. The clinicians use the following facts to 'prove' that the Daughters were willing 'partners': that Father–Daughter rape usually continues for lengthy periods; that the Daughters feel shame; that the Daughters feel enormous guilt, particularly *after* disclosure; that there are no real ill-effects; that many Daughters experience sexual pleasure in the raping situation; and that some Daughters appear to genuinely love the Father who raped them. All these strands of 'evidence' will be examined in this chapter.

In the wake of Freud's Oedipal theorising, many clinicians have assumed 'co-operation' or 'participation' on the part of the Daughters and struggled only to determine the *degree* of such co-operation. Invariably they become involved in considerations of coercion and whether or not force was used – thereby putting the Daughters in the same (sinking) boat as adult female rape victims who are deemed to have consented unless they resisted to the point of bearing the physical marks of their defeat (i.e. risked death). In no other crime of physical violence is the victim presumed to have colluded on these grounds.

The evidence from the Daughters about coercion is overwhelming. In a 1980 study of social workers' impressions of the incest cases they had dealt with, 64 percent responded that 'the threat of violence stood out clearly' as the most common way 'used by fathers to obtain sexual contact'.[10] In Tormes' study of forty Daughters the twenty 'incest' victims all 'claimed to have submitted to the fathers' sexual demands either because of personal threats to them or fear of future violence'.[11]

We have already seen that the Fathers, as adult males, have all the power of adult-to-child as well as male-to-female, over the Daughters. *Of course* the Daughters are scared of the Fathers.

Many women [and girl-children], when faced with a sexual attack and realizing their psychological and physical inability to protect themselves, are immobilized with fear . . . *The victim's reaction time will be especially prolonged if she knows the offender and trusts him not to harm her.*[12] [My italics.]

The expectation that 'Daddy will protect me' means that most Daughters trust their fathers over and above any other man. Only a 'small' amount of coercion is needed by a Father to rape a Daughter.

Unable to see this social reality, many researchers enumerate the 'characteristics' of the Daughters in an attempt to determine why these particular girl-children 'became' victims of rape by a Father. By means of this exercise the Father's 'coercion' becomes the Daughter's 'passivity'. Thus we find the social workers describing the Daughters as 'quiet, withdrawn, subservient, emotionally dependent, and passive'.[13] Tormes found that:

The children from incestuous families . . . may generally be described as 'socially compliant'. Prior to referral to the agency for the present event, only two children (two victims) had come to the attention of public agencies because of behavioural problems at school. The mothers often referred to the victims as 'quiet', 'obedient', 'good' girls, and 'very helpful in the home'.[14]

The Daughters appear, on these grounds, to fit the male supremacist stereotype of a 'good daughter': the pre-pubescent female eunuch. That the Daughters may have been 'withdrawn' and 'socially compliant' because they had been repeatedly raped by a Father and because they were in a social worker 'treatment' environment which was probably experienced as threatening, appears to fall outside the conceptual scope of studies such as these which prefer to take the patient/victim personality as the true one. The many other Daughters who run away from home, get charged with EMD (being 'exposed to moral danger'), and placed in custody, are not available, of course, for such family-based Father–Daughter incest studies, and so the clinical picture is biassed accordingly, presenting a picture of more 'passivity' than is actually the case.

The presumed passivity and social compliance of the Daughters is the manifest behaviour of all oppressed peoples who are not in a state of open rebellion.

The man in a position of higher social status relative to the woman is particularly able to use moral blackmail. He can use his position of power to coerce the woman into consenting. This is facilitated since subordinates are accustomed to relating to superordinates with deference and expect them to be trustworthy . . . without regard to her compliance or lack of it, *her dependence upon him as a powerful person keeps her from reporting and opens the door for further exploitation.*[15] [My italics.]

We have seen that the Daughter is, for very good reasons, powerless before the Father; that she has, most likely, the attributes of withdrawal and compliance that characterise powerless people; and that she is dependent upon him precisely because he is a powerful person in her world.

In one study of six cases, the researchers apparently probed a little deeper and found that:

They perceived their assignment as substitute mothers as due to their sex and viewed boys as freer to be children . . . All of these girls viewed woman's role as depreciated and self-sacrificing, requiring very much with very little in return.[16]

These six Daughters, having experienced one of the most profound forms of the oppression of women, are able to verbalise some of the socio-political dimensions of the relationship between the sexes, expressed in terms of sex-role expectations.

Central to the female sex-role is love. Many professionals talk or write of the frequent cases of 'incest' in which the Daughter really loves the Father. Some have put to me the question, 'What does that mean? What do you do about it if she really loves him?' My answer is that fear, compliance and dependence can produce the *semblance* of love. They almost certainly produce a *desire* for love, of which a semblance of love may be the manifestation.

. . . in incest cases, the ego defence of reaction-formation may cause the victim to love the hated person since she may be unable to deal with the feelings of hatred and the ramifications of expressing them directly . . . Victims of oppression may react by inviting further exploitation, when the line between love and hate becomes blurred. If the phenomenon is operative in the rapist–victim relationship, it should not lead to false assumptions about the degree of consent in the original rape.[17]

In the stories in this book, we have seen how Kim and Jude occasionally went willingly on outings with the Father, in the short-term hope/belief that it had 'all changed'. Depending (for existence) on your rapist creates a desperate, *everyday* need to disbelieve what has been occurring – the abuse and exploitation of your own being. 'Surely if I'm nice today (and he hasn't "done it" for a week now), everything will be all right?'. Having no escape from the family, the Daughter's only escape is to dream that the horror will go away.

Workers at the Single Women's Refuge in Sydney have found that many of the Daughters they provide shelter for, have explained to them that the Father who raped them often expressed 'love', as in 'I'm doing this because I love you', as an integral part of the actual raping. For many of these victims 'love' and rape have therefore become synonymous. Thus many of the Daughters seek an 'escape' in early marriage, or establish a pattern of relationships with men in which they are searching for love: what they often get is violence and exploitation, a repetition of the relationship they experienced with the Father.

The Daughters' desire (need) for love is often used against them, as it is for many adult women. 'Love', for females, begins to change very early in life from a physiological need for nurturance and reassurance, to the giving of nurturance (in keeping with the female role stereotype under male supremacy), in the (usually) mistaken belief that we will be repaid in kind. For example, one Daughter was able, unlike the mother,

> . . . to help her father over acute aggressive outbursts merely by talking with him . . . The daughter enjoyed being able to help her father whenever he was agitated, but preferred that she keep her role in this category. She recognized that *she saw her father more as a sick child than as a father*.[18] [My italics.]

Feeling 'guilty' about punishing your oppressor is a classic response of oppressed peoples, particularly females, whose oppression is based in putting others before themselves. It is one of the reasons that many adult women do not proceed with legal action against a man who has raped them.

The trouble with seeing the 'sick boy' within the Father is that as women (of whatever age), we know that we will love a sick child no matter what it does because, after all, we understand that it doesn't know any better, 'it can't help itself', and ultimately, *it is not*

responsible for what it does (it is only a child). So the Daughter/
Little Mother often experiences a great deal of guilt if the
repercussions after disclosure are unpleasant for the Father. The
Daughter referred to above

> . . . indicated that she felt much more comfortable after her
> father was out of the home, but even so she felt guilty about her
> part in placing him in a state hospital.[19]

The clinicians, in finding that guilt is the most widely experienced
emotion in the Daughters, especially *after* disclosure, assume,
simplistically, that the guilt arises out of having been a willing
'participant', and that it is particularly apparent after disclosure
because that is when the Father *may* be punished. The guilt is seen
as emanating from the fact that she has put the Father at risk: the
assumption is that if she were guiltless, she would not feel that way.

The 1980 study of social workers' impressions of 'incest participants' gave a response of 82 percent of strong guilt feelings being
present in the Daughters.[20] Kaufman (1966) found that 'depression
and guilt were universal as clinical findings in these girls' and that
'their verbalized guilt, as far as our clinical material demonstrated,
was in connection with the disruption of the home and not over the
incest itself'.[21] In keeping with the line of argument that says the
Daughter only becomes guilty when she 'sees the result of her
actions', a 1969 study observes that 'massive acute anxiety in the
first instance may be aroused because of the closeness of the
external event to the unconscious fantasy'.[22] Thus the clinicians
argue that the Daughter feels 'guilty' because of her participation in
(if not initiation of) the 'sexual relationship' (raping).

Guilt is self-destructive, because it is anger with nowhere to go
except inwards. Guilt is internalised resentment. So-called 'guilt',
therefore, is an extremely convenient 'emotion' for male supremacist society to refuse to demystify: keeping 'guilt' alive and well
means that women, in taking on responsibility for the real tangible
guilt of men, in the guise of nurturance, tear themselves apart with
the invisible rage elicited by being oppressed as a woman. Women
and girl-children most often turn that rage inwards because
expressing it outwardly is frightening (since it is so big) and
unwomanly (since it is not 'nice').

Katan (1973) gives a clinical account of this process. She found, in
a psychoanalytic study of women raped as children, that a crippling
degree of 'excitement', meaning a compulsive desire to repeat the

experience growing out of the 'overstimulation which continues as a central problem in their lives', afflicted these women. She argues that this form of 'excitement', in its clinical sense, produces guilt feelings:

> The tremendous excitement of these six women focused on the fantasized acquisition of the penis and identification with men. *Only in this identification and excitement could they escape the unbelievably low self-esteem they all had in common* . . . The tremendous excitement that was aroused in all these patients made all their conflicts extraordinarily intense; hence the abnormal amount and quality of guilt they were forced to cope with . . . *Their aggression was turned against the self in a savage form.* If turned against the outside world, it had a strange quality to it that I can only describe as raw, not really fitting their personalities.[23] [My italics.]

The 'fantasized acquisition of the penis' is, of course, a desire to take in, have access to, the power (symbolised by the phallus) that men have, *so that they are allowed to be angry*. But as females, such behaviour is not allowed, is unfeminine: so it manifests itself as 'guilt': 'Their aggression was turned against the self in a savage form'.

Other clinicians have posited explanations of the Daughters' 'guilt', such as psychiatrists Sloane and Karpinski (1942):

> . . . that the guilt feeling stemmed not from society's condemnation [as if that would not be enough!] but from within the girl herself, and that it had to do with hostile designs (death wishes) against the mother.[24]

This theory devolves from the reverse-Oedipal theory which holds that the girl-child desires her mother's death so that she can assume her place as her father's sexual partner – and that having had an 'incestuous affair' (been raped by her father) she feels guilty about her degree of success in removing her mother from the scene.

Kaufman *et al.* (1954), in discussing 'delinquent' behaviour in some adolescent Daughter-victims, actually blame the sexuality of the Daughters, able only to see the female-as-temptress component of the stereotypic view of women:

Since the sexuality of these girls led to the arrest and incarceration of the father and disruption of the home, they had the experience of seeing their destructive, omnipotent fantasies come true.[25]

So here the Daughters are seen not only as desiring the mother's death (the destructive, omnipotent fantasy), but also as carriers of an innately evil weapon – their own sexuality – about which they are naturally expected to feel guilty since it was the cause of the Father's 'incarceration'.

Freud's 'discovery' of sexual fantasy in children and the 'adjustments' made by Freudians like Abraham and others can be heard chiming distortedly down the decades in these blaming-the-Daughter statements. It is a curious fact that it is generally conservative thinking which regards children as innocent non-sexual vessels who must be coddled and protected (as opposed to the radical social view which encourages children to be self-directed and to take responsibility for their actions), and yet it is the same conservative view which treats the Daughters as She-Devils in the guise of children – especially when the public reputation of the Father is threatened. Some clinicians become quite vitriolic in their phrasing about the girl-children who have become Daughters – and thereby 'surrendered' the protection due to them as children. The oft-quoted Bender and Blau study of 1937 says 'these children *undoubtedly* do not deserve completely the cloak of innocence with which they have been endowed by moralists, social reformers and legislators'[26] (my italics); and weiner in 1962 observes that there is much to show 'that the daughters, like their mothers, are not merely innocent pawns of their father's will'.[27]

Most considerations of 'guilt' in the literature feed into the still-prevalent attitude that repetition-proves-participation, as well as the even more outrageous daughters-are-female-so-they-probably-caused-it-all-anyway. These two theories may be connected, as in:

Most studies of father–daughter incest reveal that some daughters accept or even provoke incestuous activity. This would be expected as so many father–daughter liaisons go on for so long.[28]

That so many 'liaisons' go on for so long is often merely another measure of the Daughters' misguided love (nurturance), and is certainly a measure of the power of the Father over a Daughter within the family situation.

Not only is she acting out the female cultural tradition in loving and/or forgiving the Father, but also taking on the emotional load of protecting the whole family from the knowledge of what is happening to her:

> To truly understand the passivity of the daughter, one needs to imagine the situation as it is perceived through the eyes of a child. Especially in a paternalistic family, the daughter has been taught to obey her father in all situations, to anticipate punishment for any show of defiance, and to believe that what her father does is unquestionably in her best interests . . . But even if she knows that incest is socially reprehensible, *the real and implicit threats in the situation are often sufficient to secure her passive co-operation in the absence of any reasonable alternatives.*[29] [My italics.]

Part of the 'real and implicit threats in the situation' is the knowledge that significant other adults, particularly her mother, will have their lives profoundly affected if she succeeds in 'disclosing' the rape situation with which she is living. Many Daughters take on the weight of this responsibility for other people's feelings to a paralysing degree. They then choose to protect the family, rather than themselves.

For many of those who do succeed in disclosing the situation, the result is enormous extra emotional trauma caused by being made to feel responsible for the fall-out: that is, it becomes the (raped) Daughter's 'fault' that the Father is imprisoned, or sent for 'treatment'; that the family loses a breadwinner; that her mother feels ashamed and represses knowledge of what has happened among relatives and friends; and that the family may go through the upheaval of moving to another town or city in an attempt to escape the opprobrium visited on the whole family.

The Daughters' powerlessness and female-nurturance (love) thus set them up to be total victims. The nexus between their powerlessness and love becomes, in the rape situation, (coerced) acquiescence, which the male supremacist clinicians and researchers misname 'participation'. Sloane and Karpinski show some of the reasoning which results in the 'participation' theory:

> In each [of five cases] the man appears to have been the active seducer. It is evident, however, that the girl was more or less

149

compliant, despite her protestations of innocence, since sexual relations took place at frequent intervals over long periods. The third girl, for instance, continued to live at home, where she claimed she was being coerced into incest, even after her two sisters had left in order to avoid their father's advances.[30]

The Daughter who 'continued to live at home' may have felt too fractured, in innumerable ways, to contemplate the world outside; she was also probably trying, by staying, to salvage something of value in her life. She may:

> . . . feel emotionally bound to the rapist because of the conjoint knowledge about the encounter and the shared guilty secret. This will often occur *when she fears that knowledge of the event will hurt others or seriously damage other existing relationships which she values*.[31] [My italics.]

Many clinicians, not able to see this aspect of being a powerless and embattled being, argue that the (raped) Daughter has *chosen* to play a role whereby she keeps the whole family together by 'replacing' her mother (who is seen to have 'abandoned' her role in some way) with herself. Some Daughters do indeed play this role, but in a structural sense, as opposed to a freely chosen power-trip. She may 'keep the family together' by being the buffer of the Father's rape-aggression; by protecting her mother and siblings from this knowledge, she prevents the break-up of the family and the subsequent pain of dispersal and change for everyone concerned. I have heard several women who were Daughters speak of having done this, with the added rider that they extracted a promise from the Father to leave their younger sisters alone, in return for which they 'acquiesced'. Several finally broke the silence when they found out the Father had broken his promise.

A Daughter who has been raped by a Father, and then carries a sense of responsibility for having broken up the family or caused 'scenes' or caused her Father to be imprisoned, has great reason to feel rage. It is not her fault that Fathers rape Daughters, or that Mothers get upset, or that her family has been shattered. It is in no way her fault, but she feels as though it is – hence her guilt/rage.

Another common finding is that the Daughters feel 'shame' about the rape involvement. The dictionary (Concise Oxford Dictionary) definition of shame is (1) 'Feeling of humiliation excited by consciousness of guilt or shortcoming, of having made oneself or been made ridiculous . . .'; (2) 'Restraint imposed by, [or] desire to avoid, such humiliation'; (3) 'State of disgrace or ignominy or discredit; person or thing that brings disgrace'. The clinicians have mostly assumed that the shame of the Daughters is caused by 'consciousness of guilt'. However, since we have seen that the 'guilt' of the Daughters is internalised rage, this simplistic connection does not answer. Shame is also 'desire to avoid humiliation', and the experiencing of a 'state of ignominy': thus, shame is a logical response to being raped.

The Daughters, in expressing shame, are speaking of *what has been done to them*. They are speaking of humiliation, of powerlessness. They are speaking of the effect of having a Father use and abuse their very bodies against their will. They are speaking of an invasion of privacy and integrity carried out in hatred. There are two kinds of shame: the one that comes from self-criticism of an action, such as 'I shouldn't have spoken so sharply to you'; and the other which is the shame that is taken in when something is done to us, when we are humiliated. The Daughters who feel shame have been humiliated, in gross physical and emotional forms, as well as experiencing, at close hand, the Father's hatred. I say hatred because there is no love in rape; I say hatred because it is obvious that rapists are full of self-hatred. Only existential emptiness, alienation from what it means to be human, i.e. self-hatred, can produce the act of rape. The Daughters as the objects of rape are young, dependent, and constantly accessible: it is not unreasonable to assume that the Fathers, in raping a Daughter, are forced, more than in adult rape, to confront (except that they repress) the inhumanity of their power. For the Daughter, the nexus between the hatred coming at her and the humiliation resulting from it produces a feeling called 'shame'. But, as with guilt, if a Daughter digs deeply enough under this shame, she will find rage.

Yet another reason which is advanced by the clinicians as an explanation for the Daughters' passivity is that it is a pretence designed to disguise their own active sexual enjoyment of the situation. For example, one Daughter who is described as having experienced real pleasure in sexual contacts with her father, also managed to appear quite passive. Weiner, a psychiatrist (1962), presents the case like this:

> . . . in spite of her eagerness, she had always assumed a role of passive acquiescence, had purposely admitted none of her pleasure to him – as a means of assuaging guilt and deflecting

accountability onto him. It is quite likely that many incestuous daughters [sic] avoid guilt feelings by denying their enjoyment of the sexual experience and behaving in an outwardly passive manner during sex contacts.[32]

To say that the Daughter 'had purposely admitted none of her pleasure to him' completely begs the larger question of whether he was remotely interested in her pleasure, as opposed to his own. Leaving such carping aside for the moment, the fact is that to have the sensation of genital pleasure in a rape situation is a mind-splitting experience.

Kim experienced such pleasure (and hated it) during two years of genital manipulation by her de facto father. Sonia, too, experienced sexual pleasure, and hated the ambivalence it produced. That some Daughters (and some adult women rape victims) suffer pleasure within a rape experience is a key element in rape crisis counselling, because a 'mind-split' comes from the feeling that the body is betraying us. This happens because knowledge and *acceptance* of female sexuality is still widely (and wildly) suppressed in our culture. Knowledge of her own erogenous zones and likely genital reactions is rarely explained to girl-children. Thus a girl-child who is being raped by a Father and experiences 'pleasure' feels her will (which does not want this contact) separating from her body. If it feels good, it can't be rape, can it?

Oh yes it can. If the will is not united with the body, then pleasure (of the body) is experienced either as a betrayal (by the will) and denied, or as a discrete other element which belongs to the victim who knows her body well and can accept her physiological sexual responses for what they are. Neither of these reactions bear any resemblance to the psycho-social mutuality of shared love-making where body and will are in harmony. When sexual pleasure is experienced as betrayal by the body, the Daughter (or woman) will probably decide it was not rape, because she has been taught that rape equals unpleasure and that pleasure equals participation.

Here is an account (1966) of one Daughter's experience of this split and how she responded:

She stated that she would occasionally become excited when her father would have intercourse with her. She felt at the time that it was probably a natural reaction, that, after all, she was human, and even though she didn't want to experience any pleasure, it happened anyway. She then began to have severe anxiety and insisted that her mother do something more drastic to prevent her father from having sexual contact with her. She wanted her mother to stay with her more of the time. When the mother refused, the child went to the school psychologist and told him.[33]

Passivity (being coerced) can thus co-exist with the experience of pleasure. As the stories in this book testify, and also those in Armstrong's book, *Kiss Daddy Goodnight*, most of the Daughters appear to be passive – like the 'subordinate' people they are – whether pleasurable, painful, or indifferent sexual responses are elicited. What else can a Daughter do?

So, out of all this consideration of passivity or participation, and acquiescence or coercion, comes only one result as far as many of the clinicians (and therefore general public) are concerned: blame the Daughters. Some studies have been carried out to try to determine what, if any, are the short- and long-term effects of Father–Daughter rape on the Daughters. Many of these studies deduce the victim loved it because they find very few, if any, ill-effects at all:

Their emotional reactions were remarkably devoid of guilt, fear or anxiety regarding the sexual experience. There was evidence that the child derived some emotional satisfaction from the experience.[34]

Despite the calm generalisations of this statement, which pervade the whole study (Bender and Blau, 1937), we find that this remark is, in part, preceded by a horrifying account of some of the effects:

Some of the children show immediate harmful effects on their personality development. The infantile stage is prolonged or reverted to in the younger child, and the so-called latent stage with its normal intellectual and social interests is sacrificed. There appears to be mental retardation in some cases, and school accomplishments are thwarted. Anxiety states with bewilderment concerning social relations occur especially in children who are seduced by parents.[35]

Experts like these authors who maintain, in the face of the above information that they themselves wrote, that the Daughters were not particularly affected (in spite of the fact that most of the girls and boys in their study were living in mental institutions), leave me

153

wondering if they themselves had ever been children.

Similarly, Kinsey (1953), the original 'sexologist', found in his large sample of the normal population that 24 percent of females 'had been approached while they were pre-adolescent by adult males who appeared to be making sexual advances, or who had made sexual advances, or who had made sexual contacts with the child'.[36] He found that 80 percent of these females 'had been emotionally upset or frightened by their contacts with adults' and that 'a small proportion had been seriously disturbed'. He then goes on to interpolate his own qualitative judgment, which he makes absolutely no effort to substantiate, of these findings:

> . . . in most instances the reported fright was nearer the level that children show when they see insects, spiders, or other objects against which they have been adversely conditioned . . . It is difficult to understand why a child, except for its cultural conditioning, should be disturbed at having its genitalia touched, or disturbed at seeing the genitalia of other persons, or disturbed at even more specific sexual contacts.[37]

Lukianowicz (1972), in a study of twenty-six victims who had entered out-patients' for 'nervous complaints', found that six of them had 'no ill-effects'. From this proportion of 23 percent, he deduces that:

> This group of girls would rather confirm Bender and Blau's (1937) observations that *most* children who have had sexual contact with adults do not come to any real harm.[38] [My italics.]

In this study, the remaining twenty victims were placed into three other categories in terms of the effects Father–Daughter rape had had on them: 'girls who became promiscuous', 'girls who became frigid' and 'girls who developed neurotic symptoms'. And yet Lukianowicz, the Father-supporter, decides that 'most' of them were not affected: when dealing with this kind of logic, we know that we are up against something other than reasoning power.

Lukianowicz's category of 'girls who became promiscuous' is an indicator of the fact that some of the Daughters act out the sexual object role they have been given within the family. These Daughters will typically run away from home; live on the streets (if they escape welfare homes/prisons); and often eventually become prostitutes. Such behaviour is often seen by judicial and therapeutic

154

professionals as utterly reprehensible: they will use it as proof that such girl-women were sexually motivated in the sexual activity with the Father, and argue that they probably initiated it or at least co-operated happily. Another way of viewing such behaviour is to see it as (apart from desperation) strength, self-assertion: an attempt to gain control over their lives, and to obtain some power in the public world.

> That some incest victims become overt and clever manipulators who actively attempt to turn their enforced sex object status to their own ends is not surprising and might be seen as a vigorous and healthy grab for power, rather than 'pathetic'. *Their behaviour flaunts the real status of women*, which is precisely why it is considered threatening, embarrassing and unpalatable.[39] [My italics]

Feminist theorists O'Donnell and Craney accurately pin-point the logic of such 'promiscuous' behaviour. These Daughters, who have been repeatedly raped by their Fathers and received little or no support from their Mothers, know (a) who has power, (b) that they are given male approval primarily as an object of male sexual desire, and (c) that they do not want to repeat, in themselves, the wife-mother role with its obvious lack of power. But in thereby acting out, in a very public form, the quintessence of patriarchal sexual relations, they become social pariahs. They are not playing the game of Happy Families: just as it was not played for them by their Fathers.

From my own experience with girl-child rape victims, and from reading the literature, I have collected the following list of possible 'effects' of Father–Daughter rape: bed-wetting, pants-soiling, sleep-lessness, fear of the dark, excessive washing, learning problems, school phobia, street phobia, running away, hypochondria, uncontrollable crying, indirect outbursts of anger, low self-esteem, hatred of women, nightmares, somnambulism, suicidal desires, a desire to commit murder, withdrawnness, loss of appetite, overeating, clinging behaviour, all forms of regressed behaviour, 'precocious' or 'inappropriate' sex-play, tics, sleeping all the time, stealing, compulsive lying, muteness, loss of breath, vomiting, speech disorders, self body-loathing, separation anxiety, hyperactivity, fear of death, fear of suffocation, claustrophobia, lowered performance levels at school or work, giving energy only to schoolwork, fear of friendship, 'irrational' fear related to objects such as the smell of alcohol, and fear of men (being raped again).

Some theoreticians have argued that the effects are bad only if the Daughter is young;[40] some have argued that adolescents suffer most ill-effects and that young Daughters are virtually unaffected.[41] Some, as we have seen, try to argue that there are usually no ill-effects. This kind of professional attitude may actually help to cause many of the long-term behavioural outcomes listed above, since the Daughter, in the process of being 'helped', is explicitly or subliminally being faced with the same controlling, belittling, disbelieving behaviour which accompanied the rape, and which is integral to so much behaviour meted out by adults to girl-children.

> Following sexual victimization the most salient attitude of the child is distrust of the adult world. The child's behaviour is characterized by such clinical symptoms as bad dreams, restlessness, and a marked tendency to be withdrawn and hostile – especially to parents, teachers, and adults, including protective service caseworkers who seek to help the child.[42]

An example of such a caseworker might be Lindy Burton who, in spite of being a woman, is one of the most viciously anti-Daughter practitioners in the child abuse field. She conducted a study of sexually abused children with a control group and found that the only difference was that the raped children displayed more 'affection-seeking behaviour'. But rather than grant the victims even this need, she writes:

> The possibility cannot be ignored that the affection-seeking behaviour observed in the study might also indicate an attempt on the part of the child to replace the adult with whom he [sic] had a sexual relationship . . . many children may gain considerable comfort from thinking themselves loved and wanted by an adult.[43]

Burton was apparently dealing with many children who had not yet arrived at a position of widespread distrust of the adult world, but her myopic, adult-centred thinking, which cannot distinguish between rape and a desire to be loved (protected?), would certainly ensure that the victims in her care were driven to a position of distrust.

The victims' distrust of the adult world will often manifest itself as withdrawal. 'Withdrawal' – the appearance of no ill-effects – can hide enormous horrors from non-sensitive 'helpers'. Peters (1975), in a comparative study of adult, adolescent and child rape victims, found that 'children of 12 years and younger are so withdrawn that they cannot be comparably evaluated by a social worker'.[44] He (sensitively) surmises that:

> Perhaps child victims react with less perceptible emotional response because the incidents were less severe, less brutal, and far less life-threatening than those involving adults or adolescents. *It is more likely, however, that the child is unable to express her reaction and may retreat into emotional withdrawal, which then is misinterpreted.* We must recognize that we are using overt behavioral or psychologic changes as response indicators.[45] [My italics.]

Withdrawal, of course, is one of the most difficult responses for a clinician/caseworker to deal with, because in offering no measurable indicator of interactive behaviour, it leaves the professional helper with a feeling of having constantly failed. Withdrawal is fear: the drawing of a blank screen to hide the horrors inside, in case they are not sensitively handled by other people.

The more recent clinical literature is replete with advice about how to counsel the Daughters, how to successfully cure or therapise the Daughters, how to minimise the traumatic effects of court proceedings (without doing any judicial 'injustice' to the Father who must be presumed innocent until, etc.), and how to conduct medical examinations with the minimal level of repeat-of-the-rape being experienced by the Daughter. Some of this advice is good, within traditional 'helping' frameworks. Much of it, however, is couched within a cobweb of the same old blame-the-victim mythology:

> Incestuous relationships always reflect poor family functioning. The pediatrician, *with his concern for the physical and emotional well-being of his patients* and families, should be aware and informed of this relatively common problem . . . Although public and professional sentiment is generally empathetic toward the daughter and negative toward the father [sic], *there are indications that the daughters may play an active and initiating role in the incestuous relationship* . . . the daughter is usually the passive participant who seldom complains or resists.[46] [My italics.]

157

The schizophrenic approach of such clinicians, who are trying to sound as though they understand at least some of the attendant horrors in the situation for the Daughter, but who are actually supporters of the original rape ideology which produced the victim, is further illustrated by this pragmatic advice from the same writer:

> If the pediatrician suspects incest (sexual abuse) he should feel comfortable to say to the child 'I have a feeling that maybe (or I wonder if maybe) your father or brother may have touched your body or private parts and that may have frightened or confused you?' The openness and comfort on the part of the physician generally helps to make the child more comfortable, less guilty, and aware that someone knows the secret and is not shocked or frightened away.[47]

Coming from a doctor who believes Daughters may 'play an active or initiating role', and that the Daughters automatically feel 'guilty', such 'comfort' sits very ill indeed. *He* may be comfortable, but will she, the Daughter whom he is 'helping'? No amount of 'trying' to be comfortable is going to lessen a Daughter's mistrust if that professional is inclined to believe that it might well have been her fault anyway.

Two child psychiatrists, Poznanski and Blos (1975), purporting to give advice and information to professionals about 'helping' incest victims, reveal their own particularly vicious method when they write:

> At initial examination the adolescent may not show any evidence of guilt. But when, *in the course of psychotherapy the youngster's own active participation and pleasure are exposed*, tremendous guilt, remorse, depression, and resistance become evident . . . It is as though [these girls] have the emotional needs of 2 or 3 year olds, but every time they are touched or held sexuality is aroused.[48] [My italics.]

The Daughters certainly do not need 'help' from such omnivorous misogynists as these.

What the Daughters want most is to be believed and *therefore* protected. They have much to be protected from: Summit and Kryso have written of the four 'levels of betrayal' suffered by many Daughters. First there is the raping itself:

158

The child feels used and betrayed by her father, and feels she has no worth except as a sexual object. She is alternately courted and demeaned, loved for her attraction and then hated for her power, often labeled as bitch, slut, or whore.[49]

The second level of betrayal occurs when she turns for help – to be heard and protected – and is spurned. For many, this is the most frightening moment of all. It is the point at which many Daughters switch into a life-long pattern of resignation. Some persevere, speaking to different persons in their lives, until someone 'hears' and the situation changes. The 'lucky' Daughters, of course, are heard when first they speak.

The third level of betrayal, for many, occurs if she, and/or the family, become involved with 'helping institutions' of any kind.

The girl is punished by the demand for explicit, incriminating testimony and by being regarded as depraved and ruined through her participation . . . In her own mind, she comes to feel guilty and responsible.[50]

Even if the 'helping' and/or judicial systems treat her more humanely than this, for all Daughters, following disclosure, there is the possibility of the fourth 'betrayal':

A bizarre spinoff of the labeling process is the fascination the girl presents to others. She may be regarded by relatives as dangerously attractive . . . Publicly deflowered as she is, she is regarded as no longer deserving of respect or protection. We know of at least four cases where male relatives have attempted seduction after a girl has admitted [sic] intercourse with her father.[51]

For many of the Daughters then, one of the results of having been raped by a Father is that other Fathers think she is 'fair game'. The hunting analogy in such a metaphor does not come about by cultural accident. Many of the Father-rapists give 'keeping her away from those other men out there' as the reason why they raped her in the first place: the reasoning being that if the 'game' lives in his fields, then it is his to use for himself. The other Fathers who 'attempt seduction' after they find she has been a victim of Father–Daughter rape, are reasoning that the 'game' has changed its nature from a passive farm animal (innocent child) to a free-range animal at large (a fallen female), who can be hunted at will.

As well as the need to be heard, and the need to be protected from the initial raping relationship, as well as any others which come as a result of it, the Daughters need oceans of affirmation and reassurance that they are not responsible, that they are not 'bad', and that they have nothing to feel 'guilty' about. For several of the victims I have met that reassurance has only come from rape crisis or women's refuge workers. Occasionally victims have found a truly caring, affirming professional 'helper', but usually only when they are adult and in extreme crisis from the effect of negative feelings about themselves which they have carried for years. Far too many professional 'helpers' are still carrying a headful of the anti-victim mythology which abounds in the clinical literature and within our culture generally.

Given the fact that Father–Daughter rape is now being perceived, even by the most conservative professionals and by politicians, as a recently 'discovered' phenomenon about which *something must be done*, we are undoubtedly going to see a plethora of new services being offered by every kind of medical and social 'helping' agency. Amongst the personnel involved in these endeavours will be those who do this specialised counselling under duress (directed from above) and carrying with them all of the worst prejudices possible; and there will also be those who can listen and care profoundly, affirming the victims' being and worthiness; and there will be all shades of helping in between.

> Only those professionals who see rape as an act of violence are able to empathically relate to victims. Professionals who perceive the assault as being primarily sexual are often seen by the victims as voyeuristic, chauvinistic, and unbelieving.[52]

The culture of rape ideology holds that rape is sex, sex is fun, and therefore, in simple syllogistic logic, rape is fun. Any 'helper' who believes that 'rape is sex' is automatically embarked on promoting this male supremacist syllogism. Rape ideology does not see any difference between rape and sex because it is incapable of perceiving rape through a woman's (or girl-child's) eyes.

> Because of their different symbolic involvement in their sexual experiences, a man is unable to understand why a woman can become so upset, and he is particularly puzzled when the traumatization period is prolonged. No matter how hard she may try to communicate, the fact that he cannot identify with her

160

experience nor understand it, except perhaps on a cognitive level, adds measurably to her trauma.[53]

Not only can male 'helpers' not really identify with the Daughter as a female rape victim, but there is also the additional fact that many of the Daughters are actively experiencing an utterly reasonable fear of men at the precise time when they are being offered 'help'. In most cases, the Father was 'a trusted acquaintance or a respected figure'[54] – and now the Daughter is being asked to 'trust' another respected male figure. No wonder the victims may 'continue to be confused and troubled about trusting men'.[55]

Ideally, then, professional helpers should be women who have demonstrated an ability to identify with girl-children as rape victims. (Male helpers who are genuinely anxious to work in the field could work with boy-victims.) Whatever the kind of 'help' being offered, it must centre on the Daughter and her needs. Quite apart from the fact that she has deserved at least that after what she has been through, if, at this most crucial point of disclosure, she does not get what she needs, she may well withdraw into life-long patterns of self-destructive behaviour and massive distrust of the rest of the world.

The Santa Clara programme workers have found that the most pressing need, for almost all the Daughter-victims whom they see, after removal of the Father (protection), is reassurance from her mother or mother-figure. To that end, they first 'work' with the Mother–Daughter dyad, aiming to assist these two in supporting and caring for each other. Axiomatic to such work is their belief that the Father bears full responsibility for what has happened:[56] through assuring the Mother and Daughter of this, the tendency for the Mother and Daughter to blame one another is mitigated.

In the stories in the Exposition, we saw how both Kim and Vicki stayed with their mothers while they cried during the days following disclosure. (The fact that many Mothers find it difficult to grieve with their Daughters is discussed fully in the next chapter.) I see such behaviour as female solidarity: as the Daughter sinking into the relief of pain shared at long last and, at the same time, supporting and caring for a Mother who is feeling shock and shame and grief. For there is grieving to be done by Mothers and Daughters who share this most intimate knowledge – the visitation of rape-aggression by a Father within the family – for it means that they, as women together, have seen through the rape mythology which dichotomises the Father-as-Protector and the male-as-Rapist.

161

5   The Mothers –
Bound and Blamed

If we speak of motherhood at all, we are inevitably speaking of
something far more than the relationship of a woman with her
children. And even this relationship has been shaped long
before the first child's birth. All women are daughters of
women – is this an obvious, a simple-minded statement? or
does it reach through the layers of the weaving to inner
chambers only now beginning to be explored by women?

Adrienne Rich,
'Motherhood: The Contemporary Emergency
and the Quantum Leap',
On Lies, Secrets, and Silence

A woman's main role in life is presented as the
reproduction and production of a Happy Family. This prescriptive
role flourishes still, in spite of the modernistic ideal view of
marriage as a 'partnership of equals'. Modernism arrives slowly in
the suburbs and towns where most people live. And even the trendy
'ideal' view of marriage has not yet begun to probe the depth and
intensity of the power relations that exist between men and women
as a result of sex roles and the sexual division of labour.

The father in the family is still seen as the breadwinner: the
person whose function is to go out to paid work somewhere in the
marketplace. The wife-mother is the nurturer – of him, and any
children they may have. Her function is the unpaid provision of
emotional, social, and physical caring for everyone else in the
family. This role includes being sexually available to her husband. If
she works in the paid workforce through necessity or preference or
a mixture of both, she is not significantly relieved of any of the
burdens of her primary unpaid role – that of wifing and mothering.

The wife-mother role also assumes emotional mediation between
her husband and their children: ensuring that the father is seen as a

'good man' by his children, and, at the same time, that the children do not put too many demands on him. She is also expected to mediate within the child's personality development so that her children are, and are seen to be, 'good'. It is seen by others, and felt by her, as a measure of failure if anything goes wrong in the complex web of balancing acts required to create the reality and/or image of the Happy Family. It is always her fault.

Throughout the literature on 'father–daughter incest' or 'child sexual abuse', the mother is blamed. She is blamed principally for *causing it*; she is also blamed for maintaining it, for not stopping it, for 'pretending' that she didn't know it was happening. This blaming of the mother often occurs at length and in depth in articles which are ostensibly studying the Daughters or the Fathers. I have been able to find only one study which sets out to examine the Mothers;[1] yet in spite of the dearth of hard data, the mythology of blame aimed at the Mothers pervades the whole body of literature. The lack of research specifically on the Mothers is particularly significant given the pejorative nature of the statements made about the Mothers. In reading the literature it is obvious that many of these statements have become 'self-evident truths' in the minds of many researchers. In speaking with professional and community-based volunteer helpers, it is clear that these 'truths' have also become part of popular folklore about Father–Daughter rape.

The mothers are blamed basically on two grounds: collusion or abandonment. These two words recur over and over again. There are several descriptions advanced as to the different types of 'collusion' or 'abandonment'; over-arching both these types of reasons, the mothers are blamed for fulfilling too literally the 'feminine' sex-role stereotype, or for not fulfilling it. They are blamed for behaving like traditionally stereotypic women – with passivity and insecurity; or for behaving non-stereotypically – such as going out to work. Either of these swings of the pendulum may be seen as a causative factor in the Fathers' actions. The Mothers are set up to be losers, whatever they do. 'Colluding' behaviour is usually seen as passive and fearful, but may be assertive; 'abandoning' behaviour is seen as active and aggressive (i.e. assertive), but may result from non-coping (weak) behaviour too. Either way, she has failed to fulfil her 'role': something has gone wrong with the family so it's her fault.

The most enduring myth of all is that the mother 'colludes'. Recently I was present at a workshop on 'child sexual abuse' as part of a women's refuge workers' conference: everyone involved held the attitude that the Fathers were baddies, and the Daughters were victims, but many participants believed (mostly because they had 'heard') that the Mothers were to blame too. The argument is that the Mother *must know*, at some level, that it is happening, since she is presumed to be an integral (if not the central) part of the family structure and interaction. She is seen as guilty of 'collusion' if she does nothing to confront the situation and stop it happening, even when she insists that she did not know it was happening. Not-knowing is no defence to the hardline proponents of this view, who will argue that she must have known 'subconsciously', if not consciously.

A plethora of *superficial* evidence does exist to support the unilateral 'collusion' theory. As we have seen, many Daughters try, directly or indirectly, to tell their Mothers, who often either reject the information outright, or belittle it by not 'hearing' the gravity of the situation. Many Mothers actually literally see some of the evidence of the Father's sexual access (power) over the Daughter, and yet are able (have a need) to rationalise away the witness of their own senses. One researcher comments that when a Daughter is raped,

> The mother may be struggling with denial of her own anger for having been raped literally or figuratively by adverse life circumstances . . .[2]

The discovery that one's husband (or son or father or brother) had raped one's Daughter would indeed seem like being raped 'figuratively'.

In keeping silent about the Father, the Mother betrays herself: herself as female, reflected in her Daughter. To that extent, the Mother too, *is* being raped. In her experience of her powerlessness, in her humiliation at bearing such a socially unacceptable 'family secret', and in her identification with her daughter (or any girl-child), the Mother shares with her Daughter the horror of rape exploitation. But the Daughters, in their desperate need for understanding from the Mother, often feel angrier with their Mothers than with the Fathers. They feel their Mothers have deserted them, failed them. In a sense, they are right.

The Mothers have many reasons for not being able to 'see' or 'hear' (and thereby being charged with 'collusion'). No woman, except one who was a girl-child rape victim herself, has *any* information on which to base belief in such an event. All the cultural baggage about marriage, motherhood and Happy Families contains absolutely no information about the possible need to protect our daughters from men within the family.

The 1982 pamphlet handed out to schoolchildren by police in Australia says 'Beware of Strangers' in large type on the front and back; in between are pages of pictures of places (parks, alleyways, storm-water channels, street-corners) that are 'dangerous', and more large type saying '*Strangers* are people who *do not visit your home* and whose house *you and your parents do not visit*'.[3] [original italics]. The girl-children who receive this leaflet with its accompanying 'friendly lecture' are not only being given a gut-thudding lesson on Stranger Danger (and subliminally told to stay inside all the time); they are also being taught that their parents (which includes mother) do not know, let alone live with, anyone who would sexually assault a child. For generations, Mothers have been kept apart from their Daughters by this kind of misinformation. For the Daughter who is being raped at home, she has learnt (knows) that her mother probably won't (won't want to/be able to) believe her; and the Mother has learnt that 'it' doesn't happen at home.

For many women there is also a very real economic (survival) imperative. At the moment of disclosure (of 'seeing' or being made to 'hear'), she must choose whom to believe. Most women are economically dependent on their husbands' incomes: to confront such an horrendous reality as Father–Daughter rape automatically raises the instantaneous spectre of a shattered family which means going 'on welfare'. The ideal concept of marriage as an equal partnership is revealed in all its deception when it comes to separation, division of property, and maintaining an income on the part of the woman. In discussion after I gave a lecture recently, a student recalled an incident when she was quite young, in which the milkman had tried to kiss her. She had gone immediately to her mother, wanting protection, but her mother had brushed the information aside: 'She definitely didn't want to know', the student said. In later years, she realised that her mother urgently needed to stay on amicable terms with the milkman because he allowed her to have milk on credit, which was an essential factor in her low-budgeting organisation. This example is, in microcosm, a picture of the economic reality of most women.

Very many women also derive much of their sense of identity from the class status and/or personality of their husbands. They have been taught that being a 'good woman' means being a subservient wife, and they have built their daily actions around this

165

role. Women are encouraged to give allegiance to 'their man', from the television commercial about the best washing powder for 'his' shirts, to not confronting any inadequacies he may have (Quick Quiz: Are You a Good Wife?).

I believe there is another reason why so many Mothers repress stories of sexual harassment from the Daughters: such stories touch all women in terms of our own suppressed childhood memories, and in terms of our lifelong existence as potential rape victims (fear of men). We ourselves fall victim to the myth of childhood purity (protected doll-like creatures), because to do otherwise would tap our own enormous wells of fear, and, most overwhelming of all, theaten the whole fabric of male supremacy and the sanctity of the family. On this level, the desire not to know is instantaneous, involuntary. For these complicated reasons many women feel they have no choice: *their very sense of survival* is predicated on keeping going with what they have got, since the unknown yawns like a void. They choose food, shelter, their own precarious sense of identity, and a spurious peace over the ultimate confrontation with rape, in the form of 'their man'.

The 'colluding' theory is transformed in the face of this awareness of the Mother's position. To the extent that she colludes, she does it for the following reasons: she is economically and socially dependent; she is blinded and deafened by male supremacist mythology about rape; she is full of fear at the prospect of confronting the ideology and practice of rape, alone, in her own home; and she is aware, however subliminally, that she will be blamed by the world of experts Out There. She senses that ultimately she will have no support at all.

The charge of 'abandonment', on the other hand, goes further than the charge of 'collusion', in that it holds that the Mother *caused* the Father to rape a Daughter. The 'logic' behind this charge is that if the Mother is absent (for *any reason*), some Fathers will 'naturally' approach whatever other female is around, in a sexual manner. *Therefore* the Mother is guilty of *causing* the rape by virtue of having absented herself. Forms of abandonment that are commonly mentioned are going to work, going out, having friends outside the home, being hospitalised, becoming pregnant, being sick or depressed. When we recall that 'incestuous' Fathers are often found to be classical patriarchal tyrants who attempt to control all movements and contacts of other family members, it would seem that these forms of 'abandonment' are, in fact, any type of behaviour on the part of the Mother that upsets the smooth flow

166

of the Father's life which is predicated on a wife being constantly in the home, in her 'role'. Occasionally, the Mother's death is proposed as the form of 'abandonment' which caused the Father to rape the Daughter(s):

> In only one case [out of twelve] was a wife not a part of the family constellation, her death having occurred before the time of incest. (In this case *the father was able to verbalize openly his anger towards his dead wife for abandoning him.*)[4] [My italics.]

In no other context have I come across the fact of death as almost an act of will on the part of the deceased. Her death 'caused' the 'incest': the invisible assumption behind such twisted thinking is that of course a man will need to use whatever sexual outlet is available if his wife is 'not there'.

This brings us to the key component of the 'abandonment' charge, the element known as 'sexual estrangement', which invariably means sexual withdrawal *by* the wife. As investigator Herman remarks:

> Professional authors do not say that the mother is 'no good in bed', but the language of many of them barely disguises the same judgement.[5]

'Bad' sexual relations are regarded by most professionals as axiomatic in cases of Father–Daughter rape, and the active person in the 'estrangement' is always the Mother:

> . . . the mothers in cases of father–daughter incest often encourage such activity by frustrating their husbands sexually, deserting them in some fashion, and leaving the daughter to assume the maternal role . . . In Reimer's sample, almost without exception the incestuous father had been barred from intercourse with his wife, usually because of childbirth or her absence, just before the onset of incest . . . Kaufman's study found that incest usually began when both father and daughter felt the mother had abandoned them, either by giving birth to a new child, turning to the maternal grandmother, or developing some new interest outside the home.[6]

The mother, as wife, is expected to be always available for her husband's sexual 'needs'. The age-old sexual double standard flaps healthily in the hot air of the clinicians' (and Fathers') judgment that a wife has failed in her duty if her husband feels sexually 'frustrated'. Sometimes there is evidence that it is the husband who has withdrawn, but only at the expense of a vicious attack on the wife as sex object: one writer tells us that 'in some cases she had become unattractive because of obesity or personal neglect'.[7] With sexist guidelines such as these operating, it is no wonder that the Mothers get such short shrift.

She is frigid and wants no sex with her husband. This is another way of *bowing out of her role as a wife and giving reason to the husband to look elsewhere for sex . . . the mother feels relief when the daughter substitutes for her.*[8] [My italics.]

The statement that 'she is frigid and wants no sex with her husband' is closed, allowing no questioning, analysis or caring. The way such information is presented in clinical studies such as this one, implies that the Mother is capriciously choosing to withdraw sexual access to her body. There is also, of course, the underlying assumption that she *should* be sexually available to her husband: it is part of her role as wife. The idea that a woman has the *right* to decide what should happen to her body does not even enter the conceptual framework of writers who operate from such an assumption. The wild judgment that the Mother 'feels relief when the daughter substitutes for her' is made within the original (male supremacist) assumption: the Mother may not want to do it, but she knows that the Father must be supplied with a female body for his use – this is a stunning example of how male supremacist attitudes are attributed to the minds and mouths of women.

It seems quite likely that many of the men who become Daughter-rapists are probably not 'good in bed' themselves. Such a deduction seems logical in view of their choice of a sexual partner who is, by definition, not able to respond with any mutuality. From what we know of their behaviour with the Daughters, the Fathers are almost always concerned only with their own pleasure, whether it be ejaculation, touching erogenous zones, or some form of fetishistic sexual expression. It is not unreasonable to assume that they approached their wives in the same way: most women find this ignorant and selfish form of male sexual behaviour repugnant, if not insulting. The Mothers who had sexually estranged themselves from the Fathers may simply have been protecting themselves from this form of degradation.

168

I could find only one study which had apparently bothered to ask the wives of offenders why they had sexually 'abandoned' their husbands. Not surprisingly, all of the reasons given were connected to the Father's actions: their withdrawal was a *reaction* to his behaviour:

Alice's mother refused to have sexual relations with her husband, claiming his love for little girls disgusted her. Betty's and Carol's mothers also refused to participate in sexual activities with their husbands once they found that their husbands had become sexually involved with their daughters.[9]

Assertive acts like these undoubtedly happen more often than we know. Most Mothers who 'hear', even a little, probably do *something*. To withdraw from sexual activity with the Father as a consequence of his raping his (and her) Daughter seems a most logical emotional response. Another study mentions that 'most [out of fourteen] mothers responded to the incest by separation from their husbands'.[10] Apart from these two brief remarks in the literature, the negative (male) view of the Mothers' sexual abandonment as the *cause* of Father–Daughter rape reigns supreme.

The charge of 'abandonment' on the part of the Mother has absolutely nothing to do with the *cause* of Father–Daughter rape. Whether the Mother is seen, or felt, to be abandoning the husband or the children physically, emotionally, socially, psychically, or sexually, is not, in itself, a cause (or even an excuse) for the Father's actions. If it were it would mean that all men needed a keeper all the time, for who could determine which men are liable to fantasise 'abandonment', or which men are liable to react to any of the multifarious forms of abandonment they might feel, by raping a Daughter? To blame the Mother in this way successfully removes from the Father any responsibility for his actions. The implication is that he 'can't help' what he does. Male supremacist social structure seeks to impose on women the role of moral arbiter, since it abjures women to be blamed for dereliction of duty when men 'fall by the wayside'. In reading the 'incest' literature, I have found that part of the role of mothering is an expectation that Mothers will in fact be God's police within the family – over her husband as well as her children. A 1966 psychiatric study of six cases found that

the need to maintain a minimum level of individual and family

169

tension through reliance on a maternal figure was central in each of our cases.[11]

Rather than deduce from this that something might be wrong with the societal structure of families, these researchers use the Mothers' failure to provide a 'maternal figure' on which *everyone else* could rely as further evidence of her active involvement in the raping situation.

Many clinicians find that the Mother 'failed to protect' her Daughter from the Father: a subtle variation on the charge of collusion.

Whether she is genuinely unaware, is concealing, or refusing to see, the mother is no longer able to fulfill her function in the family and protect the daughter.[12]

In real life this piece of patriarchal information (that one of her functions *in the family* is to protect her daughter(s)) is only given to women after the event, and then it comes in the form of a judgment because they have failed to do it. (Feminist Quick Quiz for Mothers: Have You Been Told Everything You Need To Know?)

The 'failing to protect' charge is also used to embellish the 'abandonment' theory:

In another case incest took place when the patient [the father] was unable to be gainfully employed and the wife, who *had to support the family*, had *relegated the husband to the role of a babysitter*.[13] [My italics.]

In the utterly reasonable expectation that her husband would look after their (his) children while she went to work, this wife is accused of emasculating him by 'relegating' him to be merely a 'babysitter'. In his angst (identity crisis) at this (presumably) unsought role reversal, he rapes a Daughter, but the clinician clearly sees it as at least partly the mother's fault. She has not only failed to protect her daughter: she has also failed to massage the Father's ego into a suitably masculine reflection.

In rare cases, it is clear that a mother has literally failed to protect her daughter in situations which have been consciously known to her.

One mother of a seven-year-old girl left the room for some

170

incidental [sic] shopping while her live-in boyfriend was ordering the little girl to strip and mimic her mother's coital posture. The man raped the child on that occasion, and for the next year and a half imposed physically traumatic vaginal, anal, and oral intercourse. The girl pleaded for rescue but could not gain her mother's sympathy or protection. Neighbours reported hearing screaming and seeing discarded bedsheets stained with blood and faeces. Both of the mother's two subsequent partners also molested the girl until she began to run away from home at age eleven.[14]

The writers describe the man and the mother involved in situations like this in these terms:

This sort of chronically antisocial, potentially violent man is often found as a surrogate father living with a woman who is passive and self-punishing. He is not the sort of man a mature, well-adjusted woman selects as the father of her children.[15]

This is ostensibly an 'analysis' of the situation; in fact, it is a series of statements that are closed. One gets the impression that men may be 'chronically antisocial, potentially violent', as though it were a fixed entity; similarly, women may be 'passive and self-punishing'. Any real analysis would be asking Why? and How are people to interact with such constructed characteristics? and Does this balance of power have anything to do with sex roles? economic factors? rape ideology?

To contemplate the degree of powerlessness and dependence on men felt by a Mother such as this is a deeply enervating exercise. Why is a woman often 'self-punishing'? How is it that a woman can become so dependent? and so powerless in the face of rape aggression? The internalisation of passivity by women differs in degree along a spectrum: it is a direct result of a male supremacist cultural system that indoctrinates women to exist only as the playthings or nurturers of men. Female sex-role conditioning, fostered within the rape ideology which inculcates fear of men as a way of living, has inevitably led women to respond 'inadequately' in the face of Father–Daughter rape.

Even when a Mother does meet the situation adequately at the point of disclosure, she is still not immune from the theorising that brings the blame back to her for having caused it all in the first place. There are several Freudian-based theories which zoom in on

171

the Mother, or the Mother's mother, or the Father's mother, and charge her with being 'cold', 'hostile', 'rejecting', etc., and by this failure to provide the *warmth* expected of Mother-love, to have caused the raping. The first of these theories was proposed by Kaufman *et al.* (1954) and is particularly popular with several of the clinical authors, presumably because it not only blames the Mother-wife but also her mother. Kaufman and his colleagues found that the victim's maternal grandmothers 'were stern, demanding, controlling, cold and extremely hostile women' (maybe they were angry?) and that they were 'hard workers and masculine in character'.[16] Kaufman describes the Mothers and makes the connection between them and their mothers like this:

> The mothers . . . when first seen for interviews . . . were described as hard, careless in dress and personal appearance, infantile, extremely dependent and intellectually dull. Most of them were poor housekeepers, panicky in the face of responsibility, and seemed on the surface to be satisfied to live in disorder and poverty [sic]. However, on closer study, they emerged as brighter than average with a potential for achievement far beyond their actual performance. They married men who were also [sic] dependent and infantile. If they married a second time, the second partner was even more irresponsible and unsuccessful than the first. *This was a repetition of the pattern set by the maternal grandmother.*[17] [My italics.]

By blaming, originally, the Mother's mother, Kaufman establishes a profile of the Mothers based on an 'unresolved oedipal conflict' which they attempt to resolve by creating, out of their Daughters, a 'mother-figure', so that they can have another go at being a Daughter. This is 'abandonment' and 'collusion' all rolled up into one.

One of the later exponents of this theory[18] writes more succinctly:

> It has been shown that such a parent often has been rejected by her own mother, with whom she had identified; she thereby may develop a hostile attitude toward her female offspring and *make them targets for the sexual advances of the father.*[19] [My italics.]

The apparent passivity of the Fathers is highlighted again when, as a result of this 'problem' of the Mothers, the Fathers 'become

172

involved with' their Daughters, or use them as 'targets' of their irrepressible sexual urges, as though such actions on the part of the Fathers were mere side-effects of the 'real' issue which is the Mother's rejection by her own mother. Beneath such exhaustive efforts to trace the blame back to female ancestors lies the unspoken collaboration of the clinicians with the apparently will-less Fathers.

A parallel theory blames the Father's mother; this theory holds that Father–Daughter rape is 'the father's ultimate act of hostility or hatred towards the mother'[20] – meaning his own mother. This theory starts with the 'evidence' (which we saw in The Fathers chapter was utterly inconclusive) that the Fathers have unresolved Oedipal problems in relation to their own mothers:

> Classical psychoanalytic theory suggests that seductive and over-possessive mothers, by provoking incest fears, tend to produce guilt-ridden sons vulnerable to sexual deviation.[21]

The argument goes that such men will hate women, seeing them as alternately seductive and uncaring[22] ('seductive and over-possessive mothers'), so they react to their wives as though they were the same (especially after the birth of children) and rape ('become sexually involved with') the Daughter as a means of punishing the wife who has also become Mother. (Remember that the Fathers are almost universally found to be not psychotic.) Thus the Daughter is reduced to a pawn in a sick game being played out by the Father against his Mother: 'therapy' at the hands of such a theorist would presumably render the Mother and Daughter invisible, while the expert focussed on the Father's 'problems' as a result of his mothering.

Another version of the theory of inadequate mothering in its multifarious forms is that the Daughter is reacting to maternal deprivation:

> An additional unconscious motivation when the daughter sees the mother as cruel, unjust, depriving and rejecting is the use of incest as a means of getting revenge.[23]

Here again, the Mother is the 'cold' person; as well, the Mother and Daughter are seen as competitors, using sexual 'control' of the Father as a way of getting at each other. Such a view plays straight into the world of male sexual fantasy which likes to think that all women desire all men all the time.

Another of the endless Oedipal permutations which blame the Mother holds that the Mother has 'unresolved' feelings in relation to her father:

> . . . in this case, we have *a mother who rejected a feminine role for herself* as a result of hurt and disappointment at the hands of her father. *She acts out her oedipal wish for her father through her daughter.* The daughter serves as a perfect instrument for such a function, since she has learned to turn to men for security and affection because of intense affectional frustration at the hands of women . . . she can turn to her father and gain satisfaction of her needs. This takes place through a sexual channel that is most appropriate in terms of how the fathers satisfy their needs.[24] [My italics.]

Again we see the Mother and Daughter as the active agents: the Mother 'rejecting' her own femininity and using her own daughter to act out her own repressed desire to have intercourse with her father; the Daughter 'turning to' her Father to find satisfaction of the affectional needs which her mother has (purposely) denied her. The meaning of the last sentence of this quotation, taken in the context of actions on the part of the Mother and Daughter, actually points out that it is the Father who chooses a 'sexual channel'. He does this because that is what he does. It is 'appropriate' for Fathers to do because that is what they do. The language used to express this tautology is suitably impersonalised: the Father has no responsibility; he simply reacts as he has been programmed to – that is, sexually, as in rape.

These writers (sociologists) would no doubt say that the feminist view that rape ideology controls many of our social relations was far-fetched, even ridiculous. They themselves, however, display its rigid hold on society by their subtle, but ultimately dishonest, use of language. The point is, of course, that even if a Daughter does experience her Mother as rejecting, neither she nor the Mother are asking for the Father to rape her.

With theories like these around that saddle the Mother with the pivotal causal role in Father–Daughter rape, it is no wonder that when we turn to the 'profiles' of the Mothers, we find mainly negative characteristics. Selby's (1980) study of social workers' impressions of the characteristics of the individuals in families where Father–Daughter rape has occurred, gives the following information on the Mothers, which I have set out in table form:

Traits of the Mothers for which more than 50% of social worker respondents indicated either 'frequently' or 'always':

remote	52%
submissive	50%

Traits of the Mothers for which over 50% of social worker respondents indicated either 'never' or 'occasionally':

warm	82%
nurturant	79%
overprotective	74%
reliable	72%
dominating	67%
impulsive	57%
hostile	56%

Selby notes that:

> While this pattern of responses seems generally consistent with that reported in the literature, it is interesting to note that as with the daughters there appeared to be greater consensus among the present respondents in those traits which *do not* characterise the mothers than in those which do.[25] [My italics.]

Since the statistically 'positive' characteristics attributed to the Mothers in this study were remote and submissive, it is worth pointing out that the same study found that the positive characteristics of the Fathers were manipulative (66%), impulsive (60%), dominating (58%), and unpredictable (54%). When confronted with manipulative, impulsive, dominating and unpredictable husbands, most women find that remote and submissive behaviour is their only option, since conditioning into passivity is the basic *modus operandi* of the female sex-role.

There is a subterranean theme running through some of the clinical literature which holds that the Mothers *choose* men as husbands who are pre-inclined to be rapists of Daughters. Here is one such researcher who apparently has a humanistic approach:

> The women who accept misogynous, imperious, or rapacious partners deserve enlightened attention, not only for their own needs but for the protection of the children in their care.[26]

175

Apart from the assumption that Mothers 'accept' such partners, as opposed to being stuck with them, there is also an assumption of Mothers being only worth helping *because* they are Mothers – that is, the children are really the focal point. And behind all these assumptions there is complete failure to address the problem of why these Fathers *are* 'mysogynous, imperious, or rapacious'.

The only study which specifically focusses on the Mothers (entitled 'The Wives of Rapists and Incest Offenders') was predicated on the hypothesis that these women would be experiencing 'unsettling kinds of social and psychic burdens', and on a 'suspicion' that such women 'could use the criminal act of her husband to raise her own status or reestablish a superiority over him'.[27] Not surprisingly, the study found that the wives appeared to obtain 'considerable satisfaction' from the hospitalisation of their husbands and their own social position as 'martyred wives'.[28] While the tone of this 'finding' prevails throughout the article, the researchers also found quite contradictory evidence which they present without discussion:

> Four [out of seven] of the incest offender wives also agreed that there had been psychological difficulties for them after the offence, but . . . their answers tended to be *general kinds of statement, such as: 'I went off the deep end for a while'*.[29] [My italics.]

The existential reality of 'going off the deep end' is not only misnamed as a 'general kind of statement', but is also utterly subsumed under the thesis of pleasurable martyrdom.

A notable finding of this study was that blaming the Daughter-victim was 'totally absent' among the wife-mothers: 'They stated that they still loved the victim or that they were sorry for her.'[30] This is a particularly interesting observation since it is in direct contradiction to many other research 'findings' and the oft-quoted belief of many professionals that the Mothers usually feel jealous of their daughters and reject them because they have become sexual 'competitors'.

Jealousy between women over a man is created by male supremacist social structures. Jealousy is experienced as a sense of missing out and/or rejection. Some mothers clearly do experience a component of jealousy in the case of adolescent Daughter-victims, in the plethora of emotional reactions which follow disclosure: the kind of jealousy which attaches to sexual rejection. Her husband, the Father, has, after all, been sexually approaching someone else. For many women the conditioning that leads her to believe she will virtually cease to exist without 'her man' has been very effective: she has also been taught that to be sexually desirable is the only way to keep him when it comes down to brass tacks. So her 'jealousy' is intermeshed with her fears that are based on economic inequity and the powerlessness of women in the public world generally.

There is another element of 'jealousy' which pervades many Mother–Daughter relationships, irrespective of whether Father-Daughter rape occurs in the family. This jealousy is founded on the Beautiful Young Woman cultural stereotype which invades every billboard, every second television image, all magazines, and a huge number of shop windows. The message that every woman receives is that all the world (men) wants to look at a nubile sex object. To be young, courted and wed is the apotheosis of this dream. After that, it's all downhill in terms of the sex-object stakes. For many women, seeing their pre-pubescent daughters change, over a year or two, into the dream-image of the magazines, reminds them of their own fleeting period of 'desirability' (in which they never felt really secure anyway), along with the concomitant 'invisibility' of pregnancy, child-rearing, and aging that has been her lot since that brief golden period. There are no affirming images of these later stages of a woman's life in our culture: those that ostensibly are positive are actually always presented about a 'famous woman': 'She's still sexy, in spite of being pregnant . . .'

> The universal sway of the feminine stereotype is the single most important factor in male and female woman-hatred. Until woman as she is can drive this plastic spectre out of her own and her man's imagination she will continue to apologize and disguise herself, while accepting her male's pot-belly, wattles, bad breath, farting, stubble, baldness and other ugliness without complaint . . . Women are reputed never to be disgusted. The sad fact is that they often are, but not with men; following the lead of men, they are most often disgusted with themselves.[31]

Only when Mothers and Daughters are not being divided against each other by the plastic image of the near-nude young woman in the evening tabloid newspapers will jealousy cease to effectively separate them into individual units.

To conclude this presentation of the blame-the-Mother literature and widely prevalent attitudes, here Lustig *et al.* (1966) say it all:

It is interesting that despite the formal innocence of the mother in the actual incestuous event, *she seems to emerge as the key figure in the pathological transactions involved* . . . Despite the overt culpability of the fathers, *we were impressed* with their psychological passivity in the transactions leading to incest. *The mother appeared the cornerstone in the pathological family system.*[32] [My italics.]

We have seen that the Mother is blamed, along a whole causal continuum which ranges from 'contributing' to its occurrence to being the 'cornerstone' in the whole sequence of events. She is blamed for her 'complicity' on a conscious and an unconscious level. She is blamed if she is passive, or if she is assertive; if she is sexually withdrawn or if she is sexually active; if she behaves so as to have her own identity in the world or if she doesn't; and she is 'blamed' for not 'seeing' and 'hearing' the unimaginable – her husband (or son or father) secretly raping her Daughter.

The facts are that some mothers never know (at any 'level') that Father–Daughter rape has occurred in their families; some mothers leap to protect and defend their Daughters as soon as they do know that it is happening; others tread a tightrope of suspicion, resulting in self-loathing because it seems so awful even to suspect such a thing – 'I must be going mad'; and others retire into remoteness, unable to cope with such horrific realities in an unsupportive world. Some are driven to murder. In a recent (1981) South Australian case the mother murdered her brutal husband when she found out that he had been raping four of her five daughters for years.[33] When she was convicted of murder (even though several members of the jury were crying at the verdict), a huge public outcry arose calling for reform of the law so that evidence of provocation could be considered for the defence. She was acquitted at an appeal trial. The facts of the case have been publicly accepted without question, thereby putting Father–Daughter rape on the public agenda in Australia in a manner which had not existed previously.

The Mother's isolation derives from the 'feminine' role model which establishes motherhood as the moral and behavioural arbiter of everyone else in the family. And therefore the keeper of secrets. The degree of the Mothers' isolation is only comparable with the Daughters' experience of lonely victimisation. The so-called 'failure' of the Mothers is rooted in their isolation, their economic non-freedom, and the ubiquitous taboo on speaking of the subject. As we start to break the taboo, Mothers and Daughters everywhere will find their isolation melting away. As the Adelaide mother said to two of her daughters, who were trying to leave home in the face of the father threatening to kill them and raping one of them at knife-point:

> I'm scared of him but if we all keep together we are stronger than what he is, but if you don't back me up I can't do anything.[34]

She did something; they backed her.

Much of the anger that the Daughters feel towards the Mothers comes from the disappointment of their desperate need for a woman in their lives who is strong. They, more than all the other Daughters in the world, need to experience women who say No to rape aggression. Feminist theorist Herman deduces from the literature that mothers in 'incestuous families' are 'even by patriarchal standards . . . unusually oppressed', and goes on to say:

> More than the average wife and mother, she is extremely dependent upon and subservient to her husband . . . Rather than provoke her husband's anger or risk his desertion, she will capitulate. If the price of maintaining the marriage includes the sexual sacrifice of her daughter, she will raise no effective objections. Her first loyalty is to her husband, regardless of his behaviour. She sees no other choice. Maternal collusion in incest, when it occurs, is a measure of maternal powerlessness.
>
> As for the question of the Mother's responsibility, maternal absence, literal or psychological, does seem to be a reality in many families where incest develops. *The lack of a strong, competent and protective mother does seem to render girls more vulnerable to sexual abuse.*[35]

Because the Mother rarely gives the Daughter the sense of female strength for which she is searching, the Daughter turns on the Mother, unable to see, in her simple urgency, that the oppression comes from the much larger cause of male supremacist social structure which controls women (her mother included) through the fear of rape, the 'solution' to the fear of rape which is marriage and a Happy Family, and rape ideology which sanctions the Father's right of access to females of any age.

The infrastructure of masculinity and femininity causes Father–Daughter rape, by creating men who see other people as possessions and objects and sex as the most masculine way of expressing that power of possession, and women who feel too alone to attempt to stop them. The agony of the Mothers lies in their powerlessness to help the Daughters from whom they have been separated and with whom they long to identify.

> In the land where the moon hides, mothers
> and daughters hold each other tenderly.
> There is no male law at five o'clock.[36]

All Mothers have been Daughters: we/they have much to share.

6   The Sons –
Oedipus, the Boy and the Man

It was never the rapist:
it was the brother, lost,

the comrade/twin whose palm
would bear a lifeline like our own:

decisive, arrowy,
forked-lightning of insatiate desire

It was never the crude pestle, the blind
ramrod we were after:

merely a fellow-creature
with natural resources equal to our own

Adrienne Rich, from 'Natural Resources',
in *The Dream of a Common Language, Poems, 1974-77*

In the typical scene of intra-family rape involving the Father and the Daughter, we have found that the Mother is also seen in an important role as far as the Father, the Daughter and the clinicians are concerned. How do Sons relate to the triangle of relationships formed by the Mother, the Father and the Daughter? Psychiatrist Cormier writes of the Fathers:

They . . . try to separate the sons from the daughters and the wife. In this kind of familial relationship, the sons undoubtedly become resentful and hostile to the father. In some . . . cases the son was the one who disclosed incest, and occasionally a son has attempted incest himself, following the father's example.[1]

In a family where the Father is raping the Daughter(s), the Son has the ultimate patriarchal model. Some attempt resistance; some repress the knowledge; some, however, follow suit. Just as the Daughters in these families are receiving the most thorough conditioning into rape-passivity, so too are the Sons learning the male counterpart of that conditioning: an absolute sanction on the right of males to rape, based on a belief in the ownership of young females within the family. This element of sex-role conditioning for Sons is not, of course, addressed in the clinical literature on the dynamics and effects of Father–Daughter rape.

We find that the Sons are usually only mentioned in terms of 'mother–son incest'. In this form of incest, the Mother is presumed by most researchers to be the initiator, and the participants have been labelled and dismissed by the clinicians before the event occurs. This is accomplished in generalisations such as this, by the psychiatrist Sarles:

> Mother–son incest is so rare and the taboo so great that when it occurs one or both of the partners may be assumed to be severely disturbed or psychotic.[2]

Meiselman points out that 'no such dire predictions' of disturbance or psychosis are assumed in the case of 'father–daughter or sibling incest'.[3]

What of the Mothers and Sons who do engage in sexual activity? It is difficult to draw many conclusions because the clinical literature deals with only a very small sample: often the same half-dozen or so cases appear over and over again. They appear to be the only ones that have, until very recently, been fully presented clinically. Meiselman has usefully divided the phenomenon into two categories: son-initiated incest and mother-initiated incest.

Taking the latter first, we find that the case histories may vary from sexual activity which the 'mother may cloak with pretenses of personal hygiene', such as bathing her son's penis until age the age of fourteen,[4] to a situation where, at the age of four, his mother 'took him into her bed one night and rubbed her genital organs against his in order to masturbate'.[5] In one case which is presented with unusual thoroughness, psychiatrists Yorokoglu and Kemph were treating a youth whose mother coerced him, from the age of ten to twelve, into having intercourse with her, as well as making him and her daughter (slightly younger) stimulate her sexually in a variety of ways. The mother was gaoled, the children taken into state homes, where Jim proceeded to 'adjust well'. Interestingly, Yorokoglu and Kemph conclude that:

> There seemed to be an absence of sadistic elements in this relationship, in contrast to the typical father–daughter incest cases in which frequently the child is threatened by the parent.[6]

They further mention that during the two years of sexual activity with his mother, Jim had 'no adjustment problem or any scholastic difficulties' which, as we have seen, is not the norm for girl-child victims of rape by a Father.

Meiselman deduces that mother-initiated incest with a son often causes disturbance in the son *after* the event, but not during it.[7] She explains this delayed disturbance syndrome in the same 'pathological' terms as other clinicians when she writes that where severe reaction in the son occurs afterwards, she believes

> . . . that the long-term pathological relationship between mother and son that preceded the consummation of the incest, plus other genetic and environmental factors, was the major cause of schizophrenia and that overt incest was only 'the last straw'.[8]

Thus we find that in cases of mother-initiated incest with a boy-child, both parties are presumed to be locked into a sick symbiotic relationship of which incest is only one manifestation. This formula for diagnosis automatically means that the protagonists will be separated and institutionalised for 'treatment'.

The cases of son-initiated incest that are accessible in the literature present a very different picture. In these we see a pattern: an adult son rapes his mother. Wahl, a psychiatrist, presents an instance in which the son, in his early twenties, found his mother 'naked and in an alcoholic stupor and, according to the patient and another informer [a watching male friend], he had intercourse with her'.[9] Wahl, having established this son as an extremely disturbed ex-Korean war veteran who had already been hospitalised for a 'psychotic' condition, turns the tables in time-honoured misogynistic fashion by concluding that 'loss of maternal control, as in alcoholic stupor, operates as an unconscious seduction on the part of the mother'.[10] And so we return (having never really left) to the blame-the-mother syndrome.

Similarly, the sociologist Weinberg outlines a case in which the mother (aged 54) and son (aged 27) were still living in the same house. After returning home together from a party with friends and relatives, the son burst into her room and 'demanded intercourse':

> She pleaded with him, but he threatened to kill her if she were not quiet. He then had relations with her. Later she ordered him from the house, while she went to her other son's home and reported the affair.[11]

In spite of the fact that the police were called straight away – that is, the mother made no attempt to hide what had happened – Weinberg interprets events like this:

> Although the facts in the case are scant, *the attitudes of the mother are underplayed.* Whether the mother was *tacitly seductive* in this whole process is unknown. At any rate *the intense guilt manifested by the mother* and son after the affair is apparent.[12] [My italics.]

This is a case of outright lying by Weinberg. While he does present evidence of the son's ensuing remorse, there is absolutely nothing said about the mother after she ordered him from the house, as quoted above. So, having told us that she 'pleaded' not to be raped, and went for help and support as soon as she had been, Weinberg attempts to leave us with a sense of her 'co-operation' in his concluding remarks about the case.

Weiner, a psychiatrist, reports a case in which the father was the instigator. In what is clearly a group rape situation, the mother is again held to be, in part, responsible:

> This man forced his two teenage sons to have intercourse with their mother while he watched. This man had become impotent after an initially good sexual adjustment in his marriage and watching his sons have intercourse with his wife stimulated him to the extent where he was able himself to copulate. The father was schizophrenic and the mother, although not psychotic, *was partly responsible for the incestuous relationship.*[13] [My italics.]

So we arrive at the inevitable: when 'mother–son incest' is clearly a case of forcible group rape, it is labelled an 'incestuous relationship' and the mother is still held to be (partly) responsible. Sons in a family situation of this type are, of course, literally being made into rapists by the Father: a very blatant form of initiation into the world of male supremacy.

Workers at the Sydney Rape Crisis Centre have observed that Son–Mother rape is being increasingly reported.[14] Whether this is a new phenomenon or the emergence of a relatively common, but hidden, practice, we do not know. The workers at the Centre have encountered examples of the Son copying the Father as intra-family rapist. One mother sought their aid when her son began raping his four sisters, as her husband had been doing for years. It was only after several contacts with this woman that they found that the son was also raping her. The workers deduce from this and other cases in which they have been involved, that Son–Mother rape may be the most difficult thing of all for women to talk about. To acknowledge that a Son has raped her, a Mother risks all: apart from the likelihood of being disbelieved, she risks not only universal condemnation for being such a Bad Mother that she could have produced such a Son, but also the shattering recognition that in spite of the travail and ecstacy of giving birth and nurturing him, this is what he finally thinks of her. Woman/cunt/bitter hatred.

Other workers from the Centre cite a woman who was raped by her husband's brother whom they had raised as their own from a young age, and whom she regarded as her son. When he was twenty-six he returned home and not only raped her but also mutilated her. Her husband supported his brother (her Son), so she left the marital home. She eventually committed suicide, leaving a message for the Rape Crisis workers explaining that she could no longer live, now that she perceived what hatred men may have for women.

The rape of a Mother by a Son would seem to be the quintessential expression of misogyny: hatred for the female who gave him birth. Insofar as rape, in theory and most often in practice, is directed at women's genitals, the Mother would be a logical target. Her genitals, after all, he once knew inside out, the source of his birth, the spring of life from which he descended into a hate-filled planet. Is this why men rape? Is the Mother the true object of their hatred? The clinicians who surmise that for a rapist-Father his Daughter represents his own mother, would appear to be contributing support to such a theory.

Summarising the literature, we find that Mother–Son sexual relations are apparently extremely rare. If initiated by the Mother, it tends to happen when the Son is a child, and the sexual activity may be experienced by him as pleasurable and is usually non-sadistic, in that it is not accompanied by violence or threats. If initiated by the Son, it tends to happen when he is an adult, and its execution carries all the hallmarks of rape. When this occurs, we can say that the Son has become a Father: a grown male with the power of authority vested by male supremacy, and the physical and psychic strength to rape.

The nexus of Mother and Son is of particular interest when looking at the incest 'taboo' which is held to operate throughout our society in terms of all sexual relations among family members. We have seen that the incest taboo is merely a vaporous obstruction to perceiving reality when applied to the common occurrence of Father–Daughter rape. However, we find a different picture if we look at Mother–Son incest.

An anthropologist, Needham, maintains that in terms of any universality about the pattern of incest taboos:

> The most that might be claimed is that they characteristically include certain minimal prohibitions, e.g. that of sexual intimacy between mother and son.[15]

A typical finding in any anthropological fieldwork on incest is that 'among all peoples incest with one's own mother is considered the greatest sin'.[16] And French anthropologist Moscovici writes:

> The form of incest most generally condemned is undoubtedly that between mother and son; between fathers and daughters it is most easily tolerated . . . Though exemption is not official, in most cases an incestuous father is seen as merely reprehensible whereas a mother is condemned outright.[17]

The usual justification/explanation for the incest taboo is that 'in-breeding' is more likely to produce deformed/retarded children. Meiselman points out that the Mother–Son relationship would be less likely to produce any offspring than the other two primary combinations (brother–sister and father–daughter), since the mother would often be past her period of 'optimum fertility' by the time her son had matured, 'yet this union is by far the most strongly condemned'.[18] In arguing thus, she intimates that there are variables operating which have nothing to do with genetic considerations.

A sociologist, Parsons, developed a socialisation theory of the incest taboo which partially indicates how the separation between

186

Mother and Son comes about. He argues that the child's erotic needs must be controlled/repressed within the biological family as a precondition for effective maturation and the wider social good.[19] Thus, manipulation of childhood sexuality is perceived as the means by which society is maintained in a stable state. With its unstated ambience of behaviour modification, this theory is currently understandably popular, fitting comfortably as it does into popularised psychology by appearing to explain the functional reason for Oedipal severance from the Mother.

Just as Freud's Oedipal theory does describe some realities for boy-children within a male supremacist society, so too does Parson's socialisation theory of the incest taboo describe, partially, how the taboo operates. The repression exerted on the Son's sexuality means that sex/sensuousness are separated out, declared apart from the love which is experienced as security, mother, dependence. Thus we have Sons growing into men with an internalised experience of patriarchal cultural and emotional forms: the split between mind and body, spirit and matter, male and female. Although Parsons purports to be describing a 'human' taboo, he eventually reveals, after describing the thorough and profound steps by which the repression and redirection of sexuality takes place, that he is really writing only about what happens to the Sons:

Only mother–son incest is as such directly involved in the constellation I have sketched.[20]

So from Freud to modern sociological theory, and throughout the field of anthropology, we find that Mother–Son incest is the 'real' taboo. And in spite of male sexual fantasy as acted out in films like *La Luna* and *Murmur of the Heart*, which are mistily romantic representations of son–mother sexual relationships, we find that in real life the clinicians declare such Mothers and Sons to be psychotic, severely disturbed, and in need of hospitalisation. So Mother–Son incest is, in actual practice, the most condemned form of incest: the real taboo in practice as well as in theory.

The real function of this taboo is to remove sons from the world of women, thereby drawing them in to the only other world there is, that of men. Boys become men by being declared taboo for their mothers. The taboo means that all women hold back from their sons, saying a psychic-sensual No from the moment of birth. Having been rejected at birth, the Son develops a deep hatred for his mother, whose womb promised all, in terms of safety and love. By the time he is grown up the hatred is usually utterly repressed, expressing itself in the form of disgust at the thought of sexual relations with her, even if he genuinely loves her.

The taboo operates even more profoundly in relation to mother–daughter ties. The homosexual strand of the incest taboo is literally implicit: it is never even mentioned. Mothers also reject their daughters – more thoroughly than their sons insofar as that they are not even aware that they do it. Chodorow, a sociologist, has written an exhaustive analysis of how mothers differentiate in terms of female and male children. She argues that children of both sexes are originally 'matri-sexual' in that their first and most important sensuous, gratifying contact is with their mother, but that during the maturation process mothers more or less consciously push their sons away, knowing that they must join the other-gender world of men, who are distanced from the home/family. In contrast to this process, Chodorow argues, mothers identify with their daughters, keep them closer to them and their world, and in so doing probably give them *less* sensuousness but *more* gender-training for their presumed future role as mothers.

In discussing the functional role of the incest taboo, Chodorow points out that:

> . . . given the organization of parenting, mother–son and mother–*daughter* incest are the major threats to the formation of new families (as well as to the male-dominant family itself) and not, equivalently, mother–son and *father*–daughter incest.[21] [Original italics.]

Chodorow thereby gives us a key to the real role of the incest taboo. Father–Daughter incest (rape) does *not* threaten the 'male-dominant family'; nor does Son–Mother incest (rape) when the Son is an adult, since he is then 'male-dominant' instead of, or as well as, the Father. But Mother-to-Son or Mother-to-Daughter incest would threaten the existing male supremacist forms since the Father would become comparatively irrelevant to the emotional fabric which determines the relationship within the family.

When we see the incest taboo as the means by which the 'male-dominant family' is maintained, then Oedipal theory shifts its emphasis from the (repressed) sexual nexus between Mother and Son to the more pertinent connection between Father and Son: the reproduction of male dominance. Seen in this light, the Mother's

188

role in the Oedipal triangle is the agent who delivers the Son (an embryonic Man) up to the Father.

Like women, Sons have to jump to anticipate the desires of the Father. Freud mentions 'how often little boys are afraid of being eaten up by their father',[22] which is a recurrent mythological theme in many cultures. A Monster (Dragon/Father) is slain by a youth (Son) who thereby becomes a man (Father). He is usually given a Princess (Daughter) as a reward as well. A woman I know who teaches primary school pupils has found that if a group can be encouraged, through a Unit on Ghosts or Spooks or Dreams, to talk of their greatest fears, the girls will almost invariably name 'bogeymen' (rapists), while the boys will own to a fear of being eaten by a monster. The girls of course are being literal, naming a fear they already feel, with which they will have to live out their whole lives. The boys, I suspect, are being more metaphorical in the expression of their very real fear, since they cannot name the Father, because their only chance of salvation lies in becoming one.

To become a Father, a Son has to repress his deep emotional attachment to his mother, and repress the fear/rage/contempt he may feel for his father. The 'complex' which results from the apparent resolution of this process could well be guilt: guilt caused by deserting the world of women, which the Son recalls in the form of an ancient memory as a place where women (Mother) walked tall and free, sexual and unafraid. The sense of 'guilt' is easier to cope with than its true origin: rage at the Father for determining that life should be ordered in this way.

The psychoanalyst Rank writes of the role of the Father, in setting up 'social father-organization' (patriarchy), as being to 'sever the sons from the mother' and goes on to claim that:

The systematic social depreciation of woman from her original heights finally results in a reaction against that infantile dependence on her, which the son, now become father, can no longer bear.[23]

The Son-become-Father, with all the concomitant power implied by such a transition, is bound over for the rest of his life to deny the 'original heights' of the Mother.

To ease the passage of this frightful denial, there are the initiation rites of male bonding which bear witness to the absolute difference between the worlds of women (Mother) and men (Father). In western society, the bastions of training for ruling-class Sons, fee-paying schools and selective University colleges, have unofficial initiation 'tests' which involve rites of passage into the male world characterised by cruelty and authoritarianism. The initiate may be stripped naked and taken to a distant destination and left alone to make his own way 'home'; he may have his testicles painted black or various painful things done to his penis; he may be induced to get helplessly drunk and taken to a brothel; he may be made to breast-stroke, naked, along a gravel drive and then thank the Fathers who are 'initiating' him. The point of all such 'games' is to prove that (a) he doesn't show his feelings, (b) he accepts the authority of the male world, and (c) he has left the mothering world of women behind forever. The same purpose is achieved for middle-class and working-class Sons, by 'boys nights' on the town, by stag parties, by the particular rituals of bikey gangs, by men taking a pimple-faced apprentice to the pub and getting him drunk, by a Father winking at his Son's 'wild oats', and by the institution of war: the Father telling the Sons to go out there and kill. These rites of initiation are truly binding: ask any man who has been affected by feminism and is trying to change.

The religion of the Fathers, the spiritual representation of patriarchy, with its stern male God who allowed his Son to be nailed to a dead piece of wood, offers little comfort: shape up or ship out. The only reprieve is offered by the Catholic female figure of Mary, the tortured, distorted female remnant of the original Earth-Goddess. She stands in Catholic churches, larger than life-size, hands out-stretched, with an expression of absolute understanding and forgiveness on her face. The Eternal Mother – rendered powerless, a symbol of the lost nurturance, confined within the walls of a building which is a monument to inhumanity, where only the blood dripping from the Christ-figure (her Son) is brighter than her eyes. The respite of those who kneel at her feet is brief indeed, because her very femininity is a travesty of the strength for which the supplicants are searching. The male supplicant is touched by the softness of the Marian Mother, but she has no power with which to *do* anything, even forgive; the female supplicant sees only her own powerlessness deified.

This ineffably sad distortion of the female principle – the Virgin Mary of established Christian religion – is one of the main symbolic forms of Woman/Mother experienced in western society. For many Sons, it faithfully depicts the image of Woman created for them by the Mother and Daughter(s) in their family, where the Father holds all the power that matters. The Son(s) in a family where the Father is raping the Daughter(s), is apparently in a unique position, insofar as he is not an object of the Father's physical or rape-aggression, in that he is male and relatively free of the power dynamics that the Father is using to manipulate all the females. His relative freedom would suggest that he might be the agent who could object to his Father's actions, support his sister(s), seek outside intervention and assistance.

The Son usually does not do this because he is too deeply involved in his own effort to become a Man. Mostly, he is already identifying with the powerful, though distant, figure of his Father, even though he be still a young boy who is physically and emotionally inhabiting the world of home and Mother. Moscovici, in suggesting that the Mother–Son incest taboo is a structural bulwark of this gender differentiation in loyalties goes further, to argue that the incest taboo is integrally related to the subordination of women:

> The world of men and the world of women circle in different orbits and in opposite directions. Men inhabit a universe of signs and women a universe of significance . . . If the prohibition of incest marks the transition from nature to culture it is a transition from a state of male and female equality to a state of male dominance. The prohibition, like all forms of social intervention, creates a dual set of relationships: reciprocity for the men and subordination for the women, the second being one of the conditions for the first.[24]

Thus the incest taboo, experienced within the family along with and as part of Mother's milk, separates the Son from the Mother and *in so doing* inculcates the social imperative, within patriarchy, of the subordinate position of women.

Brøgger, much influenced by Moscovici's argumentation, says of the incest taboo:

> This prohibition is the prerequisite for male dominance, because otherwise sons would remain with their mothers and form a different group, a feminine hierarchy, and male power would disintegrate.[25]

If boy-children, and therefore men, were integrated into the female world, instead of women being placed on the periphery of the male world, then patriarchy would vanish. Instead of separation there would be unity.

By means, then, of the asymmetrical incest taboo, male supremacist/'moral' injunctions consolidate the Mother in her absolute isolation. She is given a family – her husband and their children – to look after in enforced solitude, and is then bound over to release all of them from her sensuousness and care *even though* they would all prefer to receive more of it. The Father, meanwhile, prepares for the day of initiation rites when he welcomes his Son into the world of men (the Son having 'proved himself' by repressing his tears and rage at the original rejection by the Mother); and simultaneously, the Father prepares his Daughter for her sex-object role by treating her like a doll, 'my princess', or ignores her utterly, or rapes her. Thus, within the family, both Sons and Daughters learn that women promise love but then withdraw it; and both Sons and Daughters learn that men confer rewards and punishments, sometimes arbitrarily, sometimes in proportion to social behaviours that have been extracted in the hope of approval. Deep down, both Sons and Daughters *desire* the approval/love of Mother most of all, the love that emanates from the dark of the amniotic fluid and the turn of the seasons; up-front, both Sons and Daughters *seek* the approval of Father because that determines the measure of success they have achieved in the real world, the public world, the male world – the world that is made in the image of the Father who as a boy lost his mother and will not ever let her see him cry.

The incest taboo *is* the family. The family is the incest taboo. (Without one the other would not exist.) It is this conflation of the incest taboo and the family that ensures, through severance from the Mother and the subordination of women, that Sons will feel hatred (misogyny) and desire (rape) for their Mothers (all women). In thus creating misogynistic Sons, the incest taboo/family exists to ensure male supremacy.

The incest taboo, then, obviously creates Sons who become Fathers: the Fathers who need to avenge their anger by raping the female principle in the form of helpless girl-children. The dominant power in any social structure which is hierarchical in its construction can *only* allow injunctions and roles which serve its own purpose: the incest taboo (Mother–Son) serves the interests of patriarchy.

7 The Family –
A Man's Home is His Castle

The roles available to women and men are clearly articulated in
fairy tales. The characters of each are vividly described, and so
are the modes of relationship possible between them. We see
that powerful women are bad, and that good women are inert.
We see that men are always good, no matter what they do, or
do not do.

We also have an explicit rendering of the nuclear family. In
that family, a mother's love is destructive, murderous. In that
family, daughters are objects, expendable. The nuclear family,
as we find it delineated in fairy tales, is a paradigm of male
being-in-the-world, female evil, and female victimization. It is
a crystallization of a sexist culture – the nuclear structure of
that culture.

Andrea Dworkin, *Woman Hating*

The incestuous family is a microcosmic paradigm of the
rape ideology which operates in the macrocosm of society. In the
incestuous family we find the most powerless of females, a
girl-child, has become the sexual possession of the Father, the king
in his castle lording it over his concubine. We find his wife, the
Mother of the girl-child he has appropriated for his own use, eking
out her days in cowed submission. We find the Son, a prince, either
emulating his Father or skulking in the servants' quarters playing
with other boys and trying not to see what is going on upstairs.

The Father, in his power, denies he is doing anything wrong. If
anyone doubts this, he has his courtiers, the clinical, academic and
sex-liberationist apologists, to defend him. The Mother, so cowed
as to be hardly visible, is like the Queen in many fairy stories:
absent from centre stage. She may, if she is lucky, have ladies-in-
waiting (friends) in whom she can confide and with whom she can
weep. The Daughter exists only for her Father's pleasure; allowed

no playmates, no closeness with her Mother, no freedom, she is contained within a world where to be female is to be a sexual slave.

While the analogy may appear exaggerated when rendered in fairy-tale form, the details remain essentially the same in real life.

The Fathers are variously described, even by the clinical writers who strain to exonerate them, as 'tyrants',[1] as exercising 'paternal dominance',[2] and as needing to 'appear the strong patriarch'.[3] One could justifiably argue that such men are suffering under the limitations and demands of culturally constructed concepts of masculinity – i.e. simply trying to be a 'male' as social pressures dictate. However, this line of argument, while endeavouring to understand the place of masculinity within a sexist society insofar as it affects *individuals*, does not address itself to the larger problem of the male supremacist context in which Father–Daughter rape occurs. The Fathers may be struggling to be real Men: the clinical researchers and social investigators, as we have seen, largely identify with them. The pornographers and academic sexual liberationists are concerned, moreover, with encouraging them. A sociologist, Farrel, is quoted in *Penthouse* in 1977:

> . . . few things are as powerful as a deviation whose time has come. Homosexuality, wife swapping, open marriage, bisexuality, S & M, and kiddie porn have already had their seasons. Just as we seemed to be running low on marketable taboos, the unspeakable predictably popped up . . . After centuries of restraint, incest is finally a hit.[4]

This excited pronouncement opens an article which is ostensibly concerned with the so-called sexual liberation of children. As Herman reflects:

> Such statements of concern for the well-being of children seem a bit out of place, appearing as they do in publications whose main purpose is to supply masturbatory fantasy material to men, and which generally display an attitude toward children ranging from utter indifference to the most violent hostility.[5]

The actions of the Fathers must be seen within the cultural context which aids and abets them. These Fathers are not aberrant males: they are acting within the mainstream of masculine sexual behaviour which sees women as sexual commodities and believes men have a right to use/abuse these commodities how and whenever they

194

can. The fact that many Fathers do not behave in these ways towards their Daughters, that some men do not behave in these ways towards all women, does not alter the fact that they *could*. Those men who say they want to 'help', could most pertinently demonstrate this by working for and with all the men in the world who see women as rape-bait, who use women in sexually abusive ways. Just as women have formed support environments and groups for the victims of sexual and physical abuse, so caring men could form re-education groups, de-programming groups for their brothers who cannot see beyond the actions demanded by their own alienated masculinity.[6]

Men have economic, legal, political, physical, medical and social power over women, but at the root of all these is sexual power. Sexual power is exercised at the most intimate level, the most personal level. Male sexual power over women is expressed in public and in private. It is applied to women individually and collectively. It attempts to determine how women dress, how they walk, how they sit; it maintains that every woman is good or evil; and that no matter which she is, 'All she really wants is a good fuck'. With his ramrod he will tame her, brand her, possess her.

Father–Daughter rape is the paradigm *par excellence* of this social structuring of heterosexual relations. In Father–Daughter rape we find the most powerless females being sexually used by the most powerful males. Male adult to female child.

> Children are essentially a captive population, totally dependent upon their parents or other adults for their basic needs. Thus they will do whatever they perceive to be necessary to preserve a relationship with their caretakers. If an adult insists upon a sexual relationship with a dependent child, the child will comply.
>
> Given this reality, it makes no sense to invoke the idea of consent. Consent and choice are concepts that apply to the relationship of peers. They have no meaning in the relations of adults and children, any more than in relations of freemen and slaves.[7]

The Daughters do what they must do to *survive*. They do what they do because they live in a society in which they see women being sexually harassed/teased/belittled every day: in the streets, on television, at school and in their homes.

The Mothers too, do what they do to *survive*. They have been subjected to all the everyday sexual belittlement of women that

195

their Daughters have seen, and more. They *want* to believe that the home, the family, is the one place that is safe from this institutionalised violence and derogation of women. They want *not* to see/hear that their husband, brother, father, son is bringing this horror into the home, their home. Like the Daughters, the Mothers function with a bundle of survival strategies, both conscious and unacknowledged.

Father–Daughter relations vary along a continuum from rape to complete disinterest. The disinterested end of the spectrum, however, is lightly weighted compared with the sexual and/or emotional connection between most Fathers and Daughters. In the vast majority of families in which there is no Father–Daughter rape, there is, instead, an emphasis on the Father–Daughter tie, within the family constellation of relationships.[8] Most Father–Daughter relations are characterised by an exchange: he gives her validation of her femininity (i.e. female sexuality as defined by male supremacist culture), and she gives him emotional support in the form of validation as a patriarchal figure (at least overtly – she may bitch about him covertly). This exchange, apparently mutual, is actually determined by the power balance between them: the father gives her validation *in return for* the emotional comfort she bestows on him. She thereby becomes 'a good girl'.

Most Fathers set a high price on their Daughter's sexuality: she is only a good girl if she does *not* fool around with boys. The implicit demand of most Fathers is that their Daughters be seen as attractive, sexual, and, paradoxically, hard-to-get, chaste. When a Daughter does manage to fulfil this image, other men will flatter the Father with remarks, or looks, that appraise *his* property; she's a good-looker, but it's Hands Off.

Herman, after summarising the literature on paternal attitudes to and involvement in caring for their children, states that:

> The only predictable way that fathers show interest in their daughters is in an early and strong insistence that their girls conform to rigid stereotypes of femininity.[9]

In the typical patriarchal family, then, most Daughters are being prepared, overtly or covertly, for stereotypical femininity – which is based on dislike of women and aggrandisement of men. The patriarchal family constructs Daughters who are ready, willing and able to co-operate in male supremacist society. Father-Daughter rape is merely a phenomenon at one end of the spectrum of the means by which this construction is achieved. It is no accident that the victims of Father–Daughter rape almost universally hate their Mothers. These Daughters, in being raped as children, have had more urgent and early need than any other females to break the mould of acquiescent femininity: they have looked to their Mothers for a way out. Only Mothers who are able to perceive male power can provide this form of protection; and most Mothers do not provide it because they see no way out for themselves, let alone their Daughters. When we look along the continuum of Father–Daughter relations where rape is not occurring, we can see that the Mother's role there, too, is to reinforce the Father–Daughter tie. Mothers often, for example, support the social construct that the Daughter is 'her Daddy's girl'. She will also joke about (rather than oppose) his authoritarian restriction of the Daughter's movements, his dislike of any boyfriends the Daughter may wish to see. She may nod sagely when the Father avers that, 'All young men are animals: I ought to know, I've been one myself.'

Given the psycho-sexual construction of male supremacist society, the family plays an essential role because it is the site wherein Daughters are constructed: Daughters who perform this very important function for their Fathers. They provide an ambience of burgeoning female sexuality in his home and they cause other men to envy him the love and affection he receives from a nubile woman to whom they have (theoretically) no access. In cases of sexual molestation/rape by a Stranger, many Fathers are heard to make remarks such as, 'I'll kill the bastard! *She's mine.* How dare he!'

The phrase, 'She's mine', captures the essential connection in Father–Daughter relations. as Herman points out, when Freud established a primary focus on the maturation process of the child, 'The incestuous wishes of parents, and their capacity for action, were all but forgotten.'[10] A psychiatrist, Pauncz, writing in the 50s, developed, using Shakespeare's play *King Lear* much as Freud used Sophocles' *Oedipus Rex*, a theory which he called 'the Lear complex'. What Pauncz was suggesting was that investigations of the incest taboo, and of those occasions where it was breached, had one-sidedly focussed on the presumed incestuous wishes of children, and that maybe the incestuous wishes of adults could be just as profitably examined. He writes:

The formula that 'the son kills his father and marries his mother', can be contrasted with just as an impressive formula that 'the father eliminates his wife and marries his daughter' . . . The

Lear complex is just as regular and ever-present a factor in the psyche of the grown-up man, as the Oedipus Complex is in the psyche of the child.[11]

Pauncz points out that in this theory 'we do not make the innocent child responsible (as psychoanalysis does), but the grown-ups themselves'.[12] In another paper[13] he analyses the play *King Lear*, extracting those references which specifically refer to incestuous wishes or lust in Lear towards his daughter Cordelia. He establishes this play, as outstanding in the English pantheon of 'great plays' as *Oedipus Rex* was in the Greek, as the symbolic cultural representation of a Father's obsessive sexual feelings for his Daughter.

> The introduction of the concept of the 'adult libido' tries to do justice to the instinctual cravings of the adult toward children. The concept of the Lear complex attempts to account for the specific cravings of the parents (father) towards their own children.[14]

While a few of the later researchers make passing reference to Pauncz's theory, none of them have seen fit to present it fully or to consider it in the light of their own abiding allegiance to the primacy of Oedipal factors.

When viewed through the useful lens of the Lear complex, everyday Father–Daughter ties are revealed as an essential part of the structure of male dominance. Daughters learn of this asymmetrical social pattern from their first breath, in the bosom, as it were, of the family. They thereby become mothers who co-operate in the reproduction of the same cycle. And Fathers retain their power, their primacy, in part by feeding off the approval of their Daughters and their wives, who are acting out the roles assigned to them by the only social structure they know.

Since Fathers, like other men, are imbued with the belief that sexual activity is their right (and their measure as a Man), it is, of course, only logical that we would find this right being exercised within the family, particularly with the least powerful members of it. It is only in the last hundred years that women have been allowed to keep their own property (the Married Women's Property Act 1870, UK), which was recognition of the fact that a married woman had a right to her own property. And it is only in the last hundred years that a mother's custodial rights over her children have been recognised by law. Traditional patriarchal families still flourish, however, in emotional and social terms. Within such a family, a child is seen as having no rights of her own. Herman says that the 'idea of the child's right to her own body is a radical one':[15] there is no such concept within most families nor within the popular culture, and only marginally within the law. In the traditional patriarchal family the mother does all the child-nurturing (even if she also works) and all other household work is strictly determined by the sexual division of labour, which means that she does the vast bulk of it.

It is interesting that this model of the family, re-named an 'intact family', is the concept currently being utilised by right-wing lobbyist groups to describe the ideal family, the way in which they think everyone should live. This is a truly reactionary move, since it has been spawned in response to the seemingly endless series of social truths brought to the light of day by the feminist movement: wife-beating, marital rape, economic dependency of women, inequality of divorce property settlements, spouse murder, Father–Daughter rape – all of which occur in the family.

In this family, the Father expects to be nurtured, cleaned up after, fed, comforted, admired, sexually satisfied, and respected. His word is law. He may not often lay down the law overtly, because his wife/the Mother, and often the children (especially the Daughters) as well, will anticipate his wishes: anything for a quiet life. As a result, many men go through life literally unable to wash their own socks, buy their own pyjamas, or perceive that everyone else in the family thinks that he has funny ears. Herman again points out:

> As long as fathers rule but do not nurture, as long as mothers nurture but do not rule, the conditions favouring the development of father–daughter incest will prevail.[16]

Through having ruling power, the Father is cut off from all, or most, of the humanity which swirls through the ebb and flow of daily life for women and children. He is cut off, therefore, from the emotions of daily life. He lives within patriarchal culture, wherein rape is sanctioned.

Across class, across education levels, across race, across the status of their paid work (or unemployment), men are relentlessly offered one outlet through which to escape their unhappiness and through which to prove their masculinity (thereby gaining a spurious happiness): this outlet is sex. Even men who do not act on this sanctioned behaviour – making sexual jokes, buying pornography, seducing women or raping them – will not object when other men do so in their company. To object would mean to cease being a Man in other men's eyes. And thus masculine sexual predatoriness flourishes – always with Woman as the object of its inhumanity.

Masculine sexual behaviour, as a social construct and, too often, as everyday practice, is devoid of tenderness, vulnerability and the fluid emotional mutuality which flows from shared tenderness and vulnerability. Masculine sexuality is inculcated in men and women alike as being concerned with conquering: 'getting a woman'. The colloquial language that men employ for their own sexual organ: tool, rod, stick, prick, hard-on, horn, snake, ramrod, machine – testifies to the harshness of the alienation which they feel from their own sexuality.

The phallic symbolism of towers, obelisks, war memorials, skyscrapers and modern communications facilities is something every child learns about. It may be the only thing which many people know about 'art': that artists can represent male power with a phallic object. The real subjects of phallic symbolism are those that are concerned with death and/or conquering: guns, daggers, swords, cannon, rockets, torpedoes, missiles, bombs and the machines that men send to other planets. Nuclear bombs are the ultimate symbol of the alienated horror of unfeeling male ejaculation. A phallic bomb may be released/ejaculated one day which kills us all: the final seminal spurt of patriarchy. When men begin to be outraged, disgusted, horrified by this imagery, we may be on the path to humanisation of the Earth – which will begin with the end of rape.

Feminist theorist Barry, who has written of the multifarious forms of sexual violence by men to women, places this alienation in a political context:

. . . the overbureaucratization of society and nonresponsiveness of government breed impersonality into every life, creating the condition of alienation: the individual is alienated from her/himself as well as from the larger society that seems only to absorb individuals as part of the masses. *The widespread violence we are experiencing is in part a reaction of men against that alienation, but for women living under the conditions of male domination, male violence is a further act of alienation and the source of terrorism.*[17] [My italics.]

Barry succinctly points out that the pain of alienation of men from themselves is taken out on women. Thus, while one may deplore the over-arching alienation of industrial patriachal society as it affects people of both genders, the inescapable fact is that women are on the bottom of the pile: used and abused by men who seek to alleviate a little of their own alienation by exercising power over those who have even less of it than themselves.

Fathers rape Daughters within the family; men rape women at work, in their homes, on the streets, in cars and car-parks. As long as the male principle has power to rule, at home, in the schoolyard, in the streets, at work, in culture, then we will have rape. Rape is the end result of the dehumanised authoritarian social structure called patriarchy, through which the Son becomes Father by rejecting his Mother and thereby gains unfettered access to the Daughter.

III · CODA

Action

We know there *is* a world without rape and this world is in our minds . . .

SUSAN GRIFFIN, Rape: The Power of Consciousness

Action

Navigating by chart and chance
and passion I will know the shape
of the mountains of freedom, I will know.

Marge Piercy, from 'The Perpetual Migration',
The Moon Is Always Female

The stories of women's lives
do not appear in magazines
even when they seem to

The stories of women's lives
are etched in the shadow
of a young girl's brown eyes

The stories of women's lives
are seared in the muscle
at the corners of their mouths

The stories of women's lives
weep down from the moon
in huge silver drops

carrying the siren sounds of
the stories of women's lives.

i dream

> *a world beyond rape*

i dream

> *a world where the very bodies*
> *that we live in*
> *do not incite violence against us*

i dream

> *a world where we can walk the streets*
> *or country roads, on the darkest nights,*
> *lit only by the stars*
> *and our own freedom to move*

Dreaming is useful in envisaging where we want to go, because it helps us to get there. Such dreaming, however, grows out of an awareness of how we have been constructed and abused by patriarchy. The aim of this book is to help end the silence, lift the blinds, on the subject of Father–Daughter rape. In this concluding section, as well as encouraging dreaming, I wish to emphasise the need for action. Action to change things in the world makes new dreaming possible.

1. The Speaking of Women

Women everywhere need to start talking about Father–Daughter rape. We need to talk with each other about our experiences of it, our fear of it, our confusions about it, our anger that is touched by it, and any other reactions that we have to it. We need to dredge our memories, the multiplicity of layers through which we know things, in search of our own experiences of growing up as a girl-child. We need to remember, see and understand that for girl-children there are constant messages being received about the power that men have over women. Girl-children are the receptors, as only children can be, of a multifarious network of visual, auditory and vibrationary signals about the sexual role they are expected to play in order to please men/the Father/the seat of power. Like a clean wind blowing away fog, this process of women remembering and asking and talking and validating the truth about Father–Daughter rape is the only way in which the depths of silence and blindness that have crippled most victims are going to be lifted. As Rich has written:

> One of the most powerful social and political catalysts of the past decade has been the speaking of women with other women, the telling of our secrets, the comparing of wounds and the sharing of words. This hearing and saying of women has been able to break many a silence and taboo; literally to transform forever the way we see.[1]

206

Transforming the way we see, seeing this patriarchal world and how it is structured, is both a painful and an exhilarating experience. It is painful because it means confronting the depths of the limitation, humiliation and abuse that women and children suffer within patriarchy; it is exhilarating because new thoughts, new perceptions, visions of a truly humane society become possible.

Father–Daughter rape, Son–Mother rape, Brother–Sister rape: these are rape in its most intimate (family) form. Rape is about hatred. Male supremacist hatred of such proportions has been endured within the private sphere of the family by individual women for too long. As women begin to speak of these most intimate atrocities, the face, the very being of our society will change.

2. Mothers and Daughters

As the Daughters and Mothers emerge from the shades of silenced anger, they will find each other, form groups, speak and share through the quietest night hours, and emerge into the light of day transformed by the knowledge that they each, in their aloneness, were victims, but that in their togetherness they can vision a new world into being: our world, beyond rape. Mothers will tell their Daughters, the Daughters will tell each other, on and on down the line, that some things are not to be borne.

The Daughter–Mother tie reveals a particularised form of the power that resides within the speaking of women with each other. We have seen that for the Mothers 'the eyes not seeing what the heart cannot hold'[2] has locked them off from their Daughters behind a barrier of blindness and broken hearts. When the Daughters and Mothers break through this barrier, the scales of patriarchal vision fall from their eyes and their broken hearts are mended by the love that women share – a special kind of love which occurs as women begin to acknowledge their shared identity, in suffering and in change.

The particular poignancy of Mothers and Daughters re-finding each other as sisters derives from the patriarchal injunction which blames Mothers for everything and anything – thereby depreciating Motherhood, while at the same time insisting that it is Woman's highest vocation. Daughters learn of this depreciation of Mothers, much as they breathe air: it is integral to patriarchal social forms. Daughters, nearly always, do not want to be Mothers *in the same way*: every Daughter determines to do it differently from how her

Mother did it, to do it better. But the fulcrum of patriarchal reproduction is that she has to do it: be a Mother or a Non-Mother, either way trapped in the linguistic and social imperative that a woman be defined in terms of her relationship to Mothering.

Thus Daughters reject their Mothers – and at the same time they long for them. They long for a Mother who will show them how to get out of the trap, how to be independent, whole, herself. We long for an acknowledgment of what could be possible between Mothers and Daughters.

Mothers and daughters have always exchanged with each other – beyond the verbally transmitted lore of female survival – a knowledge that is subliminal, subversive, preverbal: the knowledge floating between two alike bodies, one of which has spent nine months inside the other.[3]

The knowledge floating between two alike bodies . . . While this knowledge can be felt between any two women, it is most strongly experienced between Mothers and Daughters: one woman has created another, one's body is the same as that of the being who created it. They have known each other most intimately, in what must surely be the most intimate form of knowing experienced within the human condition: one woman created by another.

This knowing is the area that is being touched, like butterfly wings caressing (beautiful and fragile), when Mothers and Daughters speak truly, each to each.

3. Protection, Care and Change

As the Daughters and Mothers, supported by other women, indentify what has been done to them, they will, hopefully, be involved in, even initiate, changes as to the type of protection and care which are needed. Ideally, after themselves being healed as far as is possible in the miasma of horror from which they are emerging, many of these girl-children and women will become involved in supportive networks and sheltered environments which they themselves will (help) establish and operate.

The social welfare model of care which is currently the only widely available form of institutional help needs to be publicly examined and contrasted with the self-help, grass-roots validation model being offered by rape crisis centres and women's refuges. The social welfare system must undergo an internal revolution in terms of knowledge and attitudes, if it is to be capable of even partially providing the kind of care needed by the victims of Father–Daughter rape. Instead of waiting rooms, medical examinations, welfare interviews, disconnected counselling sessions and the stated or implicit moral imperatives which accompany such impersonal types of 'care', we need intense and complex systems of involvement in the ongoing process each Daughter and Mother needs to navigate in order to (re-)find a sense of integrity and belief in herself. The welfare system needs, most of all, to change its primary focus from that of family 'welder' (trying to get the family back together at all costs), to that of care and protection for the Daughter and understanding for the Mother.

Part of this process will include exposing the misuse of Freud's theory of infantile sexuality. It has been used as a blatant and outrageous form of invalidation of Father–Daughter rape. Quite apart from the vicious cruelty inflicted on individual victims by this myth, it has functioned to deepen the invisibility of Father–Daughter rape on a macro-social level. Functioning within the same cultural mode, the Fathers of the social sciences have diddled with the facts of Father–Daughter rape so as to further obscure reality. The academic interpreters of people's behaviour are just as guilty as the Fathers insofar as they purport to be 'objective' when they are in fact operating from their own subjectivity. Eschewing passionless objectivity which is, by definition, rooted in the status quo, we need to direct our passionate attention to the validation of our own senses: to believe that the worst we see and feel really is happening; and to determine what we want to do about it. In this process we will find ways to name and reject the so-called objectivity of the social scientists who have manipulated our thoughts and feelings, misnaming the reality of Father–Daughter rape.

Mothers and Daughters will also have the most pertinent input into the immediately needed reforms of the law. In every state, territory and nation, laws must be brought into existence which recognise the commonness of Father–Daughter rape, and address themselves primarily to protecting the Daughters from the now current processes of minute cross-examination and the need for evidence of corroboration, as well as the myriad effects of 'normal' rape cases.

Laws nearly always follow, rather than lead, public opinion and mainstream values. Thus the multi-faceted process of women talking, of naming, of mass publicity, of educating the silent majority, of convincing those who make and enforce laws, of involving those who deliver welfare systems and medical care, is still the first step, from which the rest will flow.

4. The Liberation of Women

The particular means by which women are kept dependent (on men) and oppressed as people, must be eradicated so that Daughters no longer find themselves with Mothers who cannot see, who cannot say No.

For women to rise out of their subordinate status, they must have economic independence. This means that the struggles for non-sexist education, non-sexist job definitions, the right to work, the right to a decent income as workers or Mothers, and truly equal pay are part of the struggle to end Father–Daughter rape.

Women must also have control of their own bodies. This means that the struggles for truly safe contraception, the right to sterilisation, the right to abortion on demand, the right to full and truthful sex education, the right to sexual partners of their choice, the right to childbirth-methods determined by the mother, and the right to full and honest information in medical matters are part of the struggle to end Father–Daughter rape.

Women must also be able to live their lives free of personal violence: the kind of personal violence which occurs because women are subordinate. This means that the struggles to eliminate wife-bashing, marital rape, street harassment, and sexual harassment on the job are part of the struggle to end Father–Daughter rape.

Ultimately, women will only be a liberated species when male supremacy ends. This means that any struggle which opposes the expression of male supremacy – expressions such as sexist advertising, pornography, the patriarchal nuclear family, rape in warfare and the use of nuclear energy and armaments – are part of the struggle to end Father–Daughter rape.

5. Sex and Sexuality Information

We must expand the embryonic attempts to educate girl-children, and society generally, about female sexuality, and about rape. The repression of information about female sexuality is clearly linked to rape in that the traditional view of women as sexually passive feeds straight into the myths about rape. Girl-children will only begin to be able to protect themselves when they (a) value their own bodies, and (b) know that they may be sexually approached by a man they know and trust.

We must teach girl-children about their own sexuality, as a base from which they can love and value their own bodies. We must teach our Daughters to recognise the experience of pleasure for what it is: their own precious bodily reactions, rather than an emotional response implying consent. We must teach them that they can and must say No to *anyone* who touches them against their will. We must teach them to exert as much control over their own bodies as is possible; and we must teach it to them as early as possible, along with walking and talking.

This mode of social-sex education, growing out of women talking together and thereby discovering what it is that girl-children need to know, is the first way in which girl-children are going to be empowered to say No. Social attitudes and availability of information which will allow them a sense of physical, emotional and sexual integrity are the obverse of the current practice of conditioned passivity based on fear induced through purposely manipulated ignorance. The very least we can ask for girl-children is a fighting chance to protect themselves by giving them as much information as we can.

6. The Patriarchal Family

The Daughters should *never* be forced, or even encouraged, to live again with the Father who has been raping them. This is the crux, and the crunch, of the change that needs to be wrought immediately. As Herman points out:

> Men cannot be expected to overcome their abusive tendencies or to develop their nurturant capacities overnight, and it makes no sense to expose children to the unsupervised care of men whose interest in them may be ambivalent at best, and perverse at worst. Women are going to have to be the teachers and the protectors for some time to come.[4]

Only an end to the patriarchal nuclear family, only a new kind of family based on complete sharing of matriarchal skills and values will bring about an end to Father–Daughter rape.

The value system of male supremacist society holds the family to be inviolable, except under the most extraordinary circumstances. It will be argued (and it is true) that there are no ideal places for the

Daughters to be removed to on a long-term basis: too often, the family is all there is. Rather than shrugging in resigned acceptance at this truism and turning away in despair, we must set about creating crisis shelters specifically for Daughter-victims, and creating or finding other living arrangements where they can live on a long-term basis. If we face the fact that most raped Daughters do *not* want to live with the person that has raped them, and believe that they should not have to, then we will find alternatives.

7. Naming Blame

The best 'alternative', of course, is the removal of the Fathers. They, after all, *are* the problem. The patriarchal power of the courts, of counsellors, of the police and the welfare system ensures that this solution is not widely possible yet. But there will come a day, not far off, when women make this utterly reasonable demand.

The Father-offenders must be named, isolated, punished. This would only be a reversal of what happens now in many instances, where the victims are the ones who feel, and are, punished. The Fathers must be named as rapists of girl-children. It must be made *socially impossible* for them to get away with it. Ostracism, public ignominy, and a complete ban on access to girl-children seems a small amount to ask in the face of the damage, suffering and pain these men have inflicted. Therapy, 'curing', counselling for individual Fathers are all very well for those who wish to deliver such services: the real problem is the social sanction of their behaviour. They must *not* be forgiven: what they have done is unforgivable.

8. The Power of Naming

In the development of the feminist movement, women have seized the power of naming. This is a revolutionary power because in naming (describing) what is being done to us (and inevitably to children and men as well), we are also naming what must change. The act of naming creates a new world view. The power of naming resides in the fact that we name what we see from the basis of our own experience: within and outside patriarchal culture, simultaneously.

We are finding forms of expression which convey the reality of Father–Daughter rape; we are finding forms of expression which reject male supremacist language – that language which presumes to tell us what is happening to us and how we feel about it. Father–Daughter rape can no longer be called 'interference', 'molestation', 'fooling around with' or 'incest'. The feelings and reactions of the Daughters must be named, described, accepted. The confusion and angst of the Mothers must be named, described, accepted. The totality of rape ideology and its integration into sex-role conditioning must be named, described, eradicated. This revolution of women naming is already under way and it is a revolution which will, one day, bring about an end to rape in all its manifestations.

We, the Mothers and Daughters, are seeing now through our own eyes. We do not forgive the Fathers. It will be said that we are uncaring; that we hate men; that we are creating a state of war. I say that the war has been declared and waged by men since the first act of rape. Whatever the reasons for men's hatred of women, we ourselves are changing the structure of the battle. We are resisting; we are strategically withdrawing; we are naming the hitherto unnameable. In doing these things *for our own sakes*, the corollary is that the Fathers have access to space in which to look at themselves: to hear what they have done, to see what they have done. The prognosis of changed behaviour on the far side of the battlefield is not promising: all types of rape statistics are rising at an alarming rate. But for us, the Mothers and Daughters, there is no going back.

*   *   *

> To dream a world into being
> is regarded by many as insanely
> impractical.
>
> *We know there is a world*
> *without rape and this world is*
> *in our minds.*
>
> As we struggle across the plains
> towards the mountains of freedom
> *we know*
>
> what to take with us and
> what to leave behind. Travelling
> light

we know when to speak or be
dumb (eyes glazed with the matt
of our knowing)

we know when to run, or to lie
in the sun. We know when to run
from danger

and circle and weave and return
from behind, clearing the plains
of the canker.

And the plains will rise up,
the mountains sink down
when we dream

this world into being.

*   *   *

A day in the future dawns still and grey. Overcast and quiet. An unremarkable day.

A small grey woman, sleeping alone, wakes in her bedsitter. Remembering. Being eight years old, sleeping alone in the small room off the verandah at the back of the weatherboard house. Remembers how she taught herself to slip into the wall, from where she watched through a crack in the woodwork when her father came to her bed.

Watched the large red roughened hands lift up the little girl's nightgown, part her legs, touch her softest tissues. While the other large red roughened hand moved to the front of his own pants, grasped at the strange red thing which she knew was hot and sticky.

But this time, this remembering, she did not stay in the wall until it was all over, to creep out and slip inside the little girl when he went away. This time she came charging out of the wall, kicking, punching and shouting, threw herself on the man, her father, with every cell in her body fighting.

The small grey woman watched this remembering with wonder. She felt a smile lifting her lips.

*   *   *

In the mountains, a fifteen-year-old girl-woman woke to the still grey day. A strand of her long black hair lay across her face. It reminded her of the night and the silent visitor who had come again to her bed. As he had been doing every week or so since she was eleven.

Her hand rose to move the hair; but it stayed, half raised to her face. The hair was speaking to her fingers: Today you will tell. Today you will speak. Today you can be strong. Today, you will stop being lonely.

*   *   *

A young married woman rose that day and did the things she normally did. She saw her husband off to work, dropped her daughter off at preschool and set out to drive to work. As she turned the first corner, the memories came again, especially the one about the first time. She found she was no longer driving to work; she was going across town to her friend's place. I have to tell you something, she said, as she sat down at the kitchen table.

She found herself speaking, telling of how her grandfather used to stick his fingers up the leg of her pants and feel her.

It first happened when I was five. I'd loved him up till then: a lovely soft, cuddly old man who cradled me in his lap and told me stories.

But that day, after my father came into the room and it all stopped happening and I started to breathe again, my grandfather's eyes met mine. I hadn't seen those eyes of grandfather's before. That was when I knew that what had happened was really as awful as it felt. You will never speak of this, they said – and in the same movement, he slid his eyes blandly round to my father and chuckled about the idiosyncrasies of an elderly old man sitting in the dusk with his princess!

I remember I ran out to the kitchen and stood near the stove to get warm because my heart was thumping so loud. My mother didn't see my eyes, or hear my heart, even though I stood there and watched her make the whole meal and then serve it. In my mind I was screaming, telling her. And saying that I didn't want to be with grandpa any more.

But I didn't say. I never have till now. But my mind has done that for years and years. Remembered. And screamed.

*   *   *

215

And as the twenty-four hours of that still, grey day rolled their gently inexorable way round the globe, all the women woke in turn, reliving their rememberings, and one by one they arose with a new new smile on their faces, and one by one they spoke. And the sound of their speakings drowned out all the other sounds in the world that day: the machines and the factories and the cars and newsreaders and doctors and priests and politicians and all the learned men were silent, because the noise of the women speaking filled up all the space. And any little places left in the silences that occurred amid the speakings and cryings and laughings of women, were filled by the noise of children playing.

Notes

Chapter 1: It Could Have Been Me (pages 77–99)

1. Herman and Hirschman, 'Father–Daughter Incest', *Signs: Journal of Women in Culture and Society*, vol. 2, no. 4, 1977, p. 756.

2. I am indebted for this use of 'imaginative' insight to Judith Long Lawe who used it in a paper entitled *Patriarchy as Paradigm: the Challenge from Feminist Scholarship*, presented to the American Sociological Association, New York, August 1976. Like many of the 'insights' of feminist thinking, this simple method of questioning the status quo of male supremacy and how it maintains itself is so obvious, that the real question is why we don't see it all the time.

3. Sydney Rape Crisis Centre workers, verbal presentation at Seminar on 'Children and Family Violence', arranged by the Institute of Criminology, Canberra, November 1979; see also Courtois, 'Victims of Rape and Incest', *The Counselling Psychologist*, vol. 8, no. 1, 1979, p. 39.

4. Gebhard *et al., Sex Offenders: An Analysis of Types*, Harper and Row, 1965, p. 219.

5. Cooper, 'Decriminalization of Incest – New Legal–Clinical Responses', in *Family Violence*, Eekalaar and Katz (eds), Butterworths, 1977, p. 519.

6. Medlicott, 'Lot and His Daughters – Parent–Child Incest in the Bible and Mythology', *Australian and New Zealand Journal of Psychiatry*, vol. 1, 1967, p. 139.

7. Australian Infantry Forces (AIF) ditty.

8. Griffin, *Rape: The Power of Consciousness*, Harper and Row, 1979, p. 7.

9. *Ibid.*, p. 21.

10. Summit and Kryso, 'Sexual Abuse of Children: a Clinical Spectrum', *American Journal of Orthopsychiatry*, vol. 48, 1978, p. 241.

11. Peters, 'The Philadelphia Rape Victim Study', in *Victimology: A New Focus*, vol. III, Drapkin and Viano (eds), Heath, 1975, p. 189.

12. Kaufman, Peck and Tagiuri, 'The Family Constellation and Overt Incestuous Relations Between Father and Daughter', *American Journal of Orthopsychiatry*, vol. 19, 1954, p. 266.

13. Cavallin, 'Incest Taboos in Adopted Children', in *Medical Aspects of Human Sexuality*, Lief (ed), Waverly Press, 1975, p. 237.

14. Chaneles, *Family Structure of Child Sex Victims*, American Humane Association Publication, 1967, p. 53.

15. Peters, 'The Psychological Effects of Childhood Rape', *World Journal of Psychosynthesis*, vol. 6, 1974, p. 14.

16. Weinberg, *Incest Behaviour*, Citadel, New York, 1955, p. 34.

17. De Francis, *Sexual Abuse of Children: Child Victims of Incest*, American Humane Association Publication, 1968.

18. Giaretto, 'The Treatment of Father–Daughter Incest: A Psycho-Social Approach', *Children Today*, vol. 5, no. 4, 1976, p. 4.

19. *Ibid.*

20. 'Incest: The Hidden Crime You Want Brought Into the Open', *The Australian Women's Weekly*, 30 April 1980.

21. R. and B. Justice, *The Broken Taboo*, Human Sciences Press, 1979, p. 16.

22. *Ibid.*, p. 17.

23. Weinberg, *op. cit.*, p. 40; Weiner, 'Father–Daughter Incest', *Psychiatric Quarterly*, vol. 36, 1962, in quoting Weinberg's 'war' findings, observes that the fluctuations occurred 'presumably in relation to the absence or presence of fathers in the home', p. 610.

24. Butler, *Conspiracy of Silence: The Trauma of Incest*, New Glide Publications, 1978, p. 10.

25. Chaneles, *op. cit.*, p. 53.

26. S. Griffin, *op. cit.*, p. 3.

27. Sgroi, 'Sexual Molestation of Children', *Children Today*, vol. 4, 1975, p. 20.

28. Chaneles, *Family Structure of Child Sex Victims*, American Humane Association Publication, 1967, p. 53.

29. Bender and Blau, 'The Reactions of Children to Sexual Relations with Adults', *American Journal of Orthopsychiatry*, vol. 7, 1937, pp. 514–6.

30. S. Griffin, *op. cit.*, p. 31.

31. Weinberg, *op. cit.*, p. 3.

32. Deveson, Anne, *Australians at Risk*, Cassell, NSW, 1978.

33. Robert Carroll, Program Administrator, Santa Clara County Child Sexual Abuse Demonstration and Training Project, in speaking to a public meeting, Canberra, 29 October 1980.

34. A. L'Estrange, 'A Report on the Lives and Deaths of the Street Urchins of St Kilda', *The National Times*, 24 February–1 March 1980, p. 13.

35. S. Griffin, *op. cit.*, p. 10.

36. Butler, *op. cit.*, p. 17. The context from which I took the quotation used in the text is as follows: 'I am writing, too, for those of us who have had no personal contact with incestuous assault. For while so many of us have difficulty in dealing with our own sexuality and while our understanding of the nature and functioning of our family lives is based upon culturally defined myths, we share similar frustrations and confusion with those families in which sexual assault is manifested. *If there is a difference among us, it is in degree, not in kind.*' (My italics.)

37. Giaretto, *op. cit.*, p. 2.

38. Weis and Borges, 'Victimology and Rape: The Case of the Legitimate Victim', in *Rape Victimology*, Schultz (ed), Thomas, 1975, p. 137.

Chapter 2: Freud and the Legacy of Mindbinding (pages 101–118)

1. Florence Rush, 'The Freudian Cover-Up', *Chrysalis*, 1977, pp. 31–45.

2. Iago Galdston, 'Freud and Romantic Medicine', in *Freud: Modern Judgements*, Cioffi (ed),Macmillan, 1973, p. 121.

3. Mary Daly, *Gyn/Ecology*, The Women's Press, 1979, p. 267.

4. Sigmund Freud, 'The Origins of Psychoanalysis –' *Letters to Wilhelm Fliess, Drafts and Notes, 1887–1902*, Imago, 1954, fn. p. 167.

5. Sigmund Freud, *The Aetiology of Hysteria*, vol. 3, 1896, p. 28.

6. Sigmund Freud, *Fliess Letters*, Letter no. 60, pp. 195–6, 28 October 1897.

7. Sigmund Freud, *The Aetiology of Hysteria*, p. 215.

8. Sigmund Freud, *Fliess Letters*, Letter no. 64, p. 206, 31 May 1897.

9. Joseph Peters, 'Children Who Are Victims of Sexual Assault and the Psychology of Offenders', *American Journal of Psychotherapy*, vol. 30, p. 400, 1976.

10. Sigmund Freud, *Fliess Letters*, Letter no. 70, p. 221, 3 October 1897.

11. *Ibid.*, Letter no. 29, p. 126, 8 October 1895.

12. J. Mitchell, *Psychoanalysis and Feminism*, Allen Lane, London, 1974; M. Montrelay, 'Inquiry into Femininity', *m/f*, 1, 1978, pp. 83–101; and J. Rose, 'Dora – Fragment of an Analysis', *m/f*, 2, 1978, pp. 5–21.

13. L. Stern, 'The Language of Rape', *Intervention*, vol. 8, 1977, p. 13.

14. *Ibid.*, Letter no. 69, pp. 215–16, 21 September 1897.

15. Hector Cavallin, 'Incestuous Fathers: A Clinical Report', in *Studies in Human Sexual Behaviour: The American Scene*, Shiloh (ed), Thomas, 1970, p. 387.

16. John Gagnon, 'Female Child Victims of Sex Offences', *ibid.*, p. 400.

17. Mitchell, *op. cit.*, p. 9.

18. Sigmund Freud, *Fliess Letters*, Letter no. 70, p. 219, 3 October 1897.

19. *Ibid.*, Letter no. 71, p. 223, 15 October 1897.

20. James Strachey, 'Editor's Note' to Freud: 'Some Psychological Consequences of the Anatomical Distinction between the Sexes', in *The Complete Psychological Works of Sigmund Freud*, vol. 1, Hogarth, 1966, p. 244.

21. Sigmund Freud, 'The Interpretation of Dreams', in *The Complete Works*, vol. 4, pp. 262–3.

22. *Ibid.* Freud, in a footnote added later (1911) to an analysis of an 'oedipal' dream: 'I have found that people who know they are preferred or favoured by their mother give evidence in their lives of a peculiar self-reliance and an unshakable optimism which often seem like heroic attributes and bring actual success to their possessors' (p. 398).

23. *Ibid.*

24. Penelope Balogh, *Freud: A Biographical Introduction*, Studio Vista, 1971, p. 46.

25. Ernest Jones, *The Life and Work of Sigmund Freud*, vol. 1 (3 vols.), Hogarth Press, London, 1961, p. 352.

26. James Strachey, Editor's Note, 1962 edition: Freud, *Three Essays on the Theory of Sexuality*, Hogarth, 1974, p. xii.

27. Beryl Henderson, born 1897: Conversation, 1972.

28. Sigmund Freud, *Fliess Letters*, Letter no. 123, p. 302, 12 November 1899.

29. James Strachey, Editor's Note to *Some Psychological Consequences*, p. 243.

30. Sigmund Freud, *Some Psychological Consequences*, p. 251.

31. *Ibid.*, p.. 252.

32. *Ibid.*, p. 253–6.

33. Sigmund Freud, Preface to 4th edition, *Three Essays on the Theory of Sexuality*, 1920, p. xvii. Later, in 1926, Freud took up the question of 'lay analysis' and wrote a defence of his friend Theodore Reik: 'The Question of Lay Analysis', *Complete Works*, vol. 20, pp. 251–2, in which he said:'the important question is not whether an analyst possesses a medical diploma but whether he has the special training necessary for the practice of analysis.'

34. Rush, *op. cit.;* see also K. Abraham, *Selected Papers on Psychoanalysis*, Hogarth, London, 1949, ch. 1, *passim*.

35. K. Horney, 'The Flight from Womanhood', as quoted in *Psychoanalysis and Women*, Jean Baker Miller (ed), Penguin, 1973, p. 5.

36. Adler, *Understanding Human Nature*, Allen and Unwin, 1928, p. 131.

37. Joseph Peters, *op. cit.*, p. 401.

38. *Ibid.*, p. 400.

39. Litin, Griffin and Johnson, 'Parental Influence in Unusual Sexual Behaviour in Children', *Psychoanalytic Quarterly*, vol. XXV, 1956, pp. 42–3.

40. Ernst Freud (ed), *Sigmund Freud, His Life in Pictures and Words*, Deutsch, 1978, pp. 114–5, shows a painting by Andre Brouillet of Charcot (Freud's original mentor in Paris) giving a lecture on hysteria. All the students are men (I could count twenty-five in the picture); the lecture is being 'illustrated' with an example – an apparently distraught woman who is being 'held' (restrained) in front of all of them, as they talk about her. This painting 'hung in Freud's consulting rooms in Vienna, and later in London'.

41. Lorenne Clark, 'The Theory and Practice of the Ideology of Male Supremacy', in *Contemporary Issues in Political Philosophy*, King-Farlow and Shea (eds), Sci. Hist. Publications, 1976, p. 49.

Chapter 3: The Fathers – Forgiven and Forgotten (pages 119–138)

1. Louise Armstrong, *Kiss Daddy Goodnight*, Hawthorn, New York, 1978.

2. Sagarin, 'Incest: Problems of Definition and Frequency', *The Journal of Sex Research*, vol. 13, no. 2, 1977, p. 135.

3. *Ibid.*, p. 127.

4. S. Weinberg, *Incest Behaviour*, Citadel Press, New York, 1955, pp. 94–8.

5. *Ibid.*, p. 97.

6. *Ibid.*, p. 96.

7. *Ibid.*, p. 94.

8. Y. Tormes, *Child Victims of Incest*, American Humane Association Publication, 1972, pp. 24–5.

9. Weinberg, *op. cit.*, p. 97.

10. E. Raphling *et al.*, 'Incest: A Genealogical Study', *Archives of General Psychiatry*, vol. 16, 1967, p. 505.

11. Tormes, *op. cit.*, p. 23.

12. *Ibid.*

13. Karin Meiselman, *Incest*, Jossey-Bass, San Francisco, 1978, p. 108.

14. R. and B. Justice, *The Broken Taboo*, Human Sciences Press, New York, 1979, p. 63.

15. *Ibid.*, pp. 64–5.

16. B. Cormier *et al.*, 'Psychodynamics of Father–Daughter Incest', *Canadian Psychiatric Association Journal*, vol. 7, 1962, p. 211.

17. Justice, *op. cit.*, pp. 67–76.

18. *Ibid.*, p. 78.

19. *Ibid.*, pp. 80–1.

20. *Ibid.*, p. 86.

21. Report in *The Canberra Times*, entitled 'Revolting Facts in Sex Case Involving Children', 20 October 1980, p. 3.

22. Justice, *op. cit.*, p. 87.

23. I. Cooper, 'Decriminalization of Incest – New Legal–Clinical Responses', ch. 34 in *Family Violence*, Eekelaar and Katz (eds), Butterworths, Toronto, 1977, pp. 519–20.

24. D. Walters, *Physical and Sexual Abuse of Children: Causes and Treatment*, Indiana U.P., 1975, p. 122.

25. Virkkunen, 'Incest Offences and Alcoholism', *Medicine, Science and the Law*, vol. 14, 1974, p. 124.

26. Meiselman, *op. cit.*, p. 106.

27. The word 'affair' occurs frequently in the clinical and sociological literature, as do terms like 'sexual relationship' and 'sexual activity'.

28. Gibbens *et al.*, 'Sibling and Parent–Child Incest Offenders', *British Journal of Criminology*, vol. 18, no. 1, 1978, pp. 40–51.

29. Ernest Jones, *Papers on Psychoanalysis*, 4th edn, William Wood, Baltimore, 1938.

30. Kaufman *et al.*, 'The Family Constellation and Overt Incestuous Relations between Father and Daughter', *American Journal of Orthopsychiatry*, vol. 24, 1954, p. 269.

31. *Ibid.*, p. 270.

32. *Ibid.*, p. 271.

33. J. Cavallin, 'Incestuous Fathers: A Clinical Report', from *Studies in Human Sexual Behaviour*, Shiloh (ed), Cass. Thomas, 1970, p. 390.

34. Gebhard *et al.*, *Sex Offenders: An Analysis of Types*, Harper and Row, 1965, p. 209.

35. *Ibid.*

36. Armstrong, *op. cit.*, p. 234.

37. Gebhard, *op. cit.*, p. 223.

38. Muldoon (ed), *Incest: Confronting the Silent Crime*, Minnesota Program for Victims of Sexual Assault, 1979, p. 14.

39. McCaghy, 'Drinking and Deviance Disavowal: The Case of Child Molesters', *Social Problems*, vol. 16, 1968, p. 48.

40. Meiselman, *op. cit.*, p. 93.

41. Gebhard, *op. cit.*, pp. 217–8.

42. *Ibid.*

43. Bromberg, *Crime and the Mind*, Lippincott, Philadelphia, 1948, ch. 4, quoted in Weiner, 'Father–Daughter Incest: A Clinical Report', *Psychiatric Quarterly*, vol. 36, 1962, p. 611.

44. Gebhard, *op. cit.*, p. 223.

45. Hersko *et al.*, 'Incest: A Three Way Process', *Journal of Social Therapy*, vol. 7, no. 1, 1961, p. 29.

46. *Ibid.*

47. Mary Daly, *Gyn/Ecology*, Women's Press, 1979, p. 257. Daly acknowledges this term as having been coined by Julia Stanley, 'Passive Motivation', *Foundations of Language*, vol. 13, pp. 25–39; and 'Syntactic Exploitation: Passive Adjectives in English', paper delivered at Southeastern Conference on Linguistics, Atlanta, Georgia, 1971.

48. Sarles, 'Incest', *Pediatric Clinics of North America*, vol. 22, no. 3, 1975, p. 635.

49. West *et al.*, *Understanding Sexual Attacks*, Heinemann, 1978, p. 8.

50. Susan Brownmiller, *Against Our Will*, Penguin, 1976, p. 280.

51. Cormier *et al.*, *op. cit.*, p. 208,

52. *Ibid.*

53. Tormes, *op. cit.*, p. 27.

54. A typical example: 'The stepfather of a 14-year-old-girl was found guilty of carnal knowledge. He was fined $150 and allowed to go home. The girl was made a ward of the State and sent away to a foster home. The man was not given any help. When the daughter came back to visit her sick mother, he tried to rape her again': Adele Horin, 'The Last Taboo', *The National Times*, 18 November 1978, p. 31.

55. Robert Carroll, Program Administrator, Santa Clara County Child Sexual Abuse Program, in a public address, Canberra, 29 October 1980.

56. Germaine Greer, 'Seduction is a Four Letter Word', in *Rape Victimology*, L. Schultz (ed), Thomas, Illinois, 1975, p. 378.

57. Tormes, *op. cit.*, p. 26.

58. Phyllis Chesler, *Women and Madness*, Allen Lane, London, 1972, p. 72.

Chapter 4: The Daughters Labelled and Libelled (pages 139–161)

1. Florence Rush, *The Best Kept Secret*, Prentice-Hall, 1980, for a history and analysis of the cultural forms in which the 'Lolita syndrome' and child-bride myths are purveyed.

2. S.M. Sgroi, 'Sexual Molestation of Children', *Children Today*, vol. 4, May–June 1975, p. 18.

3. Conversation with the mother of the child: April 1979.

4. Sgroi, *op. cit.*, p. 18.

5. M. Schecter and L. Roberge, 'Sexual Exploitation', in *Child Abuse and Neglect*, Helfer and Kempe (eds), Ballinger, Massachusetts, 1976, pp. 137–8.

6. I. Kaufman *et al.*, 'The Family Constellation and Overt Incestuous Relations Between Father and Daughter', *American Journal of Orthopsychiatry*, vol. 24, 1954.

7. Lustig *et al.*, 'Incest', *Archives General Psychiatry*, vol. 14, 1966, p. 32.

8. D. Reifen, 'Court Procedures in Israel to Protect Child-Victims of Sexual Assaults', in *Victimology: A New Focus*, vol. III, Drapkin and Viano (eds), Heath, Massachusetts, 1975.

9. R. Summit and D. Kryso, 'Sexual Abuse of Children: A Clinical Spectrum', *American Journal of Orthopsychiatry*, vol. 48, 1978, p. 239.

10. J. Selby *et al.*, 'Families of Incest: A Collation of Clinical Impressions', *International Journal of Social Psychiatry*, vol. 26, no. 1, 1980, p. 10.

11. Y. Tormes, *Child Victims of Incest*, American Humane Association Publication, 1972, p. 27.

12. Weis and Borges, 'Victimology and Rape: The Case of the Legitimate Victim', in *Rape Victimology*, L. Schultz (ed), Thomas, Illinois, 1975, p. 107.

13. Selby, *op. cit.*, p. 12.

14. Tormes, *op. cit.*, p. 27.

15. Weis and Borges, *op. cit.*, p. 121.

16. Lustig *et al.*, *op. cit.*, pp. 36-7.

17. Weis and Borges, *op. cit.*, p. 122.

18. A. Yorokoglu and J. Kemph, 'Children Not Severely Damaged by Incest with a Parent', *Journal of the American Academy of Child Psychiatry*, vol. 5, 1966, p. 122.

19. *Ibid.*, p. 121.

20. Selby, *op. cit.*, p. 12.

21. Kaufman *et al.*, *op cit.*, p. 266.

22. M. Lewis and P. Sarrel, 'Some Psychological Aspects of Seduction, Incest and Rape in Childhood', *Journal of the American Academy of Child Psychiatry*, vol. 8, 1969, p. 618.

23. Anna Katan, 'Children Who Were Raped', *Psychoanalytic Study of the Child*, vol. 28, 1973, pp. 220–2.

24. P. Sloane and E. Karpinski, 'Effects of Incest on the Participants', *American Journal of Orthopsychiatry*, vol. 12, 1942, p. 671.

25. Kaufman *et al.*, *op. cit.*, p. 275.

26. L. Bender and A. Blau, 'The Reactions of Children to Sexual Relations with Adults', *American Journal of Orthopsychiatry*, vol. 7, 1937, p. 514.

27. J. B. Weiner, 'Father–Daughter Incest', *Psychiatric Quarterly*, vol. 36, 1962, p. 613.

28. R. Medlicott, 'Parent–Child Incest', *Australian New Zealand Journal of Psychiatry*, vol. 1, 1967, p. 182.

29. K. Meiselman, *Incest*, Jossey-Bass, San Francisco, 1978, p. 159.

30. Sloane and Karpinski, *op. cit.*, p. 670.

31. Weis and Borges, *op. cit.*, p. 120.

32. Weiner, *op. cit.*, p. 614.

33. Yorokoglu and Kemph, *op. cit.*, p. 121,

34. Bender and Blau, *op. cit.*, p. 517.

35. *Ibid.*, p. 516.

36. A. Kinsey *et al.*, *Sexual Behaviour in the Human Female*, Saunders, Philadelphia, 1953, p. 117.

37. *Ibid.*, p. 121.

38. N. Lukianowicz, 'Incest', *British Journal of Psychiatry*, vol. 120, 1972, p. 307.

39. C. O'Donnell and J. Craney (eds), *Family Violence in Australia*, Longman Cheshire, Melbourne, 1982, p. 167.

40. J. Peters, 'The Philadelphia Rape Victim Study', in *Victimology: A New Focus*, vol. III, Drapkin and Viano (eds), D.C. Heath, Massachusetts, 1975, pp. 188ff; and P. Greenacre, 'The Prepuberty Trauma in Girls', cited in Lewis and Sarrel, *op. cit.*, p. 609.

41. R. M. Sarles, 'Incest', *Pediatric Clinics of North America*, vol. 22 (3), 1975, p. 638; and Sloane and Karpinski, *op. cit.*, p. 248.

42. S. Chaneles, *Family Structure of Child Sex Victims*, American Humane Association Publication, 1967, p. 53.

43. Lindy Burton, *Vulnerable Children*, Schocken Books, New York, 1968, p. 219.

44. J. Peters, 'Social, Legal and Psychological Effects of Rape on the Victim', *Pennsylvania Medicine*, vol. 78, 1975, p. 36.

45. J. Peters, 'Children Who Are Victims of Sexual Assault and the Psychology of Offenders', *American Journal of Psychotherapy*, vol. 30, 1976, p. 417.

46. Sarles, *op. cit.*, pp. 633 and 637.

47. *Ibid.*, p. 640.

48. E. Poznanski and P. Blos, 'Incest', *Medical Aspects of Human Sexuality*, vol. 9, no. 10, 1975, pp. 61–2.

49. Summit and Kryso, *op. cit.*, p. 244.

50. *Ibid.*

51. *Ibid.*

52. B. Woodling *et al.*, 'Sexual Assault: Rape and Molestation', *Clinical Obstetrics and Gynecology*, vol. 20, no. 3, 1977, p. 517.

53. Weis and Borges, *op. cit.*, p. 134.

54. Peters, 'Children Who Are Victims . . .', *op. cit.*, p. 415.

55. *Ibid.*

56. Robert Carroll, Program Administrator, Santa Clara County Child Sexual Abuse Demonstration and Training Project, in public address, Canberra, 29 October 1980. A critique of programmes such as the one at Santa Clara appears in 'The Sexual Abuse of Children in the Home', by Sheila Jeffreys in *On the Problem of Men*, S. Friedman and E. Sarah (eds), The Women's Press, UK, 1982, p. 65. She writes: 'In such centres, the child, the mother and the father are all persuaded that they are in some way responsible for what has happened so that they can all apologize to each other in future without any repetition of the offence. Such programmes claim great success. Women and children are forced to acknowledge responsibility for a situation in which they had no power or control and their experience of reality is brutally distorted.'

Chapter 5: The Mothers – Bound and Blamed (pages 162–180)

1. Garrett and Wright, 'Wives of Rapists and Incest Offenders', *Journal of Sex Research*, vol. II, no. 2, 1975, pp. 149–57.

2. Elaine Hilberman, *The Rape Victim*, Basic Books, New York, 1976, p. 50.

3. *Beware of Strangers*, leaflet produced by The National Mutual Life Association of Australia, in conjunction with the relevant state police force and a local radio station.

4. Cavallin, 'Incestuous Fathers: A Clinical Report', in *Studies in Human Sexual Behaviour*, Shiloh (ed), Thomas, 1970, p. 390.

5. Judith Herman, *Father–Daughter Incest*, Harvard University Press, Massachusetts, 1981, p. 43.

6. Weiner, 'Father–Daughter Incest', *Psychiatric Quarterly*, vol. 36, 1962, p. 612.

7. Molnar and Cameron, 'Incest Syndromes: Observations in a General Hospital Psychiatric Unit', *Canadian Psychiatric Association Journal*, vol. 20, 1975, p. 375.

8. R. and B. Justice, *The Broken Taboo*, Human Sciences Press, 1979, p. 97.

9. Hersko *et al.*, 'Incest: A Three Way Process', *Journal of Social Therapy*, vol. 7, 1961, p. 27.

10. D. Browning and B. Boatman, 'Incest: Children at Risk', *American Journal of Psychiatry*, vol. 13, no. 1, 1977, p. 71.

11. Lustig *et al.*, 'Incest', *Archives General Psychiatry*, vol. 14, 1966, pp. 31–2.

12. Cormier *et al.*, 'Psychodynamics of Father–Daughter Incest', *Canadian Psychiatric Association Journal*, vol. 7, 1962, p. 207.

13. H. Cavallin, *op. cit.*, p. 390.

14. Summit and Kryso, 'Sexual Abuse of Children: A Clinical Spectrum',

American Journal of Orthopsychiatry, vol. 48, 1978, p. 246.

15. *Ibid.*

16. Kaufman, Peck and Tagiuri, 'The Family Constellation and Overt Incestuous Relations Between Father and Daughter', *American Journal of Orthopsychiatry*, vol. 24, 1954, p. 269.

17. *Ibid.*

18. Hersko *et al.*, 'Incest: A Three Way Process', *Journal of Social Therapy*, vol. 7, 1961. See also, *Archives of General Psychiatry*, vol. 16, 1967; Raphling, Carpenter and Davis, 'Incest, A Genealogical Study', *Archives of General Psychiatry*, vol. 16, 1967.

19. Raphling *et al.*, *op. cit.*, p. 505.

20. Walters, *Physical and Sexual Abuse of Children: Causes and Treatment*, Indiana University Press, 1975, p. 121.

21. West, Roy and Nichols, *Understanding Sexual Attacks*, Heinemann, 1978, p. 24.

22. Karpman, *The Sexual Offender and his Offences*, Julian Press, 1954, p. 192.

23. Poznanski and Blos, 'Incest', *Medical Aspects of Human Sexuality*, vol. 9, no. 10, 1975, p. 59.

24. Rhinehart, 'Genesis of Overt Incest', *Comprehensive Psychiatry*, vol. 2, 1961, p. 347.

25. Selby *et al.*, 'Families of Incest: A Collation of Clinical Impressions', *International Journal of Social Psychiatry*, vol. 26, no. 1, 1980, p. 13.

26. Summit and Kryso, *op. cit.*, p. 250.

27. Garrett and Wright, *op. cit.*, pp. 149–150.

28. *Ibid.*, p. 151.

29. *Ibid.*, p. 154.

30. *Ibid.*, p. 155.

31. Greer, *The Female Eunuch*, MacGibbon and Kee, 1970, pp. 261–2.

32. Lustig *et al.*, *op. cit.*, pp. 38–9.

33. For an account of the facts see Adele Horin, 'Murder in Adelaide', *The National Times*, 26 July to 1 August 1981, pp. 3–5.

34. Horin, *ibid.*, p. 4.

35. Herman, *op. cit.*, p. 49.

36. Marge Piercy, 'Crescent Moon like a Canoe', from *The Moon is Always Female*, Knopf, New York, 1980, p. 132.

Chapter 6: The Sons – Oedipus, the Boy and the Man
(pages 181–192)

1. B. Cormier *et al.*, 'Psychodynamics of Father–Daughter Incest', *Canadian Psychiatric Association Journal*, vol. 7, 1962, p. 212.

2. R. M. Sarles, 'Incest', *Pediatric Clinics of North America*, August 1975, p. 634.

3. K. Meiselman, *Incest*, Jossey-Bass, San Francisco, 1978, p. 299.

4. *Ibid.*, pp. 302–3.

5. *Ibid.*, p. 304.

6. A. Yorokoglu and J. P. Kemph, 'Children Not Severely Damaged by Incest with a Parent', *Journal of the American Academy of Child Psychiatry*, vol. 5, 1966, p. 119.

7. Meiselman, *op. cit.*, p. 302.

8. *Ibid.*, p. 310.

9. C. W. Wahl, 'The Psychodynamics of Consummated Maternal Incest', *Archives General Psychiatry*, vol. 3, 1960, p. 190.

10. *Ibid.*, p. 192.

11. S. K. Weinberg, *Incest Behaviour*, Citadel Press, New Jersey, 1976 (1955), p. 89.

12. *Ibid.*, p. 90.

13. I. B. Weiner, 'On Incest: A Survey', *Excerpta Criminologica*, vol. 4, 1964, p. 150.

14. Conversation, Sydney Rape Crisis Centre workers, Sydney, August 1981.

15. R. Needham, *Remarks and Inventions: Skeptical Essays about Kinship*, 1974, pp. 64–5.

16. B. Seligman, 'The Problem of Incest and Exogamy: A Restatement', *American Anthropologist*, vol. 52, 1950, p. 308.

17. S. Moscovici, *Society Against Nature*, Humanities Press, New Jersey, 1976, p. 111.

18. Meiselman, *op. cit.*, p. 24.

19. T. Parsons, 'The Incest Taboo in Relation to Social Structure and the Socialization of the Child', *British Journal of Sociology*, vol. 2, 1954, *passim*.

20. *Ibid.*, p. 112.

21. N. Chodorow, *The Reproduction of Mothering*, University of California Press, Berkeley, 1979, p. 132.

22. S. Freud, 'The Question of Lay Analysis' (1927), *Complete Works*, vol. 20, p. 211.

23. O. Rank, *The Trauma of Birth*, Kegan Paul, London, 1929, p. 92.

24. S. Moscovici, *op. cit.*, pp. 106–7.

25. S. Brøgger, *Deliver Us From Love*, Quartet Books, London, 1977, p. 218.

Chapter 7: The Family – A Man's Home is His Castle (pages 193–201)

1. R. and B. Justice, *The Broken Taboo*, Human Sciences Press, New York, 1979, ch. 1.

2. K. Meiselman, *Incest*, Jossey-Bass, San Francisco, 1978, p. 93.

3. Lustig *et al.*, 'Incest', *Archives General Psychiatry*, vol. 14, 1966, p. 33.

4. W. Farrell, in P. Nobile, 'Incest: The Last Taboo', *Penthouse*, December 1977, p. 117.

5. J. Herman, *Father–Daughter Incest*, Harvard University Press, Massachusetts/UK, 1982, p. 25.

6. I am indebted for this ingenious insight to Raylee Wilson, conversation, Canberra, April 1982.

7. Herman, *op. cit.*, p. 27.

8. The development of this idea was aided by a conversation with Teresa Brennan, Canberra, July 1982.

9. Herman, *op. cit.*, p. 213.

10. *Ibid.*, p. 10.

11. A. Pauncz, 'The Concept of Adult Libido and the Lear Complex', *American Journal of Psychotherapy*, vol. 5, 1951, pp. 191–2.

12. *Ibid.*, pp. 190–1.

13. Pauncz, 'Psychopathology of Shakespeare's King Lear', *American Imago*, vol. 9, 1952, *passim*.

14. Pauncz, 'The Concept of Adult Libido', *op. cit.*, p. 194.

15. Herman, *op. cit.*, p. 204.

16. *Ibid.*, p. 206.

17. K. Barry, *Female Sexual Slavery*, Prentice-Hall, New Jersey, 1979, p. 222.

Coda: Action (pages 202–215)

1. A. Rich, *On Lies, Secrets and Silence*, Virago, London, 1979, pp. 259–60.

2. T. Morrison, *Sula*, Bantam, New York, 1975, p. 67.

3. A. Rich, *Of Woman Born*, Virago, London, 1977, p. 220.

4. J. Herman, *Father–Daughter Incest*, Harvard University Press, Massachusetts/UK, 1982, p. 217.

Bibliography

A. Articles, pamphlets, reports

Albin, Rochelle S., 'Psychological Studies of Rape', *Signs*, vol. 2, no. 3, 1977, pp. 423ff.

Anderson, Deborah, 'Counselling the Family in which Incest has Occurred', *Medical Aspects of Human Sexuality*, April 1979, pp. 143–4.

Andrews, John S., 'Incest – Who Needs It?' *Australian Journal of Forensic Sciences*, vol. 10, nos. 1 & 2, September–December 1977, pp. 30–42.

Bacon, Helen, 'Woman's Two Faces: Sophocles' View of the Tragedy of Oedipus and His Family', in *Science and Psychoanalysis*, J. Masserman (ed), vol. X, New York, 1966.

Bender, L. and Blau, A., 'The Reactions of Children to Sexual Relations with Adults', *American Journal of Orthopsychiatry*, vol. 7, p. 500, 1937.

Bender, Lauretta, and Grugett, A., 'A Follow-up Report on Children Who Had Atypical Sexual Experience', *American Journal of Orthopsychiatry*, vol. 22, p. 825, 1952.

Bentil, J. Kodwo, 'Incest: Legislative Paternalism Below Expectation', *Solicitors' Journal* (UK), vol. 122, pp. 687–8, 13 October 1978.

Berliner, Lucy, 'Child Sexual Abuse: What Happens Next?', *Victimology: An International Journal*, 1977.

Berry, Gail, 'Incest: Some Clinical Variations on a Classical Theme', *Journal American Academy of Psychoanalysis*, vol. 3, no. 2, pp. 151–61, 1975.

Brant, Renee, and Tisza, Veronica, 'The Sexually Misused Child', *American Journal of Orthopsychiatry*, vol. 47, no. 1, 1977.

Breen, J. L., Greenwald, E., and Gregori, C. A., 'The Molested Young Female: Evaluation and Therapy of Alleged Rape', *Pediatric Clinic North America*, vol. 19, pp. 717–725, August 1972.

British Medical Journal, Legal Correspondent, 'Sexual Assaults on Children', *British Medical Journal*, vol. 2, p. 1623, 1961.

Browning, D., and Boatman, B., 'Incest: Children at Risk', *American Journal of Psychiatry*, vol. 13, no. 1, pp. 69–72, 1977.

Burgess, A. W., Holstrom, L. L., and McCausland, M. P., 'Child Sexual Assault by a Family Member: Decisions Following Disclosure', *Victimology*, vol. 11, no. 2, pp. 236–50, Summer 1977.

Bush, Peter, 'Sexual Interference or Assaults on Children', *Social Biology*

Resources Centre Bulletin, vol. 3, no. 1, August 1979.

Carlisky, Mario, 'The Oedipus Legend and "Oedipus Rex" ', *American-Imago*, vol. 15, pp. 91–5, 1958.

Carroll, Robert, *Santa Clara County Child Sexual Abuse Demonstration and Training Project*, Roneo pamphlet, 1980.

Cavallin, Hector, 'Incestuous Fathers: A Clinical Report', in *Studies in Human Sexual Behaviour*, Shiloh (ed), Cass. Thomas, 1970, USA.

Chaneles, S., *Family Structure of Child Sex Victims*, American Humane Association Publication, 1967.

Chasseguet-Smirgel, Janine, 'Freud and Female Sexuality: The Consideration of some Blind Spots in the Exploration of the "Dark Continent" ', *International Journal of Psychoanalysis*, vol. 57, pp. 275–86, 1976.

Chodoff, Paul, 'Female Psychology and Infantile Sexuality', *Science and Psychoanalysis*, J. Masserman (ed), New York, 1966.

Clark, Lorenne, 'Politics and Law: The Theory and Practice of the Ideology of Male Supremacy', *Contemporary Issues in Political Philosophy*, King-Farlow and Shea (eds), Canadian Contemporary Philosophy Series, New York, 1976.

Clarke, Michael, 'Sexual Counselling: Incest', *Patient Management*, pp. 79–81, July 1978.

Connell, H. M., 'Incest: A Family Problem', *The Medical Journal of Australia*, vol. 2, p. 8, 7 October 1978.

Cooper, Ingrid, 'Decriminalization of Incest – New Legal–Clinical Responses', in *Family Violence*, Eekelaar and Katz (eds), Butterworths 1977, Toronto.

Cormier, B. M., *et al.*, 'Psychodynamics of Father Daughter Incest', *Canadian Psychiatric Association Journal*, vol. 7, pp. 203ff., 1962.

Courtois, Christine, 'Victims of Rape and Incest', *The Counselling Psychologist*, vol. 8, no. 1, Counselling Women III, 1979.

De Francis, Vincent, 'Protecting the Child Victim of Sex Crimes', American Humane Association Publication, 1969.

Deni, Laura, 'The Sexually Abused Child', *The Journal of Nursing Care*, December 1978.

Eaton, A. P., and Vastbinder, E., 'The Sexually Molested Child: A Plan of Management', *Clinical Pediatrics*, vol. 8, no. 8, pp. 438–41, 1969.

Elonen, A., and Swarensteyn, S., 'Sexual Trauma in Young Blind Children', *New Outlook for the Blind*, vol. 69, pp. 440–42, December 1975.

Ferenczi, Sandor, 'Confusion of Tongues Between Adults and the Child', *International Journal Psycho-Analysis*, vol. 30, pp. 225–30, 1949.

Ferracuti, Franco, 'Incest Between Father and Daughter', *Sexual Behaviours: Social, Clinical and Legal Aspects*, Resnik and Wolfgang, Boston, 1972.

Flammang, C. J., 'Interviewing Child Victims of Sex Offenders', *Rape Victimology*, vol. III, L. Schultz (ed), Thomas, 1975.

Foss, Paul, and Morris, Meaghan, 'Little Hans: The Production of

Oedipus', *Language, Sexuality and Subversion*, 'Working Papers' Collection, Feral, Sydney, 1978.

Frances, V., and Frances, A., 'The Incest Taboo and Family Structure', in *Family Process*, pp. 235–44, 1976.

Gagnon, J. H., 'Female Child Victims of Sex Offences', in *Studies of Human Sexual Behaviour: The American Scene*, A. Shiloh (ed), Thomas, 1970.

Galdston, I., 'Freud and Romantic Medicine', in *Freud: Modern Judgements*, Cioffi (ed), Macmillan, London, 1973.

Garrett, T. B., and Wright, R., 'Wives of Rapists and Incest Offenders', *Journal of Sex Research*, vol. II, no. 2, pp. 149–57, 1975.

Giaretto, H., 'Humanistic Treatment of Father–Daughter Incest', *Child and Neglect: The Family and the Community*, Helper, R., and Kempe, H. (eds), Michigan State University Press, 1976.

—— 'The Treatment of Father–Daughter Incest', *Children Today*, vol. 5 (4), pp. 2–5, 34–35, 1976.

Gibbens, T. C. N., *et al.*, 'Sibling and Parent–Child Incest Offenders', *British Journal of Criminology*, vol. 18, no. 1, pp. 40–51, 1978.

Gordon, Lillian, 'Incest as Revenge Against the Pre-oedipal Mother', *Psychoanalytic Review*, vol. 42, p. 284, 1955.

Greenland, C., 'Research and Methodology – Incest', *British Journal Delinquency*, vol. 9:1, pp. 62–65, 1958.

Greer, G., 'Seduction is a Four Letter Word', in *Rape Victimology*, Schultz, L. (ed), Thomas, 1975.

Griffin, Susan, 'Rape: the All-American Crime', ch. 3 in *Rape Victimology*, Schultz, L. (ed), Thomas, 1975.

Gutheil, T. G., and Avery, N. C., 'Multiple Overt Incest as Family Defence Against Loss', *Family Process*, pp. 105–16, 1977.

Hayman, C., and Lanza, C., 'Sexual Assault on Women and Girls', *American Journal Obstetrics-Gynaecology*, vol. 109, no. 3, p. 480, 1971.

Henderson, D., 'Incest: A Synthesis of Data', *Canadian Psychiatric Association Journal*, vol. 17, pp. 299–313, 1972.

Herman, Judith, and Hirschman, Lisa, 'Father–Daughter Incest', *Signs: Journal of Women in Culture and Society*, vol. 2, no. 4, pp. 735ff, Summer 1977.

Hersko, Marvin, *et al.*, 'Incest: A Three Way Process', *Journal of Social Therapy*, vol. 7, no. 1, p. 22, 1961.

Hicks, D. J., and Platt, C. R., 'The Development of a Rape Treatment Centre', in *Sexual Assault*, Walker, M., and Brodsky, S. L. (eds), 1976.

Horin, A., 'The Last Taboo', *The National Times*, pp. 30–1, 18 November 1978.

Hughes, Graham, 'The Crime of Incest', *Journal of Criminal Law and Criminology*, vol. 55, pp. 322–331, 1964.

Jackson, Miriam, 'Incest: The Last Taboo', *Broadsheet*, no. 74, 19 November 1979.

Jones, Julie, 'Sexual Assaults on Children', *Social Biology Resources Centre Bulletin*, vol. 3, no. 1, 1979.

Journal of Family Law, 'Crime of Incest Against the Minor Child', *Journal of Family Law*, vol. 17, pp. 19–115, November 1978.

Katan, Anna, 'Children Who Were Raped', *Psychoanalytic Study of the Child*, vol. 28, p. 208, 1973.

Kaufman, I., Peck, A., and Tagiuri, C., 'The Family Constellation and Overt Incestuous Relations Between Father and Daughter', *American Journal of Orthopsychiatry*, vol. 24, April 1954.

Kluckhohn, C., 'Recurrent Themes in Myth and Myth Making', *Myth and Myth Making*, H. A. Murray (ed), Brazillier, New York, 1960.

Knight, Michael, 'Child Molesters Try Shock Cure', *New York Times*, p. 43, 21 May 1974.

Kurland, Morton L., 'Pedophilia Erotica', *Journal of Nervous and Mental Diseases*, vol. 131, pp. 394–403, 1960.

Laplanche, Jean, and Pontalis, T. B., 'Fantasy and the Origins of Sexuality', *International Journal of Psycho-Analysis*, vol. 49, p. 1+, 1968.

Largen, Mary Ann, 'History of Women's Movement in Changing Attitudes, Laws and Treatment toward Rape Victims', *Sexual Assault*, Walker and Brodsky (eds), 1976.

Lester, D., 'Incest', *Journal of Sex Research*, vol. 8, pp. 268–85, 1972.

Lester, Eva P., 'On the Pyschosexual Development of the Female Child', *Journal American Academy Psychoanalysis*, vol. 4(4), pp. 515–27.

L'Estrange, Andree, 'A Report on the Lives and Deaths of the Street Urchins of St Kilda', *The National Times*, pp. 12–13, 24 February–1 March 1980.

Lewis, M., *et al.*, 'Some Psychological Aspects of Seduction, Incest and Rape in Childhood', *Journal of the American Academy of Child Psychiatry*, vol. 8, pp. 606–19, 1969.

Libia, D., 'Protection of the Child Victims of a Sexual Offence in the Criminal Justice System', in *Rape Victimology*, Schultz (ed), Thomas, 1975.

Lindzey, G., 'Some Remarks Concerning Incest, the Incest Taboo and Psychoanalytic Theory', *American Psychologist*, vol. 22, pp. 1051–9, 1967.

Litin, E. M., Giffin, M. E., and Johnson, A. M., 'Parental Influence in Unusual Sexual Behaviour in Children', *Psychoanalytic Quarterly*, vol. XXV, p. 37, 1956.

Lukianowicz, N., 'Incest', *British Journal of Psychiatry*, vol. 120, pp. 301–313, 1972.

Lustig, N., Dresser, J. W., Spellman, S. W., and Murray, T. B., 'Incest', *Archives General Psychiatry*, vol. 14, pp. 31–40, 1966.

Mabel, 'Daddy Does Things to Me', *Mabel*, no. 5, September–October 1976.

Machotka, P., Pitman, F. S., *et al.*, 'Incest as a Family Affair', *Family Process*, vol. 6, pp. 98–116, March 1967.

Manchester, A. H., 'Incest and the Law', in *Family Violence* Eckelaar and Katz, (eds), Butterworths, Toronto, 1977.

Mann, J. L., 'The Trauma in Sexual Abuse of Children', *Washington Post*, pp. C1, C5, 24 September 1973.

Medlicott, R. W., 'Lot and his Daughters – Parent–Child Incest in the Bible and Mythology', *Australian New Zealand Journal of Psychiatry*, vol. 1, p. 134, 1967.

—— 'Erotic Professional Indiscretions, Actual or Assumed and Alleged', *ANZ Journal of Psychiatry*, vol. 2, p. 17, 1968.

—— 'Parent–Child Incest', *ANZ Journal of Psychiatry*, vol. 1, p. 180, 1967.

Messer, Alfred, A., 'The "Phaedra Complex" ', *Archives General Psychiatry*, vol. 21, p. 213, 1969.

Molnar, G., and Cameron, P., 'Incest Syndromes: Observations in a General Hospital Psychiatric Unit', *Canadian Psychiatric Association Journal*, vol. 20, pp. 373–7, 1975.

Moore, S., 'Descent and Symbolic Filiation', *American Anthropologist*, vol. 66, pp. 1308–21, 1964.

McCaghy, C. H., 'Drinking and Deviance Disavowal: The Case of Child Molesters', *Social Problems* (Society for the Study of Social Problems), vol. 16, pp. 43–9, 1968.

McClemens, J., 'To Treat or Punish', *Australian Law Journal*, vol. 43, pp. 358–66, 1969.

MacDonald, G. J., and Di Furta, G., 'A Guided Self-Help Approach to the Treatment of the Habitual Sex Offender', *Hospital Community Psychiatry*, vol. 22, pp. 310–13, October 1971.

McGeorge, J., 'Sexual Assaults on Children', *Medicine, Science and the Law*, vol. 4, p. 245, 1964.

McKerrow, Wilson, D., 'Protecting the Sexually Abused Child', Second National Symposium on Child Abuse 1972, American Humane Association Publication, 1973.

O'Neal, P., 'A Psychiatric Evaluation of Adults who had Sexual Problems as Children: a Thirty-Year Follow-up Study', *Humane Organisation*, vol. 19, pp. 32–9, Spring 1960.

Parker, Gordon, 'Incest', *Medical Journal of Australia*, vol. 1, pp. 488–90, 30 March 1974.

Parsons, T., 'The Incest Taboo in Relation to Social Structure and the Socialization of the Child', *British Journal of Sociology*, vol. 2, pp. 101–17, 1954.

Pauncz, A., 'The Concept of Adult Libido and the Lear Complex', *American Journal of Psychotherapy*, vol. 5, p. 187, 1951.

—— 'Psychopathology of Shakespeare's King Lear: Exemplification of the Lear Complex (A New Interpretation)', *American Imago*, vol. 9 pp. 57–8, 1952.

—— 'The Lear Complex in World Literature', *American Imago*, vol. 2, pp. 51–83, 1954.

Peters, J., 'The Psychological Effects of Childhood Rape', *World Journal of Psychosynthesis*, vol. 6, p. 11, 1974.

—— 'The Philadelphia Rape Victim Study', *Victimology: A New Focus*, vol.

233

III, Drapkin and Viano (eds), Heath, 1975.

—— 'Social, Legal and Psychological Effects of Rape on the Victim', *Penn. Med.*, vol. 78, p. 34, 1975.

—— 'Children Who Are Victims of Sexual Assault and the Psychology of Offenders', in *American Journal of Psychotherapy*, vol. 30, pp. 398–421, 1976.

—— 'Letter to the Editor', *New York Times Book Review*, 16 November 1975.

Poznanski, Elva, and Blos, Peter, 'Incest', *Medical Aspects of Human Sexuality*, vol. 9, no. 10, pp. 46–79, 1975.

Raphling, E., Carpenter, B., and Davis, A., 'Incest, A Genealogical Study', *Archives General Psychiatry*, vol. 16, pp. 505–11, 1967.

Rascovsky, A., and Rascovsky, M., 'The Prohibition of Incest, Filicide and the Sociocultural Process', *International Journal of Psychoanalysis*, vol. 53, pp. 271–6, 1972.

—— 'On Consummated Incest', *International Journal of Psychoanalysis*, vol. 30, 31, pp. 42–7, 1949–50.

Reifen, David, 'Court Procedures in Israel to Protect Child-Victims of Sexual Assaults', *Victimology: A New Focus*, vol. III, Drapkin and Viano (eds), Heath, Massachusetts, p. 67, 1975.

Rhein, David, 'Orestes and Electra in Greek Literature', *American Imago*, vol. 2, pp. 33–50, 1954.

Rhinehart, John, 'Genesis of Overt Incest', *Comprehensive Psychiatry*, vol. 2, pp. 338–49, December 1961.

Riemer, S., 'A Research Note on Incest', *American Journal of Sociology*, vol. 45, pp. 566–75, 1940.

Rinaldi, Fiori, 'Incest with Daughters – Sentencing Patterns', *Criminal Law Journal*, vol. 4, August 1979.

Robinson, H. A., Sherrod, E. B., and Malcarney, C. N., 'Review of Child Molestation and Alleged Rape Cases', *American Journal Obstetrics and Gynecology*, vol. 110, pp. 405–6, June 1971.

Rogers, John, and Danks, David, 'The Genetic Consequences of Incest', *The Medical Journal of Australia*, vol. 2, p. 8, 7 October 1978.

Rose, Jacqueline, 'Dora – Fragment of an Analysis', *m/f*, no. 2, 1978.

Rosenfeld, A., Nadelson, C., and Krieger, M., *et al.*, 'Incest and Sexual Abuse of Children', *Journal American Academy Child Psychiatry*, vol. 16, no. 2, pp. 327–39, 1977.

Rosenfeld, Alvin, A., 'Sexual Misuse and the Family', *Victimology*, vol. II, no. 2, Summer 1977.

—— 'Incidence of a History of Incest Among 18 Female Psychiatric Patients', *American Psychiatric Association*, 1979.

Roth, R. A., 'Child Sexual Abuse: Incest Assault and Sexual Exploitation: A Special Report', *National Centre on Child Abuse and Neglect*, 1979, Washington DC.

Royce, D., 'Crime of Incest', *Northern Kentucky Law Review*, vol. 5, p. 191, 1978.

Rush, F., 'The Freudian Cover-up', *Chrysalis*, no. 1, pp. 31–45, 1977.

Sagarin, Edward, 'Incest: Problems of Definition and Frequency', *The Journal of Sex Research*, vol. 13, no. 2, pp. 126–135, 1977.

Saperstein, Avalie, 'Child Rape Victims and Their Families', in *Rape Victimology*, Schultz (ed) Thomas, 1975.

Sarles, R. M., 'Incest', *Pediatric Clinics of N. America*, vol. 22 (3), pp. 633–42, August 1975.

Schultz, L., 'The Child as Sex Victim: Socio-Legal Perspectives', *Rape Victimology*, Schultz, L. (ed), Thomas, 1975.

Selby, James, *et al.*, 'Families of Incest: A Collation of Clinical Impressions', *International Journal of Social Psychiatry*, vol. 26, no. 1, pp. 7–16, 1980.

Seligman, Brenda, 'The Problem of Incest and Exogamy: A Restatement', *American Anthropologist*, vol. 52, pp. 305–16, 1950.

—— 'The Incest Barrier', *British Journal Psychology*, vol. 22, pp. 250–76, 1932.

Sen Cong Committee on the Judiciary Sub-Committee to Investigate Juvenile Delinquency, 95 Congress, 1st Session, Chicago, Illinois, 27 May 1977, 16 June 1977, Washington DC.

Sgroi, S. M., 'Sexual Molestation of Children', *Children Today*, vol. 4, p. 18, May–June 1975.

—— 'Kids with Clap: Gonorrhea as an Indicator of Child Sexual Assault', *Victimology: An International Journal*, vol. II, no. 2, pp. 251–67, Summer 1977.

Shainess, Natalie, 'Authentic Feminine Orgastic Response', *Sexuality and Psychoanalysis*, Adelson, E. T. (ed), Brunner, New York, 1975.

—— 'Toward a New Feminine Psychology', *Notre Dame Journal of Education*, vol. 2(4), pp. 293–300, 1972.

—— 'A Re-assessment of Feminine Sexuality and Erotic Experience', *Science and Psychoanalysis*, vol. X, J. Masserman (ed), New York, 1966.

Shengold, Leonard, 'The Parent as Sphinx', *Journal American Psychoanalysis Association*, vol. 11, pp. 725–51, 1963.

Singer, Michael, 'Perspective on Incest as Child Abuse', *ANZ Journal of Criminology*, vol. 12, pp. 1–16, March 1979.

Slater, Miriam, 'Ecological Factors in the Origin of Incest', *American Anthropologist*, vol. 61, pp. 1042–59, 1959.

Sloane, P., and Karpinski, E., 'Effects of Incest on the Participants', *American Journal of Orthopsychiatry*, vol. 12, pp. 666–73, 1942.

Stern, L., 'The Language of Rape', *Intervention*, vol. 8, pp. 3–16.

Summit, R., and Kryso, D., 'Sexual Abuse of Children: A Clinical Spectrum', *American Journal of Orthopsychiatry*, vol. 48, pp. 237–51, 1978.

Sutherland, Sandra, and Scherl, D., 'Crisis Intervention with Victims of Rape', in *Rape Victimology*, Schultz, L. (ed), Thomas, 1975.

Swanson, D., 'Adult Sexual Abuse of Children' (The Man and Circumstances), *Diseases of the Nervous System*, vol. 29, pp. 677–83, 1968.

Szasz, T., 'Freud as Leader', in *Freud: Modern Judgements*, Cioffi, F. (ed), 1973, London.

Tompkins, J. B., 'Penis Envy and Incest', *Psychoanalytic Review*, vol. 27, p. 319, 1940.

Tormes, Y. M., *Child Victims of Incest*, American Humane Association Publication, 1972.

Virkkunen, M., 'Incest Offences and Alcoholism', *Medicine, Science and the Law*, vol. 14, pp. 124–27, 1974.

Wahl, C. W., 'The Psychodynamics of Consummated Maternal Incest', *Archives General Psychiatry*, vol. 3, pp. 188–93, 1960.

Ward, E., 'Rape of Girl-Children by Male Family Members', *ANZ Journal of Criminology*, vol. 15, no. 2, pp. 90–9, June 1982.

Weber, Ellen, 'Sexual Abuse Begins at Home', *MS*, p. 64f, April 1977.

Weeks, Ruth, 'Counselling Parents of Sexually Abused Children', *Medical Aspects of Human Sexuality*, vol. 10, p. 43, 1976.

Weich, Martin J., 'The Terms "Mother" and "Father" as a Defence Against Incest', *Journal American Psychoanalysis Association*, vol. 16, no. 4, p. 783, 1968.

Weiner, I. B., 'On Incest: A Survey', *Excerpta Criminol.*, vol. 4, p. 137, 1964.

—— 'Father–Daughter Incest', *Psychiatric Quarterly*, vol. 36, pp. 1132–8, 1962.

Weis, K., and Borges, S., 'Victimology and Rape: The Case of the Legitimate Victim', *Rape Victimology*, Schultz (ed), Thomas, 1975.

W.A. Dept. for Community Welfare: Child Life Protection Unit, 'Report and Recommendations Arising from a Survey on Services Currently Available in W.A. for Sexually Abused Children and their Families', May 1979.

White, L. A., 'Definition and Prohibition of Incest', *American Anthropologist*, vol. 50, p. 416, 1948.

Whiting, John W. M., 'Totem and Taboo – A Re-evaluation', *Science and Psychoanalysis*, vol. III, 1960, New York.

Williams, Judy, 'The Phenomenology of Incest', *Social Deviance in Australia*, Edwards, Anne, and Williams, Paul (eds), 1975.

Woodling, B. A., Evans, J. R., and Bradbury, M. D., 'Sexual Assault: Rape and Molestation', *Clinical Obstetrics and Gynecology*, vol. 20, no. 3, 1977.

Williams, J. E., Hall, 'The Neglect of Incest: A Criminologist's View', *Medical Science and Law*, vol. 14, pp. 64–5, 1974.

Women's Weekly, 'Incest: The Hidden Crime You Want Brought into the Open', *The Australian Women's Weekly*, 30 April 1980.

Woodham, A., 'Sexual Abuse of Children is Increasing', *The Australian Women's Weekly*, pp. 39–40, 28 February 1979.

Wright, Richard, 'The English Rapist', *New Society*, 17 July 1980.

Yorokoglu, A., and Kemph, J. P., 'Children Not Severely Damaged by

Incest with a Parent', *Journal of the American Academy of Child Psychiatry*, vol. 5, pp. 111–24, 1966.

Zaphiris, Alexander G., 'Incest: The Family with Two Known Victims', *Child Protection*, American Humane Association Publication, 1978.

B. Books

I. Works which have a perspective similar to that found in this book

Armstrong, Louise, *Kiss Daddy Goodnight*, Hawthorn Books, New York, 1978.

Barry, K., *Female Sexual Slavery*, Prentice-Hall, New Jersey, 1979.

Butler, Sandra, *Conspiracy of Silence: The Trauma of Incest*, New Glide Publications, San Francisco, 1978.

Griffin, S., *Rape: The Power of Consciousness*, Harper and Row, San Francisco, 1979.

Herman, Judith Lewis, with Hirschman, Lisa, *Father–Daughter Incest*, Harvard University Press, Massachusetts, and UK, 1981.

Rush, Florence, *The Best Kept Secret*, Prentice-Hall, New York, 1980.

II. Further reading

Abraham, Karl, *Experiencing of Sexual Traumas as a Form of Sexual Activity*, 1907.

Amir, M., 'The Role of the Victim in Sex Offences', *Sexual Behaviours: Social, Clinical and Legal Aspects*, Resnik and Wolfgang (eds), Little/Brown, Boston, 1972.

Ardener, Shirley (ed), *Defining Females, The Nature of Women in Society*, London, 1978.

Backofen, J. J., *Myth, Religion and Mother Right*, Bollingen, New York, 1973.

Bakan, David, *Child Abuse: A Bibliography*, Toronto, 1976.

—— *Slaughter of the Innocents*, CBC, Toronto, 1976.

Balogh, Penelope, *Freud: A Biographical Introduction*, Studio Vista, London, 1971.

Bardwick, J. (ed), *Feminine Personality and Conflict*, Brooks/Cole, California, 1970.

Bourne, R., and Newberger, Eli (eds), *Critical Perspective on Child Abuse*, Lexington Books, Massachusetts, 1979.

Brady, K., *Father's Days*, Dell, New York, 1981.

Briffault, R., *The Mothers*, Allen and Unwin, London, 1959.

Brøgger, Suzanne, *Deliver Us From Love*, Quartet, London, 1977.

Brome, Vincent, *Freud and his Early Circle: The Struggles of Psychoanalysis*, Heinemann, London, 1967.

Brownmiller, Susan, *Against Our Will*, Penguin Books, 1976.

Burgess, Ann Wolbert, *et al.*, *Sexual Assault of Children and Adolescents*, Lexington Books, Massachusetts, 1978.

Burgess, A. W., and Holstrom, L. L., *The Victim of Rape: Institutional Reactions*, Wiley, New York, 1978.

Burton, Lindy, *Vulnerable Children*, Schocken Books, New York, 1968.

Chesler, P., *About Men*, The Women's Press, London, 1978.

—— *Women and Madness*, Allen Lane, London, 1972.

Chodorow, N., *The Reproduction of Mothering*, University of California Press, Berkeley, 1979.

Clouzet-Choisy, Maryse, *Sigmund Freud: A New Appraisal*, Greenwood, Connecticut, 1974.

Cioffi, Frank, *Freud: Modern Judgements*, Macmillan, London, 1973.

Clark, Lorrene, and Lewis, Debra, *Rape – the Price of Coercive Sexuality*, Women's Ed. Press, Ontario, 1977.

Costa, Joseph L., *Child Abuse and Neglect*, Lexington Books, Massachusetts, 1978.

Daly, Mary, *Gyn/Ecology: The Metaethics of Radical Feminism*, The Women's Press, London, 1979.

De Mause, Lloyd (ed), *The History of Childhood*, Souvenir Press, London, 1975.

Durkheim, Emile, *Incest: the Nature and Origin of the Taboo*, Stuart, New York, 1963.

Dworkin, A., *Pornography: Men Possessing Women*, The Women's Press, London, 1981.

Edwards, J., and Williams, P., *Social Deviance in Australia*, Melbourne, 1975.

Eekelaar, U. M., and Katz, S. N. (eds), *Family Violence: an International and Interdisciplinary Study*, Butterworths, Toronto, 1977.

Farley, Lin, *Sexual Shakedown, The Sexual Harassment of Women on the Job*, McGraw-Hill, New York, 1978.

Firestone, S., *The Dialectic of Sex*, The Women's Press, London, 1979.

Forward, S., and Buck, C., *Betrayal of Innocence: Incest and its Devastation*, Penguin, UK/NZ, 1981.

Freud, Ernst, *Sigmund Freud: His Life in Pictures and Words*, Deutsch, London, 1978.

Freud, Sigmund, 'Project for a Scientific Psychology', in *The Complete Psychological Works of Sigmund Freud*, Strachey, L. (ed), vol. 1, Hogarth, London, 1966.

—— 'The Interpretation of Dreams', in *Complete Works*, Allen and Unwin, London, 1954.

—— 'Fragment of an Analysis of a Case of Hysteria (Dora)', in *Complete Works*, vol. 7, 1905.

—— 'A Case of Paranoia Running Counter to the Psychoanalytic Theory of the Disease', in *Complete Works*, vol. 14, 1915.

—— 'Some Psychological Consequences of the Anatomical Distinction between the Sexes', *Complete Works*, vol. 19, 1925.

—— 'The Question of Lay Analysis: A Postscript', *Complete Works*, vol. 20, 1927.

—— 'The Origins of Psychoanalysis', in *Letters to Wilhelm Fliess, Drafts and Notes, 1887–1902*, Imago, London, 1954.

—— *Three Essays on the Theory of Sexuality*, Hogarth, London, 1974.

Friedman, S., and Sarah, E. (eds), *On the Problem of Men*, The Women's Press, London, 1982.

Gebhard, P. H., *et al.*, *Sex Offenders: An Analysis of Types*, Harper and Row, New York, 1965.

Gil, David, *The Challenge of Social Equality*, Schenkman, Massachusetts, 1976.

Goldstein, Michael, and Kant, Harold, *Pornography and Sexual Deviance*, A Report of the Legal and Behavioral Institute, Beverly Hills, California, 1973.

Gornick, Vivian, *Essays in Feminism*, Harper and Row, New York, 1977.

Griffin, S., *Pornography and Silence*, The Women's Press, London, 1981.

Hart, T., *Don't Tell Your Mother: A Story of Incest*, Quartet, London, 1979.

Helfer, R., and Kempe, H. (eds), *Child Abuse and Neglect: The Family and the Community*, Michigan State University Press, 1976.

—— *The Battered Child*, University Chicago Press, 1968.

Herrmann, Kenneth J., *I Hope my Daddy Dies, Mister*, Dorrance, Philadelphia, 1975.

Hilberman, Elaine, *The Rape Victim*, Basic Books, New York, 1976.

Hollis, Patricia, *Women in Public, 1850–1900*, George Allen and Unwin, London, 1979.

Honoré, Tony, *Sex Law*, Garden City Press, London, 1978.

Hunt, David, 'Parents and Children in History', *The Psychology of Family Life in Early Modern France*, Basic Books, New York, 1970.

Hursch, Carolyn, 'The Trouble with Rape', a psychologist's report on the legal, medical, social and psychological problems, Nelson Hall, Chicago, 1977.

Jones, E., *The Life and Work of Sigmund Freud*, Hogarth, London, 1961.

Justice, Blair and Rita, *The Broken Taboo: Sex in the Family*, Human Sciences Press, New York, 1979.

Karpman, B., *The Sexual Offender and His Offences*, Julian Press, New York, 1954.

Kempe, Ruth S., and Henry, C. (eds), *Child Abuse*, Fontana/Open Books, London, 1978.

Kereny, C., *Eleusis – Archetypal Image of Mother and Daughter*, Routledge and Kegan Paul, London, 1967.

Kinsey, A. C., *et al.*, *Sexual Behaviour in the Human Female*, N.B. Saunders, Philadelphia, 1953.

Klein, Melanie, *The Psychoanalysis of Children*, Hogarth, London, 1932.

Konopka, Gina, *Young Girls: A Portrait of Adolescence*, New Jersey, 1976.

Lazarsfeld, Sophie, *Woman's Experience of the Male*, London, 1938.

Lief, Harold I. (ed), *Medical Aspects of Human Sexuality*, 750 questions answered by 500 authorities, Haverley Press, New York, 1975.

Lloyd, Robin, *For Money or Love: Boy Prostitution in America*, Vanguard Press, 1976.

Maisch, Herbert, *Incest*, Stein and Day, New York, 1972; Deutsch, London, 1973.

Mannoni, Octave, *Freud*, Pantheon, US, 1971.

Marcus, L., and Francis, J., *Masturbation: From Infancy to Senescence*, Int. University Press, 1975.

Martin, Harold P., *The Abused Child*, Ballinger, Cambridge, Massachusetts, 1976.

Masters, R., *Patterns of Incest: A Psycho-social Study of Incest Based on Clinical and Historic Data*, Julian Press, New York, 1963.

Meiselman, K., *Incest: A Psychological Study of Causes and Effects with Treatment Recommendations*, Jossey-Bass, San Francisco, 1978.

Mitchell, J., *Psychoanalysis and Feminism*, Allen Lane, London, 1974.

Morris, N., and Hawkins, G., *The Honest Politician's Guide to Crime Control*, Chicago University Press, 1970.

Moscovici, S., *Society Against Nature*, Humanities Press, New Jersey, 1976.

Mueller, G. D. W., *Legal Regulation of Sexual Conduct*, Oceana, New York, 1961.

Murdock, G. P., *Social Structure*, Macmillan, New York, 1949.

MacDonald, J. M., *Rape: Offenders and Their Victims*, Chas. Thomas, Illinois, 1971.

Nelson, M. C., and Ikenberry, Jean, *Psychosexual Imperatives: Their Role in Identity Formation*, Human Sciences Press, New York, 1979.

Needham, Rodney, *Remarks and Inventions: Skeptical Essays about Kinship*, Tavistock Publications, London, 1974.

O'Donnell, C., and Craney, J., *Family Violence in Australia*, Longman Cheshire, Melbourne, 1982.

Rank, O., *The Trauma of Birth*, Kegan Paul, London, 1929.

—— et al., *Psychoanalysis as an Art and a Science: A Symposium*, Wayne State University Press, Detroit, 1968.

Reed, E., *Woman's Evolution*, Pathfinder Press, New York, 1975.

Reik, Theodor, *Psychology of Sex Relations*, Grove Press, New York, 1945, 1961 edn.

Rich, A., *On Lies, Secrets and Silences*, Virago, London, 1979.

—— *The Dream of a Common Language, Poems, 1974–1977*, Norton, New York, 1978.

Roazen, Paul, *Freud: Political and Social Thought*, Alfred Knopf, New York, 1968.

—— *Freud and His Followers*, Alfred Knopf, New York, 1975.

Rodriguez, A., *Handbook of Child Abuse and Neglect*, Med. Exam. Publication, New York, 1977.

Rubin, Isadore, and Kirkendall, Lester A., *Sex in the Childhood Years*, Fontana, New York, 1971 (imp. 1976).

Salzberger-Wittenberg, Isca, *Psycho-Analytic Insight and Relationships: A*

240

Kleinian Approach, Routledge, London, 1970.

Santiago, Luciano, *The Children of Oedipus: Brother–Sister Incest in Psychiatry, Literature, History, and Mythology*, Libra, New York, 1973.

Schmitt, Barton (ed), *The Child Protection Team Handbook*, Garland, New York, 1978.

Schreiber, Flora R., *Sybil*, Warner, New York, 1973.

Schultz, Le Roy G. and Gochros, Harvey L. (eds), *Human Sexuality and Social Work*, Association Press, New York, 1972.

Schultz, Le Roy (ed), *Rape Victimology*, Thomas, Illinois, 1975.

Sherfey, M. J., *The Nature and Evolution of Female Sexuality*, Vintage, New York, 1973.

Shiloh, A. (ed), *Studies in Human Sexual Behaviour: The American Scene*, Charles Thomas, USA, 1970.

Smart, Carol and Barry, *Women, Sexuality and Social Control*, Routledge and Kegan Paul, Boston, 1978.

Stein, Robert, *Incest and Human Love: the Betrayal of the Soul in Psychotherapy*, Third Press, New York, 1973; Penguin, Baltimore, 1974.

Stone, M., *The Paradise Papers*, Virago, London, 1976.

Sugar, Max (ed), *Female Adolescent Development*, Brunner/Mazel, New York, 1979.

Sussman, Cohen, *Reporting Child Abuse and Neglect*, Ballinger, Massachusetts, 1975.

Tollison, C. D., and Adams, H. E. (eds), *Sexual Disorders: Treatment, Theory and Research*, Gardner Press, New York, 1979.

Walker, Marcia, and Brodsky, S. L. (eds), *Sexual Assault*, Heath, Massachusetts, 1976.

Walters, David R., *Physical and Sexual Abuse of Children: Causes and Treatment*, Indiana University Press, 1975.

Weinberg, Samuel K., *Incest Behaviour*, rev. edn., Citadel Press, New Jersey, 1976.

West, D. J., Roy, C., and Nichols, F., *Understanding Sexual Attacks*, Heinemann, London, 1978.

Wilson, P., *The Man They Called a Monster*, Cassell, Sydney, 1981.

Index

Female stereotype; Freud:
infantile sexuality; penis
envy; Masturbation;
Mothers; Rape; Prostitution;
Runaways; Sex-role
conditioning; Sex roles
De Francis, Vincent, 84
Deveson, Anne, 94
Deviance disavowal, 130–1
Doctors, on rape, 23, 89, 91, 157–8

Endogamy, *see* Fathers
Estrangement, sexual, 123, 167–9

Family, 77, 88, 95–6, 97, 99, 122,
137, 199, 210–11
analogy of, 193–4
disturbancce of, 92, 188
dysfunction, 78, 94
happy family, concept of, 95,
155, 162–3, 179
as haven, 87–8, 97, 196
Fantasizing, *see* Daughters; Freud;
Rape; Sexual fantasizing
Fathers
and alcohol, 124, 125, 127, 131–
2, 133
and blaming the female
principle, 123, 130, 134, 135,
138, 173
characteristics of, 93–4, 175
classification of, 93–4, 121–2,
124
and denial of rape, 135, 136, 137
and deviance disavowal, 131–2
and endogamy, 121, 122, 123
exoneration of, 45, 81, 103, 113,
121, 130, 134, 135, 138, 173
in Freudian theory, 128–9; *see
also* Freud
identity crisis of, 126, 170
and impulse control, 124, 127,
138
initiation of sons, *see* Sons
as introverts, 124
maleness, assertion of, 58, 134–
5, 142, 196–7, 198–9
and Oedipal theories, 173; *see
also* Freud
and over-possessiveness, 8–9,
14, 122

as paedophiles, 122, 125–6
as psychopaths, 88, 122–3, 125–6
punishment of, 145–6, 211
and rape as affection, 89, 133,
145
as rationalisers, 124–5, 135–6,
137
and recidivism, 68, 136
and sex-role anxiety, 134
sexual frustration of, 21, 167–8
and sexual passion, 122–3, 125,
132–3, 172
as the Stranger, 5, 98–9, 122
as tyrants, 123, 125, 166, 194
and unhappy childhood, 131
violence of, 9, 21, 69, 123, 142,
171, 200
see also Grandfather, rape by;
Male supremacy; Rape; Sex-
role conditioning; Sex roles;
Sons; Stepfather, rape by
Female sexuality, 81, 196
Female stereotype, the, 89, 143,
145, 177; *see also* Female
sexuality; Myths: female as
temptress; Property, women as;
Sex objects, women as; Sex
roles; Sex-role conditioning
Fliess, Wilhelm, *see* Freud
Freud, Sigmund
blaming the victim, 102, 103,
115, 148
castration, fear of, 112
critics of, 112, 116–17
and effects of rape on child, 105
and Father–Daughter rape, 101–
4
and Fliess, 106, 108, 110, 112
and hysteria, 103–5
and infantile libido, male, 110,
112, 114
and infantile sexuality, 102, 110,
208
and male supremacy, 101, 102,
107, 116
and misuse of language, 103, 106
and Oedipal theories, 103, 107,
109, 110–12, 113, 116, 128,
130, 142, 147, 172, 173, 187,
197, 198
and penis envy, 108, 112, 114, 147